READING BEYOND TI

Terence Cave CBE FBA is Emeritus Professor of French Literature, University of Oxford, Emeritus Research Fellow of St John's College, Oxford, and Honorary Fellow of Gonville and Caius College, Cambridge. He holds an honorary doctorate at Royal Holloway University of London and is Chevalier dans l'Ordre National du Mérite (France). He is recognized as a leading specialist in French Renaissance literature, but has also made landmark contributions to comparative literature and the history of poetics. In 2009, he won the Balzan Prize for literature since 1500 and subsequently directed the Balzan project 'Literature as an Object of Knowledge' (2010–14). His most recent work focuses on cognitive approaches to literature.

Deirdre Wilson is Emeritus Professor of Linguistics at University College London and former co-director of the Linguistic Agency project at the Centre for the Study of Mind in Nature, University of Oslo. Her book *Relevance: Communication and Cognition,* co-written with Dan Sperber, was described in the *London Review of Books* as 'nothing less than the makings of a radically new theory of communication, the rst since Aristotle's' and in *Rhetoric Society Quarterly* as 'probably the best book you'll ever read on communication.' Translated into twelve languages (including Japanese, Chinese, Korean, Malay, Indonesian, and Arabic), it has had a lasting in uence in philosophy, psychology, and linguistics and is now regarded as a classic.

OXFORD
UNIVERSITY PRESS

Great Clarendon Street, Oxford ox2 6DP
United Kingdom

# Reading Beyond the Code

*Literature and Relevance Theory*

Edited by
TERENCE CAVE
DEIRDRE WILSON

OXFORD
UNIVERSITY PRESS

# OXFORD
## UNIVERSITY PRESS

Great Clarendon Street, Oxford, OX2 6DP,
United Kingdom

Oxford University Press is a department of the University of Oxford.
It furthers the University's objective of excellence in research, scholarship,
and education by publishing worldwide. Oxford is a registered trade mark of
Oxford University Press in the UK and in certain other countries

First Edition published in 2018
First published in paperback 2020

Impression: 1

Published in the United States of America by Oxford University Press
198 Madison Avenue, New York, NY 10016, United States of America

British Library Cataloguing in Publication Data
Data available

Library of Congress Cataloging in Publication Data
Data available

ISBN 978–0–19–879477–6 (Hbk.)
ISBN 978–0–19–886351–9 (Pbk.)

Printed and bound by
CPI Group (UK) Ltd, Croydon, CR0 4YY

# *Preface*

The primary objective of this book is to demonstrate the value, and above all the *interest*, for literary studies of the model of communication known as relevance theory.[1] Across a wide range of examples chosen from lyric poetry and the novel, nine of the ten chapters presented here use relevance theory both as a broad framing perspective and as a resource for detailed analysis. They are written by specialists in English, French, and world literature, but most of the focal examples are selected from English-language cultures to avoid the problems that can arise in the close reading of translated texts. The final chapter, written by Deirdre Wilson, the co-founder (with Dan Sperber) of relevance theory, offers a retrospective view of the volume and of the issues it addresses.

Relevance theory is a cognitive approach to communication with important implications for language. Its central claim is that human communication is rarely a simple matter of encoding and decoding messages. Communicators use utterances not as signals to be decoded, but as pieces of evidence about the communicator's meaning. These pieces of evidence must be interpreted inferentially, by combining them with background information available to the audience in order to draw warranted conclusions. The resulting interpretation may be quite rich and vague—typically, not a single proposition but an array of propositions—and some aspects of it may be more salient than others, depending on which background assumptions are most easily available to the audience. On this approach, the communicator's goal is to find a form of utterance that will activate the appropriate background information in the audience's mind, and lead on to the intended array of conclusions. Thus, communication, cognition, and inference are intimately intertwined.

This cognitive approach to language and communication is grounded in evidence about the ways humans think and behave rather than deduced from formal principles. Its frame of reference is designed to capture the everyday murmur of conversation, gossip, quarrelling, peace-making, hate speech, love speech, 'body-language', and in recent times the endlessly reverberating echo-chamber of the internet, yet it remains relevant for the whole spectrum of human modes of communication, including literature. We use the word 'literature' loosely to designate a widespread (arguably universal) human activity which includes all forms of story-telling, poetry, song, and dramatic performance, whatever the medium. At one end of the spectrum, this activity shades off into the everyday modes evoked above. At the other end, it features the kind of 'canonic' work that is prized, remembered,

---

[1] See Dan Sperber and Deirdre Wilson, *Relevance: Communication and Cognition* (Oxford: Blackwell, 2nd ed., 1995); Deirdre Wilson and Dan Sperber, *Meaning and Relevance* (Cambridge: Cambridge University Press, 2012); among other major contributions, see in particular Robyn Carston, *Thoughts and Utterances: The Pragmatics of Explicit Communication* (Oxford: Blackwell, 2002).

repeated, and inventively transformed by cultures of all kinds. Most—though not all—of the literary works referred to in this book are recognizably 'canonic' in this sense, but we do not intend to promulgate a particular canon or uphold its implied values; we wish only to appeal to the shared knowledge of those who practise literary studies in whatever form or cultural environment.

The term 'cognition' is also one that can easily be misunderstood. As we use it here, it embraces the complete set of resources that a biologically evolved creature has for perceiving, interpreting, and responding to its local ecology. It is thus not reducible to concepts such as 'intelligence' or 'reason' (as opposed to imagination, emotion, or sensation), let alone to the activity performed by computers or even advanced robots, at least as they are at present conceived.

Other attempts have been made to apply the cognitive model of relevance theory to literary study.[2] This is the first to claim that the model works best for literature when understood in the light of a broader cognitive approach, focusing in particular on a range of phenomena that have been seen as justifying an 'embodied' conception of cognition and language. This broadened perspective serves to enhance the value for literary studies of the claim that is at the heart of relevance theory, namely that the 'code model' is fundamentally inadequate to account for human verbal communication, and a fortiori the modes of communication that are proper to literature.

A further word of clarification is perhaps needed here to counter a possible objection to our title (we are grateful to one of Oxford University Press's anonymous readers for urging us to think about this). There can be no ambiguity about the claim that relevance theory offers a pragmatic, inference-based, context-sensitive model in place of the model which has been dominant in accounts of language and communication from Aristotle to Saussure, Jakobson, and beyond (see Chapter 10 in this volume). The question is whether an analogous claim can be made for a cognitive approach to literary studies. We believe that it can, with the proviso that we are not speaking here about a polar opposition. Just as no relevance theorist would deny that language involves a significant element of coding (if it did not, its users would be incapable of understanding one another), so too literary specialists of every conceivable variety would acknowledge that convention provides a good deal of the infrastructure of literary corpuses, genres, canons, and traditions.

---

[2] The following in particular are referred to in the contributions to this volume: Alastair Fowler, 'A new theory of communication', *London Review of Books* (30 March 1989), 16–17; David Trotter, 'Analysing literary prose: the relevance of Relevance Theory', *Lingua*, 87 (1992), 11–27; Adrian Pilkington, *Poetic Effects: A Relevance Theory Perspective* (Amsterdam: John Benjamins, 2000); Billy Clark, 'Before and after Chekhov: inference, evaluation and interpretation', in S. Chapman and B. Clark (eds) *Pragmatic Stylistics* (Basingstoke, UK: Palgrave Macmillan, 2014); Anne Furlong, 'A modest proposal: linguistics and literary studies', *Canadian Journal of Applied Linguistics*, 10.3 (2007), 325–47; and Ruth Rosaler, *Conspicuous Silences: Implicature and Fictionality in the Victorian Novel* (Oxford: Oxford University Press, 2016). Gregory Currie deserves special mention here, since he makes extensive use of relevance theory in his major contributions to the understanding of literature, film, and art as products of human cognition; see in particular his study *Narratives & Narrators: A Philosophy of Stories* (Oxford: Oxford University Press, 2010).

However, for some considerable time now, the dominant trends in literary criticism have arguably focused on these 'encoded' aspects of literary works, in lyric and epic poetry, prose fiction, and theatre. Whether one is thinking of the role of commonplace in medieval and Renaissance writing,[3] of generic conventions, of formal poetics and rhetorics, of the varieties of 'textuality' classified by Gérard Genette, or of a Derridean emphasis on the 'always already said', critics seem to have been reluctant to acknowledge that the whole point of 'commonplace' materials and encoded forms is to provide a rich and flexible infrastructure of affordances for freshly imaginative enactments. One of the reasons for this swing of the pendulum towards literature's encoded features and functions is no doubt an abiding post- and anti-Romantic suspicion of the individual writer's claim to 'originality', or a Foucauldian suspicion of 'the human' as an invention of modern times. To counter the refrain that language and literature can only repeat themselves, one might reasonably insist that nothing is ever simply repeated; there is always a calculus of reinvention, enormously enhanced by changes in the cognitive environment (the way individuals and groups are thinking at a given moment).

Our aim, then, is not to construct some straw target that we can easily demolish; we have for that reason among others avoided using the phrase 'code *model*' in the title itself. It is rather to recentre the discussion of literary writing, reading, and performance precisely as a dynamic cognitive activity that draws on but always surpasses coding and convention. Relevance theory, it seems to us collectively, provides the ideal model for that change of emphasis. It encourages literary studies to reconceive literary works not as formulaic artefacts, separate from the world and available for labelling and classification, but as utterance in process, as communication, and as a remarkably rich and flexible resource for going beyond the coded infrastructures that all biological entities rely on, and imagining the world in unexpected ways.

This book is the outcome of an interdisciplinary project, 'Literature as an Object of Knowledge', conducted primarily within the perspective of literary studies but with ample representation from other fields. All of the contributors were core members of the project from the start and participated in all its activities. The key topics of the book were discussed and debated in depth in a series of our project workshops, and those conversations have continued in further workshops and other meetings since the project officially came to an end in September 2013. The presence of Deirdre Wilson and other relevance theory colleagues—in particular, Robyn Carston—in these dialogues led to lively debates on questions about intentionality, agency, communication, and the extent to which non-propositional factors such as affective or sensorimotor effects may be regarded as intrinsic to what an utterance communicates. We do not claim to resolve such issues in this book,

---

[3] The founding instance is Ernst Robert Curtius's *European Literature and the Latin Middle Ages*, trans. Willard R. Trask (Princeton, NJ: Princeton University Press, 1953; original German ed. 1948); a landmark recent example is Ann Moss's *Printed Commonplace-Books and the Structure of Renaissance Thought* (Oxford: The Clarendon Press, 1996).

only to bring them into focus and, again, to show how and why they should appeal to people who are interested in literature.

It is important to make clear from the outset that the aim of our collaboration was not to develop some overarching 'theory' of literature, or to add another 'turn' to the constantly shifting theoretical agenda of literary studies, but to explore a pragmatics of close reading that would draw its energies from the extraordinarily productive work on human cognition that is currently being done across the disciplines, from neuroscience via experimental and developmental psychology to philosophy (both phenomenological and analytic) and linguistics. Within this perspective, the contribution of relevance theory was of primary importance.

Our collective aim is distinctive, if not unique, in the current state of the field. There are many cognitive approaches to literature that draw on ideas from philosophy or cognitive science, but they have for the most part not been well received in mainstream literary studies because they are perceived as reductive, erasing the special complexity of literary texts in favour of generalizations derived from evolutionary studies, brain imaging, experimental psychology, linguistics, and philosophy of language or mind (or a combination of these). The contributors to this book all believe that cognitive approaches can afford powerful new ways of reading only if they take full account of the special qualities and characteristics of the literary text as an object of knowledge. Indeed, they would argue that literary study, far from being a passive participant in the cognitive dialogue, can raise questions that are highly relevant to other disciplines, and that one of their tasks is precisely to challenge the tendency to reductivism.[4]

*Reading Beyond the Code* does not offer a systematic ('pedagogic') account of aspects of relevance theory in their relation to literary studies. For that reason, we have sometimes preferred to describe the contributions as 'essays' rather than 'chapters'. Yet each chapter contributes in particular ways to our common project, and each presupposes a sense of that project. The Introduction provides the initial frame. It raises key issues and includes a condensed account of relevance theory for those unfamiliar with that theory, but does not offer a summary of the contributions. Instead, we have inserted what we call an 'interlace', a series of comments placed before each chapter which are designed both to bring out the structure of the volume as we have conceived it, and to draw attention to key points arising from the chapter in question. Sometimes these points are those the author explicitly focuses on; sometimes they present the issues as the editors perceive them—an alternative perspective, although always a consilient one. These passages are set in italics to make audible the change of voice between the editors and the author of each particular chapter.

In short, while the individual chapters may be read as independent units, we believe that their value and interest will be enhanced if they are taken as a convergent set of explorations of a common critical and intellectual domain.

---

[4] For an outline of what such an approach might look like, see Terence Cave, *Thinking with Literature: Towards a Cognitive Criticism* (Oxford: Oxford University Press, 2016), which may be regarded as a companion study for the present volume.

*Reading Beyond the Code* is designed for specialists and students of literature and literary linguistics; for relevance theorists; and for all those interested in interdisciplinary cognitive studies, especially in their relation to literature and similar cultural phenomena. We hope that it will also be relevant to anyone who takes a serious interest in literature and its value in a wider context.

TC
DW

*April 2017*

# Acknowledgements

This book arose from the project 'Literature as an Object of Knowledge', which was generously funded by the International Balzan Prize Foundation from 2010 to 2014. The project was based at the Research Centre of St John's College, Oxford, which provided invaluable additional funding, together with use of its facilities and administrative support. All of the contributors to *Reading Beyond the Code* were active participants in the Balzan project, and we wish to express our collective gratitude to the Balzan Foundation and to St John's College for enabling us to conduct the discussions and enquiries on which the book is based in the best possible scholarly conditions.

Since the book is the outcome of discussions which began in 2010, it is also indebted to the insights of many other participants in the project. They cannot all be named here, but we would like in particular to offer our thanks to Robyn Carston, who was a member of the Senior Advisory Panel and a regular contributor to our workshops. Her deep and innovative understanding of relevance theory and her unstinting advice and support were central to the conception of the book.

We are indebted to the anonymous readers engaged by Oxford University Press, whose detailed reports on our original proposal helped to shape the book as it went through the writing-up process. We are also immensely grateful to the Press itself and its officers Jacqueline Norton and Aimee Wright for their customary professionalism and warm support for our proposal. Sally Evans-Darby was a highly focused, responsive, and humane copy-editor.

The quotation from J.M. Coetzee's novel *Slow Man* which we have used as an epigraph for the book is reproduced with the kind permission of the author and the publishers (Vintage Books for world rights excluding the USA, Viking for the USA). Excerpts from DREAM WORK, copyright © 1986 by Mary Oliver, are used by permission of Grove/Atlantic, Inc. Any third party use of this material, outside of this publication, is prohibited. All other permissions are acknowledged where the text in question is reproduced.

# Contents

# Note on Pronouns

Relevance theorists long ago established a convention for the use of third-person singular pronouns in cases where the person referred to is anonymous or gender-unspecific: feminine pronouns are used for the speaker of an utterance, masculine pronouns for the listener. We have adopted that convention here in suitable contexts. However, it is not easily extended to discussion of literary works, where the author is typically gender-specific. We have therefore invited contributors to make use of alternative ways of avoiding gendered pronouns as appropriate. We have preferred to avoid cumbersome forms such as 's/he' and (with one exception where the context requires it) 'him or her'.

# Notes on Contributors

**Kathryn Banks** is Associate Professor of French at Durham University. As a Research Lecturer on the Balzan project, she explored dialogue between literature and the modern cognitive sciences. She is currently working on cognition in Rabelais, as well as literary 'thinking with' apocalypse. She is also co-editing with Timothy Chesters a book on *Movement in Renaissance Literature: Exploring Kinesic Intelligence*. Previous publications include *Cosmos and Image in the Renaissance* (2008).

**Elleke Boehmer** is Professor of World Literature in English at the University of Oxford. She was a member of the Senior Advisory Panel of the Balzan project. She is the author of five monographs and five novels, including among the former *Colonial and Postcolonial Literature* (1995, 2005), *Empire, the National and the Postcolonial* (2002), *Stories of Women* (2005), *Nelson Mandela* (2008), and *Indian Arrivals 1870–1915* (2015), and among the latter *The Shouting in the Dark* (long-listed *Sunday Times* Barry Ronge prize), *Screens against the Sky* (short-listed David Higham Prize, 1990), *Bloodlines* (short-listed SANLAM prize), and *Nile Baby* (2008). *Indian Arrivals* won the ESSE 2016 prize for Literature in English. She has edited and co-edited numerous books, including Robert Baden-Powell's *Scouting for Boys* (2004). She was a Man Booker International judge from 2013 to 2015, and holds an Honorary Doctorate from Linnaeus University in Sweden.

**Guillemette Bolens** is Professor of Medieval English Literature and Comparative Literature at the University of Geneva. She was a member of the Senior Advisory Panel of the Balzan project. Her research focuses on the history of the body, kinesic intelligence, gestures, and embodied cognition in visual and verbal arts. She is the author of *La Logique du corps articulaire* (2000, 2007), *The Style of Gestures: Embodiment and Cognition in Literary Narrative* (2012; first published in French 2008), and *L'Humour et le savoir des corps: Don Quichotte, Tristram Shandy et le rire du lecteur* (2016). She has been the director of the Swiss National Science Foundation project *Kinesic Knowledge in Anthropology and Literature*. She is a contributor to Kathryn Banks and Timothy Chesters's forthcoming book *Movement in Renaissance Literature: Exploring Kinesic Intelligence*, and to Miranda Anderson and Michael Wheeler's book *Distributed Cognition in Medieval and Renaissance Culture*, forthcoming in 2018.

**Terence Cave** is Emeritus Professor of French Literature, University of Oxford, and Emeritus Fellow of St John's College, Oxford. His publications include *The Cornucopian Text: Problems of Writing in the French Renaissance* (1979), *Recognitions: A Study in Poetics* (1988), *How to Read Montaigne* (2007), and *Mignon's Afterlives: Crossing Cultures from Goethe to the Twenty-First Century* (2011). In 2009, he won the Balzan Prize for literature since 1500, and from 2010 to 2013 he was Director of the Balzan project 'Literature as an Object of Knowledge' at the St John's College Research Centre, Oxford. His book *Thinking with Literature: Towards a Cognitive Criticism* was published in 2016. He has also contributed to *Cognitive Confusions: Dreams, Delusions, and Illusions in Early Modern Culture*, eds Mac Carthy, Sellevold, and Smith (2016), and to *Movement in Renaissance Literature: Exploring Kinesic Intelligence*, eds Banks and Chesters (2017).

**Timothy Chesters** is University Lecturer in Sixteenth-Century French Literature and a Fellow of Clare College, Cambridge. He was a Research Lecturer in the Balzan project.

He has published a book and several articles on the relationship between learned demonology and narrative in the French Renaissance. Since 2010 he has been examining questions of social cognition (mind-reading, empathy, kinesic intelligence, inference-making) as worked through both in the modern cognitive sciences and in literary texts of the Renaissance and other periods.

**Neil Kenny** is Professor of French at the University of Oxford and Senior Research Fellow at All Souls College. He was a regular participant in the Balzan project. His work has centred on early modern French literature and thought while sometimes ranging further afield. His books include *The Uses of Curiosity in Early Modern France and Germany* (2004), *An Introduction to Sixteenth-Century French Literature and Thought* (2008), and *Death and Tenses: Posthumous Presence in Early Modern France* (2015). He has published an essay on Montaigne and relevance theory (in *Lucidity: Essays in Honour of Alison Finch*, eds Ian James and Emma Wilson (2016)). He is currently working on the relation between (a) literature and learning, (b) family, and (c) social hierarchy in early modern France.

**Raphael Lyne** is Reader in Renaissance Literature in the Faculty of English, University of Cambridge, and a Fellow of Murray Edwards College. He was a Deputy Director and Research Lecturer in the Balzan project. He is the author of *Ovid's Changing Worlds* (2001), *Shakespeare's Late Work* (2007), *Shakespeare, Rhetoric and Cognition* (2011), and *Memory and Intertextuality in Renaissance Literature* (2016). As well as several articles taking a cognitive approach to literature, he writes a blog, 'What Literature Knows About Your Brain'.

**Kirsti Sellevold** is Research Adviser at the University of Oslo and a former Associate Researcher in the Balzan project. Among her publications are *'J'ayme ces mots…': expressions linguistiques de doute dans les* Essais *de Montaigne* (2004), a book chapter on the early modern French translations of *Utopia* in *Thomas More's* Utopia: *Paratexts and Contexts* (2008), and the co-edited book (with Ita Mac Carthy and Olivia Smith) *Cognitive Confusions: Dreams, Delusions and Illusions in Early Modern Culture* (2016). She has written on fictional representations of autism (in Faulkner and Vesaas) and is currently exploring aspects of non-verbal communication in Montaigne's *Essais*.

**Wes Williams** is Professor of French Literature at Oxford University. He was a Deputy Director of the Balzan project. His main research interests are in the field of Renaissance literature: they encompass the study of genre and of subjectivity, and the intersection of medicine, law, and literature in the period. His first book was *Pilgrimage and Narrative in the French Renaissance: 'The Undiscovered Country'* (OUP, 1998) and his most recent is *Monsters and their Meanings in Early Modern Culture: 'Mighty Magic'* (OUP, 2011). Currently working on the long history of 'Voluntary Servitude', he also teaches European film and literary theory, and writes and directs for the theatre.

**Deirdre Wilson** is Emeritus Professor of Linguistics at University College London and former co-director of the Linguistic Agency project at the Centre for the Study of Mind in Nature, University of Oslo. Her book *Relevance: Communication and Cognition*, co-written with Dan Sperber, was described in the *London Review of Books* as 'nothing less than the makings of a radically new theory of communication, the first since Aristotle's' and in *Rhetoric Society Quarterly* as 'probably the best book you'll ever read on communication'. Translated into twelve languages (including Japanese, Chinese, Korean, Malay, Indonesian, and Arabic), it has had a lasting influence in philosophy, psychology, and linguistics and is now regarded as a classic. Her other publications include *Meaning and Relevance* (2012), co-authored with Dan Sperber, and a novel, *Slave of the Passions* (1991).

There are the words themselves, and then, behind or around or beneath the words, there is the intention. As he speaks he is aware of the boy watching his lips, brushing aside the word-strings as if they were cobwebs, tuning his ear to the intention.

J.M. Coetzee, Slow Man, p. 70

# Introduction

*Terence Cave and Deirdre Wilson*

## LITERATURE, LANGUAGE, AND COMMUNICATION

The relationship between literature, language, and communication is one that is intuitively taken for granted by most readers, and in most everyday discussion of fiction, poetry, theatre, and the media. Yet it is complex and by no means self-evident. This book sets out to explore a conception of language and communication that, we believe, lends itself extremely well to literary studies. What that conception offers, at the most general level, is a revitalizing account of how communicative effects are achieved; at the level of close reading, it provides a powerful and highly flexible set of critical and analytic instruments. The contributors to this study, in their various ways, think through the implications of this conceptual frame of reference, but they do it in a way that respects the power of literary language itself: they offer experiments in reading according to a cognitive perspective. One of the key claims we collectively make is that literature is anything but an inert and passive object of knowledge, offered to a philosophical–critical gaze that only seeks to use it as an illustration of a pre-formed theory. Literature is not a museum full of stuffed corpses, or a set of complex diagrams, but a living repertory of atypical and (often) exotic cognitive performances.

It is important to establish from the outset that 'literature', for the purposes of this study, is not confined to certain genres or an established canon. It is conceived in a broadly anthropological perspective, where it is assumed that all human cultures, past and present, exhibit more or less demarcated forms of story-telling, fiction-making, singing, poetic utterance, mimed performance, and the like. In modern cultures, these activities have proliferated as a result of the invention of technological supports of various kinds, from printing to the electronic media. But it is again to be assumed that such activities are not just an idle spin-off of more practical and immediately productive behaviours. They are central to the way humans think about the world and themselves. In particular, they belong to a specifically human mode of cognitive evolution that encompasses, on the one hand, the capacity to imagine alternative possibilities, to remember flexibly and comparatively, to plan ahead, to infer what others are thinking, even at times to think the virtually unthinkable; and on the other, to produce public representations of their thoughts and envisage their effects on others. In such a perspective, the phenomena we loosely call 'literary' are on a spectrum with all the other ways that humans think and communicate their thoughts. The fact that they are variously tagged, in different cultures, as distinctive is a sign that they do lie on that spectrum, and that their place needs in consequence to be marked as part of a more general exercise of cognitive calibration.

The contributors to this book would therefore agree with the view taken by relevance theorists that many modes of expression considered distinctively literary are variants of everyday uses of language, and that any theory of language and communication must apply to those variants too. Such an argument usefully brings literary studies back to the conditions of everyday life and thought, while not denying the value of the counter-intuitive strategies that literary critics have often availed themselves of.

Before looking in detail at what relevance theory has to offer to literary study, and what literary study may offer in return, we need briefly to address one further set of issues. It is intuitively obvious that many uses of language are communicative, and a great deal of human communication relies on language. However, much communication is non-verbal. You can communicate with someone by making a gesture (waving to them, pointing, shaking or nodding your head), by showing them something (a key, for example), by exchanging glances with them, or even by touching them in a certain way. Musicians often speak of their desire to 'communicate' with their audience when they play, and this does not appear to be a trivial or purely metaphorical claim. Animals, too, communicate both with other animals and with humans, and it has been argued that public ('natural') languages such as Xhosa, English, or Sanskrit could have developed only among individuals who were already heavily engaged in non-verbal communication.

On the other hand, major thinkers as widely separated in other respects as Noam Chomsky and Jacques Derrida have contested the view that the function of language is primarily communicative. Some writers (and not only modern ones) across the spectrum of literary genres cultivate a language which is difficult of access, as if they wanted to protect the frontiers of what, for them, is a sacred experience, and while one could easily argue that something is being communicated precisely by that gesture, there is a sense in which the function of poetry, if not of literature in general, is not strictly or exclusively communicative. In this volume, however, we adopt the view that, while it is important to acknowledge such arguments at the outset in order to clarify the scope of our enterprise, they are largely extraneous to the pragmatics of communication, including literary communication, which is the focus of our attention.

## REPLACING THE 'CODE' MODEL
## OF COMMUNICATION

How does communication take place? For centuries, there seemed to be a straightforward answer that applied to all varieties of communication and took the form of a code-based, or 'semiotic', model. According to this model, communicators have available a set of observable signals, a set of unobservable messages, and a code that systematically relates the two. Communication succeeds when a communicator with a certain message to convey produces the corresponding signal, which is observed and decoded by the addressee using an identical copy of the code. All animal communication and some spontaneous expressions of emotion in humans fit this model.[1]

Around sixty years ago, the philosopher Paul Grice proposed an alternative answer, which relies not on coding and decoding but on the overt expression and recognition of intentions. On this account, communication succeeds when an individual who intends to convey a certain piece of information makes it clear to the addressee that she has this intention.[2] Suppose I catch your eye as we watch a politician speak on television, and briefly close my eyes and mime a yawn. Here, there is no need for a code. Instead, I offer you a *piece of evidence* about my intentions, and by combining this evidence with background information available in the context, you *infer* that I intend to let you know that I am bored. This type of communication, involving the overtly intentional display of a piece of evidence about the communicator's intentions, is what relevance theorists call *ostensive*.[3]

Ostensive acts—common examples of which include catching someone's eye, touching them, pointing, showing them something, speaking, and writing—are designed to attract the addressee's attention and convey a certain *import*. In the simplest case this import may consist of a single proposition, but in more complex cases, to be illustrated below, it may amount to an indefinite *array* of propositions. The idea that what is communicated is invariably a 'message' or 'meaning' that can be rendered as a single proposition or a small set of propositions is an unargued assumption of the code model, and one which is particularly ill-suited to dealing with literary communication.

The import of an ostensive act can be conveyed by either *showing* or *telling*. Suppose we are out for a walk and I suddenly stop and gesture towards the view. By *showing* you the view, I provide you with direct perceptual evidence for a vast array of propositions. I might have conveyed some of the same import by *telling* you about the view: that is, by providing direct linguistic evidence not of the array of propositions itself but of my intention to convey it. Showing and telling may combine, as when I stop and gesture towards the view while describing a particular aspect of it that I want you to attend to, perhaps using a tone of voice or facial expression that reveals something of my emotional attitude. To the extent that perceptual or emotion-reading mechanisms are involved, the array of propositions conveyed by an ostensive act may be richer and more fine-grained.

Ostensive communication can occur in the absence of any code, as when I invite you to sit next to me by patting the chair beside me. However, it can also benefit

---

[1] See Tim Wharton, *Pragmatics and Non-Verbal Communication* (Cambridge: Cambridge University Press, 2009).

[2] Unless otherwise indicated, we will follow the standard convention in pragmatics of referring to the communicator as female and the addressee as male. (But see also 'Note on Pronouns' above, p. xv.)

[3] On the differences between coded and ostensive communication, see Thom Scott-Phillips, *Speaking Our Minds: Why Human Communication is Different, and How Language Evolved to Make it Special* (Basingstoke: Palgrave, 2014).

from the use of coded signals which provide clues to the communicator's intentions without pinning them down completely. In many cultures, for instance, nodding is a coded signal which indicates that the communicator agrees with some proposition salient in the cognitive environment, but leaves it up to the addressee to infer precisely what that proposition is. Utterances in public languages such as English are also coded signals which provide clues to the speaker's intended import without pinning it down completely: they are often fragmentary or incomplete, may contain ambiguous, vague, or referentially ambivalent expressions, can be interpreted literally, metaphorically, or ironically, and may carry implicit hints or suggestions ('implicatures') that go well beyond the linguistically encoded meaning of the sentence uttered. In other words, utterances in English do not fully encode the speaker's intended meaning but provide some evidence about that meaning, just as patting an empty chair may provide some evidence that the communicator intends to invite the addressee to sit down. The challenge for a theory of ostensive communication is to explain how addressees infer the intended import of an utterance on the basis of the evidence provided, together with contextual information.[4]

## RELEVANCE THEORY: AIMS AND PRINCIPLES

### Relevance, Communication, and Cognition

Relevance theory treats utterance comprehension as an inferential process which starts from an observation of the speaker's communicative behaviour (or of the traces this behaviour leaves behind in the environment) and results in a plausible hypothesis about the speaker's intended import. The inference process involved is not a deductive one, where the truth of the premises guarantees the truth of the conclusion, but an 'inference to the best explanation', where the resulting hypothesis, however plausible and well evidenced, may still turn out to be false. On this approach, utterance comprehension is essentially an exercise in mind-reading, and the challenge in attempting to build a psychologically plausible pragmatic theory is precisely to explain how utterances in a public language such as English provide effective pieces of evidence which (combined with contextual information) enable the audience to recognize the speaker's intended import.

Relevance theory starts from the assumption that considerations of relevance play a fundamental role not only in communication but in cognition. Relevance is seen as a potential property not only of utterances or other ostensive acts, but of any perceptual stimulus (say, the sight of smoke coming out of a window) or internal representation (say, the memory of what happened at dinner last night)

---

[4] What follows is only a broad outline, designed to introduce the aspects of relevance theory that are most pertinent to literary questions. For fuller accounts, see Dan Sperber and Deirdre Wilson, *Relevance: Communication and Cognition* (Oxford: Blackwell, 2nd ed., 1995); Robyn Carston, *Thoughts and Utterances: The Pragmatics of Explicit Communication* (Oxford: Blackwell, 2002); Deirdre Wilson and Dan Sperber, *Meaning and Relevance* (Cambridge: Cambridge University Press, 2012); Billy Clark, *Relevance Theory* (Cambridge: Cambridge University Press, 2013).

that provides an input to cognitive processes. Thus, sights, sounds, smells, actions, thoughts, memories, or conclusions of inferences are all potentially relevant (to an individual, at a given time).

Intuitively, new information is relevant if, when added to an individual's existing assumptions, it produces a worthwhile cognitive effect: say, by answering a question, settling a doubt, correcting a mistake, suggesting a hypothesis or a plan of action, or combining with existing assumptions to yield a 'contextual implication' (derivable from new information and existing assumptions together, but from neither alone). A single piece of new information may achieve several such cognitive effects. For instance, the sight of an empty taxi rank when I am rushing to an appointment may make me revise my assumption that I left home early enough, contextually imply that I need an alternative means of transport, and strengthen my suspicion that today is not my lucky day. According to relevance theory, other things being equal, the greater the cognitive effects achieved, and the smaller the mental (or 'processing') effort required, the more relevant this input will be to me at the time.

The central claim of relevance theory is that as a result of constant selection pressures, the human cognitive system has evolved a variety of mental mechanisms whose function is to pick out potentially relevant stimuli and to process them in the most relevance-enhancing way. This claim is expressed in the cognitive principle of relevance ('Human cognition tends to be geared to the maximization of relevance.'). Why do we notice bright lights, loud noises, sudden movements, objects looming towards us rather than veering away? Because our perceptual systems are geared to picking out such stimuli, which are potentially more relevant than anything else we might have been attending to at the time. On this approach, what makes a stimulus relevant to an individual is that it interacts with contextual assumptions she has available to yield worthwhile cognitive effects, and what makes it *maximally* relevant to the individual is that it yields greater cognitive effects, for less processing effort, than any alternative information available to her at the time.

The claim that human cognition is geared to the maximization of relevance has immediate consequences for pragmatics. To communicate, the speaker needs the addressee's attention. Since attention tends to go automatically to what is most relevant at the time, the success of communication depends on the addressee's taking the utterance to be relevant enough to be worth the processing effort required. Thus, a speaker, by the very act of addressing someone, communicates that the utterance is relevant enough to be worth the addressee's attention, and this is what the communicative principle of relevance states ('Every act of ostensive communication creates a presumption of its own optimal relevance.'). To be *optimally* relevant, an ostensive act must achieve at least enough cognitive effects to be worth processing, and must, moreover, be the most relevant one compatible with the communicator's abilities and preferences. On this approach, although human cognition and communication are both geared to the search for relevance, ostensive acts raise expectations of relevance not raised by other stimuli, and these expectations guide the identification of the communicator's intended import.

## The Explicit and the Implicit

As noted above, in interpreting an utterance, the hearer invariably has to go beyond the linguistically encoded meaning of the sentence uttered. There will be ambiguities and referential indeterminacies to resolve; there may be implicatures to identify, illocutionary indeterminacies to resolve, metaphors and ironies to interpret. All this requires an appropriate set of contextual assumptions. According to relevance theory, there is a practical procedure that hearers can use in identifying the speaker's intended import: they should consider interpretive hypotheses (disambiguations, reference resolutions, contextual assumptions, implications, and other cognitive effects) in order of salience—that is, follow a path of least effort—and stop when they arrive at an interpretation that satisfies the expectations of relevance raised by the utterance.[5] Since communication takes place at a risk, this hypothesis, however plausible and well evidenced, may still be false, but it is the best a rational hearer can do.

Suppose you ask me out for a drink, for instance, and I say 'Sorry, I have to finish a paper.' In interpreting my utterance, you have to resolve a number of indeterminacies, deciding what type of paper I have in mind, what I must finish doing to the paper, and when I must finish it. Depending on how these indeterminacies are resolved, my utterance will be relevant to you in different ways. In the circumstances, you will expect it to be relevant by helping to explain my refusal to come for a drink, and you will try to resolve these indeterminacies so that they yield an overall interpretation that satisfies this expectation of relevance. The least effort-demanding (and therefore most relevance-enhancing) way of doing this may be to assume that I have to do something more arduous than finish reading a newspaper, and that I have to do it soon enough to prevent me accepting your invitation. The interpretation process is seen as taking place in 'parallel' rather than in sequence, with tentative hypotheses about explicit content (what I am asserting), contextual assumptions, and cognitive effects being mutually adjusted, with each other and with the expectation of relevance, until they yield an overall interpretation that makes the utterance relevant in the expected way.[6]

## The Figurative and the Literal

This account of ostensive communication, where the expression and recognition of intentions plays an essential role and coding is merely an optional extra, departs from standard assumptions about semantics and pragmatics in several ways that suit it well for use in literary studies. In the first place, it suggests that linguistically encoded sentence meaning—the type of context-independent meaning carried by sentences independently of the situations in which they are uttered—is quite

---

[5] For a fuller justification and illustration of this approach, see Deirdre Wilson and Dan Sperber, 'Truthfulness and relevance', *Mind*, 111 (2002), 583–632.

[6] For a recent outline of the basic assumptions of relevance theory, see Deirdre Wilson, 'Relevance theory', in Y. Huang (ed.) *The Oxford Handbook of Pragmatics* (Oxford: Oxford University Press, 2017).

fragmentary and incomplete, and has to be inferentially enriched in order to express a definite proposition. This is illustrated by our example above, where the linguistically encoded meaning of the utterance 'I have to finish a paper' can be fleshed out in various ways, yielding different hypotheses about the speaker's intended import. In many approaches to pragmatics, inferential intention recognition is seen as playing a significant role only on the implicit side of communication, while the identification of explicit content—what the speaker is taken to assert rather than merely imply or implicate—is seen as largely a matter of decoding. For relevance theorists, explicit communication is just as rich and inferential as implicit communication, and this has consequences for the interpretation of literary works.[7]

In the second place, relevance theorists reject the assumption, derived from classical rhetoric and present in most current formal semantic and pragmatic frameworks, that there is a norm of literal, plain speaking, and that figurative utterances are departures from this norm. Instead, they have been exploring the idea that many 'figurative' uses of language arise naturally in the pursuit of relevance, and require no special interpretive rules or mechanisms not required for ordinary, literal utterances. For instance, metaphor and hyperbole are seen as arising through a pragmatic process of 'meaning adjustment', or 'lexical modulation', which fine-tunes the encoded meaning of virtually every word.

Suppose I have just given a lecture and tell you, 'The audience slept throughout the lecture.' In different circumstances, you might interpret my use of 'sleep' in different ways. In some circumstances, you might understand me as making the very strong claim that the audience was literally asleep throughout the lecture: that is, that they were physically and mentally disengaged to the point of losing consciousness. In other circumstances, you might see me as making the slightly weaker claim that the audience was, if not literally asleep, at least on the point of falling asleep; in traditional terms, my utterance would then count as an approximation. Or you might take me to be claiming, still more weakly, that the audience was, if not asleep or on the point of sleep, at least closer to losing consciousness than might have been expected or desired; in traditional terms, my utterance would then count as a hyperbole. Finally, you might take me to be making a still weaker claim: that the audience, if not literally asleep, on the point of sleep, or even closer to falling asleep than might have been expected or desired, was at least extremely bored and unresponsive during the lecture: in traditional terms, my utterance would then count as a metaphor.

How are these different interpretations arrived at? Let's assume that the word 'sleep' encodes the concept SLEEP, which denotes the property of being literally asleep. Associated with this concept in memory is a variety of 'encyclopaedic' information—about the process of falling asleep, the circumstances in which people fall asleep, what people look like when they sleep, the physical and mental consequences of being asleep, and so on—which typically applies to some, but not all, instances of sleep, and is therefore not part of the context-independent meaning of

---

[7] See Carston, *Thoughts and Utterances*; François Recanati, *Literal Meaning* (Cambridge: Cambridge University Press, 2004); Wilson and Sperber, *Meaning and Relevance*.

the word. Some of this encyclopaedic information will be activated by any utterance containing the word 'sleep', and may contribute to the contextual implications and other cognitive effects that make it relevant in the expected way.

One of the original ideas of relevance theory is that humans have many more concepts than words, and can create new concepts on an 'ad hoc' basis by adapting or adjusting existing concepts. In interpreting my utterance, for instance, you may be able to use the encoded concept SLEEP to construct a whole series of such 'ad hoc' concepts (SLEEP*, SLEEP**, SLEEP*** . . . ) which share some, but not all, of the encyclopaedic information associated with SLEEP, have successively broader denotations, carry subtly different contextual implications, and therefore contribute to relevance in subtly different ways.[8] For instance, SLEEP* might correspond to the approximate interpretation described above, denoting not only people who are literally asleep but also people who are on the point of sleep; SLEEP** might correspond to a hyperbolic interpretation, applying not only to people who are literally asleep or on the point of sleep but also those who are closer to sleep than might have been expected or desired, and SLEEP*** might correspond to a metaphorical interpretation with a still broader denotation.

Which of these possibilities should you choose in interpreting my utterance? According to the relevance-guided comprehension heuristic described above, you should follow a path of least effort in looking for contextual implications (and other cognitive effects), and stop when you have enough to satisfy your expectations of relevance. Knowing that I have just given a lecture, the most salient implication of my utterance for you would probably be that the students were extremely disengaged and unresponsive. This would in turn lead on to a range of further implications (that the lecture was not a success, that the students were disappointed, that I may need some sympathy or reassurance after the failure of the lecture, and so on) which might well satisfy your expectations of relevance without your having to consider any further contextual implications derivable from the literal concept SLEEP. In that case, a rather loose and metaphorical interpretation on which the students SLEPT*** throughout the lecture but were not physically and mentally disengaged to the point of losing consciousness would be enough to make my utterance relevant in the expected way.[9]

'Sleep' is a fairly standard metaphor, with a few salient implications (having to do with inattention, lack of engagement, and unresponsiveness) on which most hearers would agree. The interpretations of poetic metaphors vary more widely, and have an 'open-ended' quality that is sometimes seen as putting them beyond the scope of standard theories of communication. Here is the philosopher

---

[8] In this framework, lexically encoded concepts are represented in small capitals (SLEEP) and newly created 'ad hoc' concepts are indicated by the use of asterisks (SLEEP*, SLEEP**...).

[9] On lexical adjustment and ad hoc concepts, see Dan Sperber and Deirdre Wilson, 'The mapping between the mental and the public lexicon', in Peter Carruthers and Jill Boucher (eds) *Language and Thought: Interdisciplinary Themes* (Cambridge: Cambridge University Press, 1998); Deirdre Wilson and Robyn Carston, 'A unitary account of lexical pragmatics: relevance, inference and ad hoc concepts', in Noel Burton-Roberts (ed.) *Pragmatics* (Basingstoke: Palgrave Macmillan, 2007).

Stanley Cavell on the interpretation of 'Juliet is the sun' (a favourite metaphor of philosophers of language):[10]

> Romeo means that Juliet is the warmth of his world; that his day begins with her; that only in her nourishment can he grow. And his declaration suggests that the moon, which other lovers use as emblem of their love, is merely her reflected light, and dead in comparison, and so on. ... The 'and so on' which ends my example of paraphrase is significant. It registers what William Empson calls 'the pregnancy of metaphors', the burgeoning of meaning in them. (1965/76: 78)

This element of indeterminacy and open-endedness in the interpretation of many metaphors has led philosophers such as Donald Davidson to deny that metaphors have 'meaning' (as philosophers understand the term) at all:

> When we try to say what a metaphor 'means', we soon realise that there is no end to what we want to mention. If someone draws his finger along a coastline on a map ... how many things are drawn to your attention? You might list a great many, but you could not finish since the idea of finishing has no clear application. How many facts or propositions are conveyed by a photograph? (1978: 48–9)

Davidson's comments are based on the assumption, shared by many philosophers and linguists, that the 'meaning' of an utterance must be capable of being rendered as a single proposition, or at most a small set of propositions. For Davidson, though, the problem goes further: it is not just that what a metaphor communicates does not fit the standard philosophical definition of 'meaning', but that metaphors do not communicate anything at all:

> The central error about metaphor is most easily attacked when it takes the form of a theory of metaphorical meaning, but behind that theory, and statable independently, is the thesis that associated with a metaphor is a cognitive content that its author wishes to convey and that the interpreter must grasp if he is to get the message. This theory is false, whether or not we call the purported cognitive content a meaning.
> (1978: 46)[11]

As we have seen in analysing the interpretation of 'sleep' above, relevance theorists take a different view. On this approach, there is a continuum of successively broader interpretations with no clear cut-off point between them: literal use shades off into approximation, approximation shades off into hyperbole, and hyperbole shades off into metaphor. To claim that metaphor falls outside the scope of a theory of communication is therefore the tip of a slippery slope. If we exclude metaphor, shouldn't we exclude hyperbole and approximation, which also introduce an element of indeterminacy into the interpretation process? In fact, the literal meaning of virtually every word is adjusted in the course of the comprehension

---

[10] Stanley Cavell, 'Aesthetic problems of modern philosophy', in Max Black (ed.) *Philosophy in America* (Ithaca, NY: Cornell University Press, 1965); reprinted in Stanley Cavell, *Must We Mean What We Say?* (Cambridge: Cambridge University Press, 1976), pp. 73–96.

[11] For more recent arguments along these lines, see Ernie Lepore and Matthew Stone, *Imagination and Convention: Distinguishing Grammar and Inference in Language* (Oxford: Oxford University Press, 2015).

process, and to exclude all but literal meaning from the scope of a theory of communication risks leaving it with nothing to explain.

Relevance theorists set out from the start to explain a much wider range of phenomena than are typically discussed in linguistics and philosophy of language. Showing a map or a photograph is a typical ostensive act, and so is the production of a poetic metaphor. Like other ostensive acts, they raise expectations of relevance, and may yield enough cognitive effects, at a low enough processing cost, to satisfy those expectations. In this framework, there is no reason to suppose that what is communicated must be capable of being rendered as a single proposition or a small set of propositions.

According to relevance theory, the import of an ostensive act consists of an *array* of propositions which may differ from each other in strength or salience: some may be strongly evidenced by the speaker's communicative behaviour while others are less so, and some may become highly salient to the addressee while others are less so. The array itself may contain a huge range of propositions or only a few, with a continuum of cases in between. At one extreme, the array might consist of a single salient, strongly evidenced proposition, or a small set of propositions that can be individually enumerated. At the other extreme (showing a photograph of the view from one's hotel window, for instance, or saying 'Juliet is the sun'), it might consist of an indefinite range of implications that cannot be individually enumerated but may be characterized by a description ('what I can see from my hotel window', 'the impression Juliet makes on Romeo'). On this approach, showing a photograph and producing a poetic metaphor fall squarely within the scope of a theory of ostensive communication.

In explaining the indeterminacy and open-endedness of the interpretations of many utterances, relevance theorists start from the assumption that the communicator's goal is not to induce a specific belief in the audience, but to make an array of propositions *more manifest* to them. A proposition is manifest to an individual to the extent that it is salient and strongly evidenced, or, in other words, to the extent that the individual is likely to entertain it and accept it as true, or probably true. Communication may then be thought of as *stronger* or *weaker* depending on the manifest strength of the speaker's intention to make a certain proposition manifest (or more manifest) to the addressee. An example of strong communication would be answering a clear 'Yes' to the question 'Is your name on the electoral register?' Examples of weak communication *in this sense* include the metaphor 'Juliet is the sun', where the communicator has in mind a vague range of possible implications with roughly similar import, any subset of which would help to satisfy expectations of relevance. The intended import would then be an array of weakly communicated propositions—'weak implicatures'—often described as a 'poetic effect'.

It should be emphasized that the 'strong'–'weak' opposition implies no judgement of the value of the utterance in question, or of its communicative power. Readers of literature and theatre audiences will very probably judge that 'Juliet is the sun' is a powerfully communicative utterance: more so, for example, than 'Juliet is smiling' or 'Juliet is wearing a red dress', both of which would count as communicating fairly strongly in relevance theory terms. In other words, the power of the 'poetic effect' (and therefore of the communication itself) is often likely to be in inverse proportion to the strength of the implicatures, precisely because of the imaginative reach (in the hands of a skilled writer) of the 'array'.[12]

## Echoic Utterances and Irony

Throughout its history, the term 'irony' has been applied to a wide range of loosely related phenomena, not all of which fall squarely within the domain of a theory of ostensive communication (for instance, situational irony, dramatic irony, Romantic irony, and irony of fate do not). Relevance theorists have been mainly concerned with verbal irony: for instance, saying 'He's a fine friend' of someone who has betrayed us, or 'It's lovely weather' in the pouring rain. In line with the aim of showing that many 'figurative' uses of language arise naturally in the pursuit of relevance, and require no special interpretive rules or mechanisms not required for ordinary, literal utterances, they analyse irony as a type of 'echoic' utterance in which the speaker tacitly expresses a mocking, scornful, or contemptuous attitude to a thought—for instance, a hope, a belief, or a norm-based expectation—that she tacitly attributes to some other person or group of people, or to humans in general.[13]

Suppose Jack and Sue are leaving the cinema and Jack says admiringly, 'That was a fantastic film.' Sue might respond in one of three ways. She might nod and say 'Fantastic!', echoing Jack's opinion and making clear that she agrees with it. Or she might say, cautiously, 'Fantastic?', again echoing Jack's opinion but indicating this time that she is doubtful about it or unsure that she has heard it correctly. Or she might say wryly, 'Fantastic', in a deadpan, mocking, or contemptuous tone of voice, indicating that she does not share Jack's opinion and rejects it with scorn. In that case, her utterance would be a typical case of verbal irony. On this approach, irony should arise naturally and spontaneously in speakers who have the capacity, on the one hand, to produce echoic utterances, and on the other, to express their own mocking, scornful, or contemptuous attitude to the echoed thought.

Of course, not all verbal irony is a response to a thought expressed in an immediately preceding utterance, or indeed to a thought expressed in an utterance at all. In saying 'He's a fine friend', I may be ironically echoing what I have been told about my new acquaintance, but I may equally be echoing unexpressed hopes I had, or a norm-based expectation that he *ought* to be a good friend. Typically, irony is directed at the failure of human hopes, or the violation of moral norms which are endemic in a social group, and are thus always available for echoing in that group. More generally, verbal irony is related to varieties of tacit quotation

---

[12] On strength of communication and strength of implicatures, see Dan Sperber and Deirdre Wilson, 'A deflationary account of metaphors', in R. Gibbs (ed.) *The Cambridge Handbook of Metaphor and Thought* (Cambridge: Cambridge University Press, 2008), pp. 98–103.

[13] For a survey of current approaches to irony, see Deirdre Wilson and Dan Sperber, 'Explaining irony', in Deirdre Wilson and Dan Sperber, *Meaning and Relevance* (Cambridge: Cambridge University Press, 2012).

or allusion that have been much studied in literary works, and benefits from being approached in that wider context.

## Processing Effort and Style

Relevance theory takes seriously the idea that utterance interpretation is a cognitive matter. It therefore assigns a central role in its account of comprehension to the notion of *processing effort*, which plays little role in formal approaches to pragmatics but has been well studied by psycholinguists.

To see the importance of processing effort in both cognition and communication, consider first the *form* in which information is presented. Imagine exactly the same information being presented to you, first in a clearly printed form; second as a faint photocopy; third as an illegible handwritten scrawl; fourth translated into a language you read only with difficulty. Each of these forms may give access to exactly the same cognitive effects, but each will differ in the amount of processing effort required to produce those effects, and this may affect your intuitions of relevance, and indeed your willingness to attend to the information at all. More generally, information may be presented in a form which makes it more or less perceptually salient, more or less legible, more or less linguistically or logically complex, and which therefore demands more or less processing effort from the individual to whom it is presented.

Some of the factors known to affect the processing effort required in interpreting an utterance include recency or frequency of use: the more recently or frequently a word, a concept, a sound, a syntactic construction, or a contextual assumption has been used, the less processing effort it is likely to require. Thus, the most frequently used sense of an ambiguous word, and the most recently mentioned potential referent for a pronoun or other referential expression, is likely to be most salient, and therefore the first to be considered by a hearer following the path of least effort. By building the notion of processing effort into the definition of relevance, we therefore make it possible to take all these factors into account in explaining how speakers and writers choose to formulate their utterances, how the resulting utterances are understood, and how their stylistic felicity is assessed.[14]

According to relevance theory, a speaker who wants to be understood should aim to make her utterance *optimally relevant*: that is, it should be at least relevant enough to be worth the hearer's processing effort, and moreover, the most relevant one—producing the greatest cognitive effects for the least processing effort—compatible with her own abilities and preferences. It is perhaps worth emphasizing here that this does not entail minimizing processing effort at all costs. The claim is not that speakers should choose the utterance that makes the fewest possible demands on the addressee's processing effort: it is that, however rich and complex the intended import, they should avoid causing the addressee *gratuitous* processing effort, and this is equally true of everyday utterances and literary texts. An

---

[14] As noted above, other things being equal, the greater the cognitive effects achieved, and the smaller the processing effort required, the greater the relevance.

utterance can be as difficult as you like, as long as there was no more economical way of conveying exactly the intended effects. Thus, the 'difficulty' of many religious texts and some literary and philosophical works is quite compatible with the search for optimal relevance.

## RELEVANCE AND LITERARY THEORY

What makes an approach based on relevance theory different from prevailing trends of literary study, and indeed from some other kinds of cognitive approach to literature? The most far-reaching premise of relevance theory is its insistence that a code model is inadequate on its own to account for the pragmatics of communication. A good deal of literary theory since the mid-twentieth century has been nourished by the assumption (derived, broadly speaking, from the linguistics of Saussure and Jakobson) that language is a code; from that assumption has arisen in turn the notion that literary form may be regarded as a second-order code. Many varieties of such arguments have been proposed, but they all have as their corollary a marked tendency towards formalism, in the spirit of the pioneering work of the Russian formalism of the earlier twentieth century, together with the Prague school, and the preoccupation with code-like features—conventions, devices, and the like—has been an enduring aspect of literary criticism since the days of structuralism. A perspective based on relevance theory would not deny that language is a code, but it would argue that what it encodes is much too fragmentary and incomplete to *make sense* on its own. Linguistic devices are the instruments of the labile, ever-shifting, temporally and culturally unstable flow of communicative language use across the whole spectrum from casual throw-away remarks between individuals who know each other well to the extraordinary extended utterances, preserved by technologies of memory, print, and electronic media, we know as literature. It is that flow, ceaselessly enriched and adjusted by mainly unreflective processes of inference, that is the object of the readings in this book. It lends itself to the vocabulary of salience and emergence (properties that emerge out of or fade away from a dynamic cognitive context, itself constantly reconfigured) and to notions such as the reflective pause, the 'passing theory', the array of implications or implicatures.

We may mention in passing here that relevance theory's idea that every ostensive act is interpreted in a cognitive context constructed in the course of the comprehension process applies not only to acts of everyday conversational exchange, but also to utterances that have been set adrift in time and therefore require a continuing process of contextual resuscitation at any number of levels, whether linguistic, factual, political, ideological, religious, ethical, or aesthetic. Such recontextualization is the staple goods of literary criticism and literary history. Relevance theorists would also agree that the contexts of communicator and audience rarely overlap entirely. Some aspects of the intended interpretation may remain permanently hidden from the audience; others may suddenly become so salient that they take up all the attention one can muster at a particular moment, and thus risk skewing the picture. The downstream conversation in which literary works continue to be re-read and rediscussed will in such cases foster 'corrections' (in something like the 'market' sense of the word), although never a definitive account.

One of the predominant trends of literary theory over the last fifty years has been the removal of the author as a living person from the interpretative scene, whether via Barthes's famous 'death of the author' or Foucault's equally famous essay on what he calls 'the author function'. These moves have been qualified in recent decades as the shift towards ethical questions (for example, in gender studies and postcolonial studies) has brought human agency back into prominence. According to the perspective offered in this book, language is indeed a remarkable instrument of human agency, affording its users vastly increased possibilities of cooperation, social organization, mutual intelligibility, memory and planning operations, and (not least) alternative modes of thought, including literature in the broad anthropological sense of the word indicated above. As a vehicle of communication, it is flexible, dynamic, always reaching after new ways of capturing the nuances of perception and experience. That perspective, however, is by no means naively optimistic: as we remarked earlier, the view of communication offered by relevance theory is one that always acknowledges the possibility of uncertainty, dysfunction, and downright failure. As Wilson and Sperber put it, 'Failures in communication are common enough: what is remarkable and calls for explanation is that communication works at all.'[15]

The corollary of the 'death of the author' was the erasure of intention from the vocabulary of literary criticism, a disappearance which had in fact already been foreshadowed in the New Criticism, with its emphasis on 'the words on the page'. Likewise, in various modes of later twentieth-century literary study, intention has emerged as a stumbling-block, to the point in some quarters of being banned from the critical vocabulary.[16]

The contributors to this volume readily accept that literary utterances are not immediate, face-to-face communications: as we have already remarked, they soon begin to move away from their originator and from their context of enunciation. What is more, the status of what they are designed to communicate is very different from much everyday conversation, since in most cases they are not meant to deliver informative or useful propositions in the everyday sense. One might be tempted to say that their *relevance* is of a kind quite different from that of everyday communication. It would be a mistake, however, to argue that this functional difference suggests some radically other cognitive regime, or that the intentional aspect of an utterance is thereby disabled or irrecoverable. Humans spend their time making subtle discriminations to calibrate and recalibrate the relation of their cognitive representations to the real world. In ordinary conversation, speakers routinely employ rhetorical strategies which are of a kind with those used in fiction and indeed in poetic imaginings. They play with language to make their intentions

---

[15] See 'Truthfulness and relevance', p. 606.

[16] For a historical survey and discussion, see John Farrell, *The Varieties of Authorial Intention: Literary Theory Beyond the Intentional Fallacy* (Basingstoke: Palgrave Macmillan, 2017).

clearer (and sometimes to disguise them); and a good deal of casual conversation is also removed from any immediate 'external' relevance to the world 'out there'. Conversely, the production of a work of literature is an ostensive act which raises expectations of relevance, whether through its linguistic register or its generic framing: it seeks to convince the reader that something valuable is being expressed, perhaps all the more so because it is free from the criterion of immediate, practical relevance. It *remains* relevant, one might say; its very function is to achieve a higher-order relevance which can inflect the cognitive environment of future readers in unexpected ways. Those are not effects of accident, or of a neutral textuality operating in a medium of pure relativism. Readers continue to assess what they think literary works mean, and in order to do so they make inferences about what kinds of meaning are intended. Otherwise there would be no point in annotating historically distant works in order to inform readers about linguistic and context-ual matters: Shakespeare's intentions are not directly observable, but most people who watch his plays find themselves caught up in the activity of inferring the intentions of the human agent who wrote them. It's true that a director and a company of actors will have intervened, with intentions of their own, to deflect the way the play is experienced towards another mode of relevance. Yet even in that case, the audience knows that there is an interplay between what they are watching and a set of utterances deeply informed by an earlier intentionality.

In that light, declarations of the death of the author and of intention seem premature. The reading of literature presupposes the agency of an author, or a group or series of authors (whether identifiable or not), and this presupposition constrains in variable degrees the act of understanding. On the side of the reader or audience, the assessment of intentionality may well be automatic and unreflective—if it were not, the communicative flow would be constantly interrupted. In literary studies, it is true, the critical act of understanding is distinctively reflective, and in many fictions (including dramatic ones), the whole point may well be that the intentional calculus of the characters is made explicit. This does not mean, however, that liter-ary criticism and interpretation must work with a determinate, transparent model of intentionality. As in everyday situations, what the character or author thinks she intends may well be porous to pre-intentional vectors, emotionally grounded or indeed psychologically duplicitous, and literary works often derive powerful effects from these endemic features of human communication.

The remarks made above about intentional 'drift' in historical works of literature already begin to provide an answer to a further question that is often asked by people encountering for the first time approaches such as the one adopted in this book. The assumption relevance theory makes is that the cognitive and communi-cative principles of relevance apply regardless of the particular language and culture of speakers and hearers. Would a literary methodology inflected by relevance theory not erase the cultural and historical differences, the local singularities, which are the lifeblood of literary works?

The first answer is that relevance theory not only allows for but actually depends on the notions of context and cognitive environment, both of which necessarily depend in turn on the cultural resources and general knowledge available at the time of utterance. Later readers may to a greater or lesser extent take the trouble to equip themselves with at least some of these resources: if they read Chaucer, for example, they will need to learn some Middle English. They will also draw inferences from the text itself about the intended interpretation of references or other semantic elements which are historically or culturally obscure to them. That kind of practice is not confined to literature, of course. If a born-and-bred citizen of the UK takes a holiday in Australia (a fortiori Saudi Arabia or Nigeria) and reads a local newspaper, a good deal of what they find there will require some elucidation by inference (or online searches), not only for news items, but also for lexical items, cartoons, headlines, and other underspecified materials.

The second answer is that relevance theory seeks to uncover deeper cognitive strategies which largely pass unnoticed in ordinary communication because most cognition is extremely rapid and unreflective. The analytic instruments offered by relevance theory can reach features of a literary text which otherwise remain hidden for the same reason. They don't offer a hermeneutics as such, but they provide a powerful propaedeutic for interpretation. As we have already indicated, far from erasing or bypassing the culturally embedded aspect of the text, they can in fact only be deployed in conjunction with historical protocols of the kind literary scholars commonly use. One of the consequences of such analyses will be to uncover evidence of how the cognitive affordances[17] studied by relevance theorists are realized in different cultures and historical periods. That evidence in turn might help to enlarge the archival repertory of relevance theory, if not to inflect or refine the theory itself.

One further distinction may be useful here. The cognitive attentiveness (whether reflective or unreflective) which is fundamental to the relevance theory model of communication is quite different from the 'hermeneutics of suspicion' (also known simply as 'critique') which has been such a central aspect of literary theory since the later twentieth century and remains a defining point of reference in gender studies, postcolonial studies, and related fields where ethical and ideological critique is regarded as essential.[18] The hermeneutics of suspicion is based on the assumption that writers (or 'texts') are ideologically or psychologically blind to at least some of their own fundamental assumptions. That may be so in certain communicative situations, but those situations are not the ones that a theory of ostensive communication is primarily concerned with. The question of how such factors are dealt with in literary instances has already been raised in this Introduction, and will form an intermittent thread in the essays that follow. Broadly speaking, however, what one might call the ideological imperative that is intrinsic to the hermeneutics of suspicion is regarded here as only one historically and culturally bound variant of a more comprehensive cognitive alertness to potential error.

---

[17] Affordances are the opportunities a given environment affords to the creatures that inhabit it; or in the context of human cultures, the means devised by users of a culture to pursue their various purposes; see Cave, *Thinking with Literature*, ch. 4.

[18] For a counter-argument, see Rita Felski, *The Limits of Critique* (Chicago, IL: University of Chicago Press, 2015).

The phrase 'epistemic vigilance' has been coined by Dan Sperber and his colleagues in discussing how hearers deal with the problem of misinformation (deliberate or accidental) which inevitably arises in communication.[19] Verbal communication enormously increases the ability of individuals to mislead one another, either in order to gain an advantage for themselves or because their own sources of knowledge are imperfect. An epistemically vigilant addressee has the capacity to assess the trustworthiness of the speaker and the reliability of the communicated information, and a constant monitoring of this type is (in principle) required if the threat of deception is to be averted. The activity we call 'criticism' (as in the phrase 'literary criticism') may be seen as an instance of epistemic vigilance in reflective mode. It should be noted, however, that epistemic vigilance is not a constraint on the cognitive fluidity of the imagination. On the contrary, it licenses imaginative activity within the domains that are appropriate to it (scientific insight, historical reconstruction, prediction of future possibilities, thought-experiments, or the endlessly extensible realms of fiction). It does not imply any particular critical or ideological investment, but rather a deeply human alertness to the ways we can misconstrue the world and each other.

The view presented above of the relation between relevance theory and the literary theories of the last half-century leaves aside many complicating issues and some potential areas of agreement. Relevance theory, for example, shares with literary theory the rejection of an oppositional distinction between 'literal' and 'figurative' modes of expression and communication. It is perfectly possible to imagine, in the long run, a reconceptualization on both sides that would reduce or even remove most of the differences we have described. Meanwhile, the contributors to this volume, while broadly sharing the editors' views as outlined here, have in some cases preferred to adopt their own line of approach and their own critical vocabulary. An exemplary case is the use of the term 'intertextual(ity)', the 'strong' sense of which (a relation between texts as such, without reference to authors, influence, originality, and the like) is incompatible with relevance theory's emphasis on ostensive communication, but which, in the now widely adopted 'weaker' sense (any kind of relation between texts), arguably remains valid in the context of this book. We collectively believe that this critical flexibility will give our arguments a wider diffusion, and, we hope, promote further discussion and reflection on the underlying issues.

## RELEVANCE THEORY AND EMBODIED COGNITION

One of the principal objectives of this book is to focus not only on what literary studies can gain from adopting a relevance theory perspective, but also on how the properties of literature and the skills of literary specialists might inflect that perspective. In other words, the relationship between the disciplines is seen here as

---

[19] See Dan Sperber, Fabrice Clément, Christophe Heintz, Olivier Mascaro, Hugo Mercier, Gloria Origgi, and Deirdre Wilson, 'Epistemic vigilance', *Mind and Language*, 25.4 (2010), 359–93.

reciprocal. Literary ways of thinking and communicating are of a kind with everyday ones, but the balance is different; other effects and other segments of the communicative spectrum become salient. In addition, there is a historical factor: the interdisciplinary context in which a debate between relevance theorists and literary specialists might evolve has changed in recent decades.

Central to our debate here is that what is now often referred to as 'first-generation' cognitive research has in the last two or three decades been supplemented by a conception of 'embodied cognition' which has considerable appeal to literary specialists and which treats the body beyond the brain as playing a crucial cognitive role.[20] There are several competing versions of this approach but they all start from the assumption that human cognition is organic and has evolved biologically. The brain itself, by which cognition becomes possible, is a physical organ, albeit an extraordinarily complex one, and the way it functions is at all times saturated with and inflected by inputs from the body as a whole. In that light, cognition can no longer be conceived as primarily geared to rational thought rather than to action, or as ontologically and functionally distinct from emotion, imagination, and motor response. Nor can it be regarded as separate from the environment in which it operates, the total human ecology (which of course includes human societies and cultures). Some have indeed argued that we should regard cognition as extending beyond the body, as becoming instantiated by all the supports or instruments by means of which humans seek to survive, prosper, extend their grasp on the world they live in.[21] This notion of 'extended mind' or 'distributed cognition', like the notion of embodied cognition itself, remains controversial, but it has an imaginative reach which makes it attractive to literary specialists.

One way of thinking about cognition as embodied is to pay attention to the two-way traffic between the body as a whole and the specialized neurology of the brain. No one doubts that the human mind is capable of higher-order functions which include the ability to derive from the seemingly irreducible tangle of the perceived environment general categories, concepts, and principles which give us a huge evolutionary advantage. But it would be a mistake to believe that thinking in general goes on at a level of high abstraction, or that all the activities we think of as mental are invariably 'top-down'. The neurological evidence suggests rather that 'top-down' thinking is at all times dynamically interacting with 'bottom-up' cognition; that is to say, the flow of perceptions, proprioceptive sensations, motor responses, and emotional impulses.

Language processing is a central aspect of human cognition, and the same points apply there too. Even those who lean towards a view of language in which abstraction and conceptualization are dominant accept that language is deeply interwoven with sensorimotor processing and that natural languages, which are acquired by speakers (first in infancy, but then through a lifetime process of enrichment) in

---

[20] On embodied cognition, see Robert A. Wilson and Lucia Foglia, 'Embodied cognition', in Edward N. Zalta (ed.) *The Stanford Encyclopedia of Philosophy* (Spring 2017 edition), https://plato. stanford.edu/archives/spr2017/entries/embodied-cognition.

[21] For a comprehensive presentation of this argument, see Andy Clark, *Supersizing the Mind: Embodiment, Action, and Cognitive Extension* (New York: Oxford University Press, 2011).

concrete situations, are saturated with echoes of the contexts and activities in which language first began to 'make sense' for them. These echoes may no longer be active—consciously deployed by the speaker or resonant for the hearer—but they provide a pre-reflective grounding for the capacity of language to enhance the human species' cognitive grasp of the world. They arise from 'procedural' memories (fully assimilated and no longer conscious memories of how to do things) as well as the cultural memories that form such a large part of the context of communication. Many cognitive approaches to language have thus moved decisively away from the post-Saussurean view of language as a string of purely arbitrary or conventional signs, detached from the natural world and indeed inhibiting access to it.[22]

If this is a plausible model for everyday communication, it is a fortiori plausible for literary uses of language. Powerful sensorimotor effects are especially evident in 'poetic' diction (whether prose or verse), while situationally acquired resonances are reinforced, indeed often made explicit, by a wide range of strategies of mutual enhancement (unexpected collocation) and figurative extension.

Guillemette Bolens has explored effects such as these across a broad spectrum of literary works, and they are the focus of attention in many of the contributions to this volume.[23] Chapters 7 and 8, for example, both address in a relevance theory perspective the classic question of the relation between metaphorical and so-called literal meaning, but all the contributors to this volume have spent a good deal of time discussing the relevance of these issues to the reading and analysis of literary works, and above all the question of whether classic relevance theory is compatible with an embodied account of language. What has emerged is a consensus that relevance theory recognizes the role of the body in cognition and communication; that it is concerned with the cognitive and communicative effects of both verbal and non-verbal acts; and that it accepts that communicative acts are often laden with features which trigger sensorimotor or affective responses (or both) in the hearer. It has productively explored the attitudinal effects achieved by irony and other evocations of mood, and of course the resonances of metaphor. In that sense, there are no theoretical obstacles to a view of communication that would satisfy both relevance theorists and literary specialists. It might of course not satisfy everyone in both camps. There are differences of emphasis and perspective which can, in individual cases, emerge as uncrossable red lines. Debates among the contributors to this volume, and among the participants in the project from which it emerges, have sometimes been sharp; but they have evolved towards a sense of common understanding and common purpose. This Introduction, together with the 'interlace' (see Preface, p. viii), is designed to sketch a frame or perspective for

---

[22] This does not mean, of course, that linguistic signs are not in some sense conventional in themselves: to be intelligible at all, language must rely heavily on lexical and grammatical convention. But these conventions are acquired and used ecologically: they are grounded in perception and action within a given world. See Diane Pecher and Rolf A. Zwaan (eds), *Grounding Cognition: The Role of Perception and Action in Memory, Language, and Thinking* (Cambridge: Cambridge University Press, 2005) for a helpful collection of studies on these questions.

[23] See Guillemette Bolens, *The Style of Gestures: Embodiment and Cognition in Literary Narrative* (Baltimore, MD: The Johns Hopkins University Press, 2012); original version: *Le Style des gestes: corporéité et kinésie dans le récit littéraire* (Lausanne: Editions BHMS, 2008).

the individual contributions, which will explore in a number of quite specific cases what happens when relevance theory is adapted for the study of literature, and the consequences one might draw from that adaptive process. It is not the purpose of our book finally to close a debate which, we hope, will continue to thrive: premature closure is not the best way to investigate phenomena as complex as those studied here.

# Interlace 1

*Elleke Boehmer's reading of W.B. Yeats's 'Long-legged Fly' is designed to open a window on poetry, and thence literature in general, as a way of thinking that invites a reciprocal act of thought. The reading is 'cognitive' in that it makes salient the special mode of thought the poem reiterates as its central theme: the reflective moment that engenders a world-changing act of cognition. At the same time, in a non-intrusive way, it also begins to insist on a methodology of reading which is informed and inflected by an inferential model of communication, enhanced by a pragmatics of sensorimotor effect, widely referred to in this volume via the notions of kinesis and kinesic intelligence.*

*In literary studies, the given nature of the object of knowledge—literary specialists seldom write poems or novels of their own which they can then proceed to analyse—imposes the obligation always to consider its properties as what one might crudely call a 'package'. Lyric poems, novels, and other literary utterances are complex and to a significant extent unguessable entities. Not only are their original contexts and intentionalities often remote from us; they also typically bind together elements of meaning, affect, and kinesic response in an amalgam that cannot without loss be disassembled into their constituent parts. We can work towards them and anticipate their properties, but at the expense of a formalism that can at times pre-empt precisely that which they have to offer us. Literary reflection and analysis take us first to an intuition of how—and why— these strangely intricate artefacts are 'put together', and of the still largely unfathomable processes from which they emerge. We begin, then, with a poem that evokes in each of its stanzas a moment of hovering reflection, a cognitive pause, which might be taken as the model for any literary reading that seeks to modify and enrich the cognitive environment of the reader.*

# 1

# The Mind in Motion
## A Cognitive Reading of W.B. Yeats's 'Long-legged Fly'

*Elleke Boehmer*

That civilization may not sink,
Its great battle lost,
Quiet the dog, tether the pony
To a distant post;
Our master Caesar is in the tent
Where the maps are spread,
His eyes fixed upon nothing,
A hand under his head.
*Like a long-legged fly upon the stream*
*His mind moves upon silence.*

That the topless towers be burnt
And men recall that face,
Move most gently if move you must
In this lonely place.
She thinks, part woman, three parts a child,
That nobody looks; her feet
Practise a tinker shuffle
Picked up on a street.
*Like a long-legged fly upon the stream*
*Her mind moves upon silence.*

That girls at puberty may find
The first Adam in their thought,
Shut the door of the Pope's chapel,
Keep those children out.
There on that scaffolding reclines
Michael Angelo.
With no more sound than the mice make
His hand moves to and fro.
*Like a long-legged fly upon the stream*
*His mind moves upon silence.*

## THE MIND'S SELF-EXPERIENCE: THE POEM
## DRAWS IN THE READER

W.B. Yeats's 'Long-legged Fly' is a lyric poem that insists upon thought and upon silence; it asks for respect for thinking.[1] From its first word, the unusual and arresting purposive 'That', it pauses us, the reader or listener; it holds a finger to the lips—a finger that later, as we will see, will again point, single out, and then forestall. Quiet, the poem says, tiptoe, be still. Approach softly, 'gently'. By the third line of each stanza the opening purpose clause has shifted into an imperative that then modulates into a scenario, a demonstration. Why must we be still? In brief, to make space for 'thought', or so that thinking may take its course. More particularly, so that Julius Caesar may ponder the further course of Roman history. So that Helen, later of Troy, may perfect her beguiling grace. And so that Michelangelo, here 'Michael Angelo', may paint transformative beauty on the Sistine Chapel's ceiling.

Quietening us in this way, 'Long-legged Fly' stages across its three stanzas three states of meditation or reflection, each one represented as a process, taking up time, and yet also as stillness, an arrested moment in time. In each case the reader is presented with the physically still mind that is nonetheless in some sense in motion, reflecting—a complex sensory and cognitive state that is then captured or encapsulated in the poem's repeating simile of the long-legged fly. The still mind in motion is compared to a fly suspended on the still surface of a moving stream, held poised by the surface tension of the water, yet at the same time moving as the current moves, and itself moving, ever so slightly, imperceptibly adjusting its balance, shifting leg to leg on the surface of the water.

Observe, even in this brief account, an element of 'Long-legged Fly' that will inform my reading throughout. The process of making thought manifest in language that takes place in the poem, we immediately see, is not carried out only at an explicated, meta-textual level; that is, a level at which we readers objectively watch the process being demonstrated and worked out in the writing. This is the more conventional way in which 'thought' might be represented and discussed in literary critical writing. Instead, in this poem, we are as reader-participants drawn into the thinking process even as we observe it. Our thinking about thinking finds its shape through the unfolding poem as we read, and as we project ourselves imaginatively into the meditative scenarios presented to us. As we read through, each one of the three stanzas presents to us a state of contemplation, each considering how the mind in deep thought might be experienced from the outside, and at the same time rendering something of the experience of that mind thinking, enacted in the figure of the fly. As this suggests, the different modes of reflection interact concentrically throughout, held in tension the one beside the other—the reading mind, the observing mind contemplating other minds, and those different minds in states of reflection.

---

[1] This reading draws on the Everyman's Library edition of Yeats's poems: W.B. Yeats, *The Poems*, edited by Daniel Albright (London: Dent, 1992).

Unfolding in time and yet captured in an arrested pose or a repetitive movement: thinking in the three stanzas thus manifests as at once diachronic and synchronic; as a process and as a fixed image (Caesar's hand upon his head, the pattern of Helen's shuffle dance, Michael Angelo's hand painting back and forth). Suggestively, the same interplay of flow and containment is highlighted in the account that relevance theory gives of the comprehension process; that is, of its ongoing mutual adjustment of hypotheses as to content, implications, and context. According to relevance theory, as an utterance proceeds, the addressee is involved in a continual balancing of inferences concerning 'the communicator's informative and communicative intentions', a balancing not unlike that moving to and fro of Michelangelo's hand, or of the fly's steadying legs.[2] The spreading proliferation of possible meanings that the utterance generates is repeatedly and sequentially constrained by the addressee or reader as they process new elements (reference assignments, contextual assumptions, implications) that unfold as part of the same communicative flow. So, too, in 'Long-legged Fly', thinking involves the dynamic, even cantilevered, balancing of oppositions: of fluidity and stasis; of openness and restraint; of plenitude (as of the dance) and emptiness ('nothing'); of the mind-animated body (Helen dancing, Michelangelo's hand) and the embodied mind (Caesar's hand, the awareness driving Helen's feet). Pause and attend, the poem requests, or, more precisely, attend to attention (its suspended energy, its poise); and then, in each stanza, and within each described scene, the poem creates a space or affordance for such attention; it induces focus and draws the reader in.

In these and other ways, 'Long-legged Fly' creates an exemplary occasion for reflecting on how cognition might be made manifest in poetic language. Activating various oscillating processes now of expression and now of implication, the poem presents cognition in effect by making the reader aware of doing it, going along with it in a self-aware way (what Coleridge called 'the mind's self-experience in the act of thinking', as will be seen). Reading the poem we at one and the same time contemplate a body in thought (or at thought), and we contemplate ourselves thinking. Invited in, invited to step closer, we imagine ourselves creeping in or along to watch Caesar, or Helen, or Michelangelo in a meditative state. The imperatives 'Quiet', 'Move', 'Shut', 'Keep' draw attention at once to the disposition of their thoughtful (or thought-full) bodies, and to ours. This distinction could be related to how, on a walk or a train-ride, even as we look around at our surroundings, and respond to them with pleasure or interest, our thoughts at the same time wander, review past experiences, compose anticipated images of tonight or tomorrow. The 'mind's eye' runs through memories, speculations, propositions, expectations, a host of internal images, even while taking in perceptions from the outside world. Two screens, we could say, external and internal, play in our thoughts at once. As we will see, relevance theory's 'framework for analysing the imprecise and the elusive', in the words of Kathryn Banks, or its 'loose' sifting of literal and other meanings, in Deirdre Wilson's, allow us to become aware of these two concurrent

---

[2] See Chapter 10 in this volume.

processes. It provides us with the tools to distinguish between them, not only in this poem, as here, but in other forms of literary expression also.

Yet, as the precisely realized image of the titular fly might suggest, 'Long-legged Fly' is not a poem on thinking only. It is also a poem about those suggestive moments when thought attaches to what we call reality, culture, the world, and transforms it; those moments when the course of history radically changes, when Caesar crosses the Rubicon, Troy falls, or the Renaissance gets underway. The poem involves the reader imaginatively in its own emergent thought processes in order to talk about the mystery of mind becoming world, or the impact of human thought in time, in terms that are appropriately at once concrete and allusive. It understands that contemplation can move history but cannot quite say how, settling at the end of each stanza on the simile of the fly that is at once still yet moving, the stream that holds yet flows, the simile that stills even as it passes. The repeating image in each case arrests the poem momentarily, holding it in suspension even as the lines move on.

## INFERRING THOUGHT PROCESSES: THE LYRIC IN A COGNITIVE FRAME OF REFERENCE

On several levels, surface and in-depth, Yeats's 'Long-legged Fly' invites a reading informed by relevance theory and kinesic analysis working together within a cognitive frame of reference; that is, by an attention to the processes through which meaning is activated and propelled in language, such as we find described in the relevance theory work of Dan Sperber, Deirdre Wilson, and others,[3] and, more recently, in respect of literary language, of Terence Cave and Adrian Pilkington.[4] The at once contemplative and performative aspects of the poem encourage a reading that acts out (or simulates), while it also acts upon, the three named minds-in-motion, those of Caesar, Helen, and Michelangelo. Their thought processes can be inferred from their embodied movements, their contemplative (now still, now moving) hands and feet that we in turn look at and think about. As we already began to see, their thinking is at once witnessed and enacted. For relevance theory, the poem's various sensorimotor mechanisms stimulate a range of both inferential and non-inferential procedures concerned with the mind at work, both ours and those of the three historical or mythic characters.

Harmonizing with the complex thought-world of the poem, the reading that unspools here takes on two closely interrelated tasks. It considers, first, how the poem might work in tandem with cognitive and especially 'relevance' approaches to literary language in ways that animate and give dynamic expression at once to those approaches and to the poem. Second, concomitantly, but more indirectly,

---

[3] Dan Sperber and Deirdre Wilson, *Relevance: Communication and Cognition* (Oxford: Blackwell, 2nd ed., 1995).

[4] See Terence Cave, *Thinking with Literature: Towards a Cognitive Criticism* (Oxford: Oxford University Press, 2016); Adrian Pilkington, *Poetic Effects* (Amsterdam: John Benjamins, 2000).

it considers how these considerations might widen our understanding of how cognition works in the reading of any lyric poem. Throughout, difficult as this may be in a linear account, the reading attempts to acknowledge the complexity of the aesthetic experience that occurs when we encounter any text as readers. It touches on an array of cognitive effects, which work in conjunction, more or less at the same time, and hence to a considerable extent defy linear enumeration or ranking (as Terence Cave analyses in Chapter 9).

But before we begin to look closely at the poem, I should enter one or two caveats (demurrals that are also deferrals, pauses, not unlike the stays of time that the simile-refrain brings about in Yeats's poem). First I want to say from the outset that my reading, like many of the other readings in this collection, is not intended as a definitive application of any particular theory of language or cognition, and also does not aim to produce a single, discrete interpretation, one interpretation amongst others. Throughout, it tries to avoid giving a demonstration, whether of relevance theory or kinesic analysis, processing the poem like raw material through a machine, producing at the other end a neat, self-contained 'cognitive' reading. For the purposes of my reading, a cognitive approach does not constitute a new literary theory, or involve a new theoretical turn, one that might in due course be organized into a 'discourse' or set of protocols, and might be explicated and applied in the way of so many other late twentieth-century theoretical approaches (post-structuralist, Marxist, feminist, New Historicist, etc). Though our training in literary criticism powerfully conditions us to approach any poem or text through one or other such framework, in a detached way, we might forestall ourselves before doing so by remembering that the interpretation activated here involves an inferential rather than a code-based model of communication. That is, it is as interested in implications or 'implicatures' as in what is explicitly encoded in the text.[5] As others in this book also acknowledge, this approach is markedly different from the symptomatic reading, or reading as decoding or deconstruction, that is core to much post-1968 literary theory, whether historical materialist or post-structuralist.

How then does this essay 'read' reading? Of central importance here as elsewhere in this book is the idea that reading or interpretation is not something done to a poem or other text; it is not an invasive or aggressive act, a dismantling, unmasking, or unpicking. Instead, comprehension and interpretation are what happen within the course of reading the poem, emerging through its play of inferences even as the poem presents itself to the reader, as we will observe. According to this approach, a reading does not attempt to extract some secret or latent meaning in a text, a deeper interpretative code or repressed message that lies behind the linguistic codes operating at its surface. Rather, reading sets different currents of suggestion and implication running, with which the reader engages, now with interest, now delight, now concern, now curiosity, their responses modifying and adjusting as the communication, here the poem, unfolds. Reading, therefore, is simultaneously an internalized and an embodied process. As all the contributors to this volume in their different ways explore, the reader is not confined to a position

---

[5] Sperber and Wilson, *Relevance: Communication and Cognition*.

outside the text, but rather works mentally, emotionally, and sometimes physically with it: opening their imagination to the meanings the poems activates; exercising their sensorimotor knowledge; sometimes even enacting in their mind its expressive motions, as we might experience in our slowing and stilling responses to this poem's injunctions, to be quiet, to tiptoe, to shut the door. In this sense, reading is itself not unlike the fly moving upon the stream, not penetrating its surface, yet aware at every moment of the semantic currents, eddies, and flows that run beneath.

In a second caveat, my reading of 'Long-legged Fly' is not particularly interested in re-presentation or signification in the established deconstructive sense. It is primarily concerned with the processes of searching for and sifting propositions, inferences, background knowledge, and other relevant pieces of information that are activated by the poem (as relevance theory has it), and less so with the more conventional and well-charted critical task of decoding the poem's complex symbolism. At the same time, it recognizes that such symbols can tap powerfully into readers' cultural repertoire, as part of the array of semantic possibility the poem makes available to them. Moreover, reading Yeats, we cannot omit to deal with symbols, or indeed Symbols. As such, he provides an interesting limit case for the kind of cognitive reading based on linguistic implication and inference we are developing, and hence for how we approach a writer's intentional or unintentional intertextuality, or their range of echoic allusion, as Terence Cave and Raphael Lyne also discuss (Chapters 9 and 2, respectively).

Throughout his career as a poet, Yeats strained against the limits of what can be said, even in a poetic language that is by its nature allusive. As he elaborates at length in his book *A Vision* (1925), for him the formal and symbolic accumulation permitted by mystical signs and emblems alone could grant access to the realm of higher signification, the 'Anima Mundi', he believed existed. In his view, this universal Anima Mundi (or Spiritus Mundi), the world seen as instinct with spirit, contained the ideal form of the thoughts, images, and processes that animate human life and shape our minds across time, such as might be captured in poetic symbolism.[6] His spiritual quest better to understand this myth-system drove all his writing but attains particularly advanced if also at times recondite expression in his late poems, which include 'Long-legged Fly' as well as 'Lapis Lazuli' and 'Among School Children'. In these works we find suggestive distillations of Yeats's wide reading in both western and eastern esoteric thought, and of his life-long interest in the interactions of the body, mind, and soul.

In short, Yeats's symbols bring an extensive—intertextual or, in relevance theory terms, echoic—network of cultural, spiritual, and literary reference into his poetry, by conscious design. His symbolic figures on one level invite decoding, consciously appealing to our reading memory or biography as readers. In my own

---

[6] On the Anima Mundi or Spiritus Mundi in Yeats, see Richard Ellman, *The Identity of Yeats* (New York: Macmillan, 1954), especially p. 163; Northrop Frye, *Spiritus Mundi: Essays on Literature, Myth and Society* (Bloomington, IN: Indiana University Press, 1976); R.F. Foster, *W.B. Yeats: A Life*, vol. 2 (Oxford: Oxford University Press, 2003), pp. 161, 313, 345; Ken Monteith, *Yeats and Theosophy* (London; New York: Routledge, 2008).

case, my responses to Yeats are strongly informed for example by my interests in the English and French literature of the *fin de siècle* (Symons, Johnson, Verlaine), those contemporaries and near-contemporaries with whom he was constantly in dialogue. More broadly, however, Yeats wants his readers to be aware of the inter-connections that dynamically link their experience of his poetry to larger bodies of literary and philosophical work (some might say traditions or canons). For him, symbols and structures in one work evoke, whether consciously or unconsciously, other occurrences in other works, immeasurably widening and enriching their range or array of reference or resonance. No symbol, therefore, could be broken down into a set of a few finite points of signification. In the first stanza of 'Long-legged Fly' this can be demonstrated, for example, in the reference to Yeats's 'gyre' theory of dialectical historical change; that is, of the constant rise, 'battle', and 'sinking' of civilizations that he developed from his knowledge of Theosophy, Swedenborg, and other esoteric philosophy. In the second stanza, at the point where the poet conjures an unnamed dancing girl the beauty of whose face caused (or, here, proleptically, would cause) 'topless towers' to be burnt, we find a direct quotation that we might more readily pick out of our stock of reading memory. 'Topless towers' refers us to Christopher Marlowe's Faust encountering the shade of Helen—'Was this the face that launch'd a thousand ships, / And burnt the topless towers of Ilium?' (*Doctor Faustus* V.i.). From this echo, we begin to build an impression of Helen of Troy's fateful beauty that, not unlike Caesar's decision, would spark conflicts and political upheaval, a 'great battle lost', and we do so whether we clearly or only partially recall it.

And yet, to return to my caveat, even as these different forms of intertextual or textually resonant awareness inevitably shape our reading, perhaps in particular our reading of Yeats, our responses to the Yeats poem in hand need not be delim-ited by them. Other chains of reference released by its lines also mould our reading experience in various ways. While readings that aim to decode are not without interest and validity, at the same time they form part of a contextualizing and poly-phonic approach to the interpretation of Yeats that, though it may powerfully work in tandem with the reading mobilized here, is also operationally distinct from it. Indeed, I would go so far as to say that in reading 'Long-legged Fly', even as we register the significance of the figures of Caesar or Helen or 'Michael Angelo', as we would the lexical meaning of words like 'maps' or 'mice', at the same time we need not be primarily concerned with the corresponding archetypes of the warrior, the lover, or the artist as they figure in Yeats's myth-system. While these traditions and symbolizations willy-nilly impact on our responses, and choreograph the spreading processes of meaning activation that our reading sets in train, they need not—or, more forcefully, they do not—shape it in any final or definitive sense.

To round off my point, I offer a demonstration of the limits of intertextual refer-ence that arises, aptly, from the notes to 'Long-legged Fly' we find in the Everyman's Library edition of Yeats's *Poems*. The editor Daniel Albright writes that Yeats's simile of the long-legged fly is related to a passage in Coleridge's *Biographia Literaria* VII in which he, Coleridge, compares 'the mind's self-experience in the act of thinking' to how 'a small water-insect' '*wins* its way up against the stream by alternate pulses of active and passive motion, now resisting the current, and now yielding to it'.[7] It is, Coleridge observed, 'no unapt emblem' for this self-experience. With this we might willingly concur, especially after observing both in Coleridge's description, and in Yeats's apparent borrowing, the attention at once to self-aware thought and to the delicate yet relatively decisive (*win*ning) movements back and forth (the fine balance) that the image of the water-suspended long-legged fly evokes.

However, even as we do so, and even as we acknowledge that Yeats was in all likelihood a reader of *Biographia Literaria*, sensitive to even if perhaps not directly aware of its influence on the making of his similes, we recognize, too, that the reference is ultimately not material to our cognitive experience of the poem, and in particular of the refrain. It enriches of course the range of semantic affordance that the repeating couplet makes available to us, and it deepens our cognitive context, yet we don't *need* to know about the Coleridge passage to process the simile. Much more significant and telling for our imaginative processing at this point are the poem's kinesic effects: most obviously, how the repetition of the 'Like a long-legged fly...' simile holds up or stills the poem's lyrical momentum forwards—a stilling that is reinforced by the evocative and echoic repetition of the directional preposition 'upon', as we saw. We might notice how the 'upon... upon' recurrence creates a semantic tension within the refrain that in some sense mirrors the surface tension of the stream. That is to say, the word prompts us to think at once *up* and *on*; at one and the same time of something *on top* of a surface, *up*on it, yet also exerting pressure, even if infinitesimally so, up*on* it, as on the meniscus of the water. And we might then, if we have read our notes, recall in some subterranean (or sub-aquatic) way the strong propulsion forwards across the surface of the stream of Coleridge's small water-insect, but we do not have to do so to grasp the full potency of the image.

Against these extended caveats, this reading offers Yeats's poem as a case study in how relevance-related approaches might deal with the language of poetry. It sets about tracing some of the multiple chains of inference that the poem produces, including inferences rising from its echoic effects. Simultaneously (re-)activating and weighing the poem's meanings, the reading also goes back to observe and reflect on that activation, through a series of repeated returns or circlings back. However, though my approach is shaped by concepts derived from relevance theory as to how language is used to communicate, it also recognizes that the poem, *this* poem, remarkably, theorizes thought, the mind's self-experience, in Coleridge's term. The poem (and so the reading) itself seeks to conceive how we understand thinking, and how language interacts with—indeed, sparks—thought. My reading proposes therefore that 'Long-legged Fly'—wonderfully, in some senses uniquely—demonstrates to us the dynamic instrumentality and 'adaptive inventiveness' that all literary form affords, in Terence Cave's description: the ways in which it encourages the reader to reflect (back) *in the moment of reading* upon the cognitive

---

[7] W.B. Yeats, *The Poems*, edited by Daniel Albright, p. 831. Emphasis in the text.

processes that are both generated and simulated in literary reception.[8] It suggests that 'Long-legged Fly' provides ways of illuminating poetic communication, which is to say, the reader's stage-by-stage interaction with the poem's shifting inferential effects.

## A DELICATE BALANCE CONJURED: READINGS

Let us turn now to 'Long-legged Fly':

To the purpose clause, 'That civilization may not sink …', that at once opens the poem and pauses that opening.

To the ten-line stanzas each comprising two ballad-like quatrains and a repeating simile—the simile-refrain that each time briefly holds the poem in suspension in our minds, like the fly on the surface of the stream.

To the loose on-running ballad rhyme scheme *abcb* that is eighteen times (of a possible thirty) infinitesimally paused by end-stopping.

To the short declarative sentence, 'She thinks', placed at the heart of the middle stanza, two words around which the rest of the poem pivots.

And to the interplay of movement and constraint to movement, of balance and imbalance, extending throughout, that these combined effects engender.

Mimicked here in my own repetitive phrasing, the reiterating structures of 'Long-legged Fly' draw the reader into a complex braid of inferences that intersect and reinforce one another across the length of the poem, repeatedly, though at different levels, returning us to the poem's core questions: How does thought emerge from silence?; How does the mind impact the world?; How might something arise from apparently nothing? Though it is artificial to draw out these links and connections in a linear way, since they in fact emerge, spread, and modify each other simultaneously, the exercise of doing so, prompted by the relevance theory heuristic, can at the same time shed light on their different criss-crossing and inter-flowing effects. Indeed, separating out the poem's different strands or streams of meaning allows us to revisit the poet's own sense of what he is making available in the poem, and through what means, and so consider why he might have directed the syntactic and semantic flow of his lines as he did. Moreover, paradoxically, by ceaselessly distinguishing, revisiting, and reassessing in this way, we ultimately succeed in holding the poem's shifting array of inferences in our minds more or less at the same time.

So we notice, for example, the poem's alternating verbs of movement and stillness—'sink', 'Quiet', 'tether', 'move', 'move', 'shut', 'moves': how several of them are in the imperative mode, demanding compliance; and how one or two refer to movement that pauses or stills. And alongside this we notice, as we did earlier, the poem's motions of going back on itself each time it returns to its refrain, as if to its fulcrum, as befits a meditation on balance and equipoise. And besides this again, we notice how the fly's legs steadying back and forth are mirrored in Helen's

---

[8] See Cave, *Thinking with Literature*, p. 31 in particular.

dancing feet, that describe at once a rhythm and yet stillness, and in Michelangelo's hand moving 'to and fro' like a pendulum, making barely a sound.

Yet, even as we observe these alternating moments of movement and of stilling, we notice also the poem's unsettling torsions and off-balances. Operating at different syntactic and semantic levels, these effects include its avoidance of outright identification (its core figure is a simile, not a metaphor); its many destabilizing 'not quite' effects; its historical inversion (in the first two stanzas: Rome before Troy); and its lexical unevenness, such as its unsteadying juxtaposition of the randomly singular and the generic—which taken together enhance the atmosphere of withheld, frustrated, and at times contorted effort. Thought, it would appear, is onerous, baffling. It requires uneasy equations to be conceived in a poem. We quieten ourselves for a seeming non-event in Caesar's tent. Helen is no longer a girl, not yet a woman; her shuffle is not quite a dance. Michelangelo's painting hand is not quite silent. Insofar as Helen is a historical figure at all, rather than merely mythical, her time-period is farther back than Caesar's, introducing a chronological torsion. The mind is *like* a fly, but is not quite a fly (a simile by its nature introduces a displacement). The fly in question, as we know, seems still but is not quite still, straddling the current, balancing and counterbalancing itself imperceptibly. Structurally, the opening purpose clause, already an inversion, modulates oddly into a negative, a further forestalling: 'That civilization may *not* sink.' The refrain-simile itself feels about-face, opening and not closing with its comparative phrase, 'Like a long-legged fly …'.

The poem's lexical unevenness introduces further tension, as in the contrast in the first stanza between the abstract Latinate 'civilization' and the monosyllabic concrete nouns 'dog', 'tent', 'hand', 'head'. This jarring, even if muted, continues in the combination of high literary allusion with Helen's 'tinker shuffle' in the second stanza, and in Michael Angelo's elicitation of sexual fantasy and desire by means of a hand merely painting to and fro in the third. Coming together with the ongoing contrasts of motion and stillness, and of stepping back and pointing at or leaning towards, these insistent oppositions evoke something of the paradox of embodied contemplation. We experience thought (and thought in history) as simultaneously in motion, manifesting in time, and yet as suspended, gathered into a pose, a pattern, a symbol, captured at the end of each stanza in the two-line simile of the poised, moving-yet-unmoving fly.

Cumulatively, these various suggestions and implications bring to our attention how 'Long-legged Fly' is able to conjure delicate balances from slightly skewed, out-of-kilter effects. The repeating structures of the poem, the purposive, the imperative, and the refrain, themselves sometimes distorted, are used to inject further quirks and paradoxes. Throughout, live thought is conjured from a posthumous perspective, by reimagining a dead past. The poem's request for quiet each time requires voicing; for seclusion, pointing, and prying. The central characters, Caesar, Helen, and 'Michael Angelo', believe themselves to be secluded and out of the way, yet are gazed upon. The viewer (or reader), addressed as 'you', is placed at a distance from the core action of each stanza, yet, voyeur-like, strains forward (is incited to strain forward) to witness, observe, eavesdrop, spy.

Imagining the three main scenarios of the camp, the street, and the chapel, the reader is granted a few specifics—'the dog', 'a street'—and a few coordinates—'a distant post', 'this lonely place', 'that scaffolding'—but put together these reference points give no more than the barest illusion of setting. Oddities, some under- and some over-specified, abound: Why a *pony*? Whereabouts is the child Helen? Why is she so solitary? What strange initiation must the pubescent girls receive and why? We are shown recognizable things, but aren't given a context in which to place them, certainly in stanzas one and two. In three, the context, though it is named, 'the Pope's chapel', 'that scaffolding', is otherwise left to be inferred.[9] Consequential moments in time, that birthed empires, wars, new civilizations, converge with the apparently inconsequential—a pony tethered to a post, a tinker shuffle in the street, children crowding at a door. On the one hand we have the haphazard world; on the other, a timeless realm inhabited by unchanging forms or symbols. Local details fail to map onto the broad patterns of myth, yet, in so failing, they at the same time reaffirm the ill-sorted, granular specificity of *now*, and in the breach create new imaginative and historical possibilities.

Running through the now flowing, now pausing motions of 'Long-legged Fly', this reading has retraced and to some extent re-staged its reflections on thought in history, the shifts in mind that produce changes in time. It has done this through a repeated circling back across its interlinked and cumulative poetic inferences and effects, in a way largely choreographed by those same repeating syntactic and other structures. Potentially extending far beyond this essay's limits, the process thus set in motion can be imagined as a series of at once widening and narrowing circles, now looking out at the impacts of the mind on the world, now referring back to the motions of our own reading minds, generated within the poem.

Inevitably, my methodological emphasis on simultaneity and repetitive pattern-ing over linearity and sequence has meant that some of the meanings that might have been demonstrated through a more forensic or analytic approach have been left latent. My intention was not to consider in a maximal way the implicatures generated in the unfolding of every phrase or line of the poem. Perhaps no reading can. Rather, my approach clustered together interrelated effects, implicitly leaving open the possibility of return to these stacked figurative moments, and of a further spreading activation and re-activation of their meanings. To illustrate: alongside the kinesic response this reading already offered to the repeating preposition 'upon', a further reading might consider, in the first stanza, the lowering vector indicated by the verb 'sink' combined with the horizontal plane described by 'spread', spatial dispositions that are again captured and reinforced in the operations of 'upon' (*up*on or up*on*) within the simile-refrain. A further reading might also look more closely than I have here at the recurrence of the verb 'move' in its different modalities across the poem, as well as the modulation of 'thinks' to 'thought' from stanza two

---

[9] Yeats's drafts of 'Long-legged Fly' in the National Library of Ireland confirm that the third stanza was itself something of an afterthought and add-on, symbolically not of a piece with the two preceding scenes from ancient history and classical myth.

to three, and consider how these small shifts might evoke for us something of the repetitive shuffle of Helen's feet (or the oscillations of Michelangelo's hand).

Overall, this reading has largely bracketed and set to one side intertextual allusion, yet such cross-referencing, integral to all literary tradition, was also granted to be relevant, indeed pressing, as a key aspect of the cognitive context that readers are likely to bring to the poem. As we consider in closing allusions and implications so far left out of consideration, some mention of a further echo, whether intentional or not, might be appropriate: the resonance of T.S. Eliot's 'The Love-song of J. Alfred Prufrock' (1915) in Yeats's final stanza featuring Michael Angelo.[10] It is an illustration of how a surfeit of echoic allusion, even when highly suggestive, may ultimately be disposable. The refrain of Eliot's poem, an evocation of an alienating, over-sophisticated social world, returns in 'Long-legged Fly' as a rhyme on the same name, Michelangelo or Michael Angelo, a rhyme that refers, once again, to a repeating action. In Eliot: 'In the room the women come and go / Talking of Michelangelo.' In Yeats: '. . . reclines / Michael Angelo. / With no more sound than the mice make / His hand moves to and fro'. Though we know that Yeats read and rated early Eliot, the interest of the cross-reference at this point does not so much lie in whether it is intentional, or in its relative loudness or resonance, unmistakable as it might seem from the juxtaposition above. It resides rather in the suggestive linking of creative activity, indicated by the name Michelangelo/Michael Angelo, with repetitive and meditative movement. Indeed, when set against Eliot's couplet, Yeats reverses the name and the back-and-forth reference, as if to place further emphasis on the repetitive motion. Once again, however, the intertextual echo, specific as it is to readers of both Eliot and Yeats, need not be manifest to the reader for the point of Yeats's final stanza to be communicated. And, further, as the subject of 'Prufrock' is quite other than that of 'Long-legged Fly', the allusion may also simply be a distraction, if an evocative one.

Alongside the other contributions to *Reading Beyond the Code*, this reading-in-motion of 'Long-legged Fly' has tried out a cognitive methodology for reading poetry, or at least sketched the general shape and dynamic of such a methodology. As such, it offers an outline of sorts of how relevance theory and related approaches will be activated and developed elsewhere in this volume. As we have seen throughout, my endeavour was in many ways made possible by the self-reflections and repetitive structures of Yeats's poem itself: how it presents states of contemplation across time; how it subtly directs the reading mind in motion; and, overall, how it invites and stimulates inferential reading. In 'Long-legged Fly' we find, as if encountering something intensely familiar with the shock of first recognition, a framework for reading with relevance; an affordance for the 'self-experience' of the thinking mind; and a demonstration of some of the ways in which thought moves in, with, and through language. Cumulatively, the poem evokes and confirms for us, once again, that literature is a cognitive archive, an accumulated layering of how thought has met the world over time.

---

[10] T.S. Eliot, 'The Love-song of J. Alfred Prufrock', in *Collected Poems* (1963; London: Faber, 1974), pp. 13–17, with the two occurrences of the lines on pp. 13 and 14.

# Interlace 2

*We move now to a poem written some 300 years earlier. Yeats might have had little difficulty in understanding Herrick's poem, but would Herrick have understood Yeats's? This counterfactual imagining is a simple way of making the point that works of literature are situated contextually, and that the overlap between the contexts available to author and readers varies on a scale that runs from zero (where, for example, the language in which the text is spoken or written is irrecoverably lost) to a maximum which is always significantly short of absolute.*

*Another way of putting this is to say that all utterances are subject to entropy, decay, interference, white noise, crackle. They are vulnerable to spatial, chronological, historical, and cultural distance; speakers and addressees, authors and readers, may also lack neurological attunement, or what one might call imaginative affinity. But, and it's an important 'but', our cognitive apparatus has evolved (both phylogenetically and culturally) to allow for, and in part to compensate for, these erosions: the inferential capacities that are central to human cognition have reshaped themselves to handle underspecification in cultural domains no less than in the perceptual sphere. In the case of literary utterances, what is more, the lack of exact attunement to the cognitive environment of readers or hearers is seldom fatal, as it might be in everyday situations, or in diplomacy, for example, where it might lead to war.*

*Literary objects (utterances, works, texts) carry with them multiple signs of their provenance, including the language they are written in, the world they refer to, the assumptions they make, the assumptions they don't make.[1] Relevance theorists would expect these signs to prompt an inferential response which may be overtly intended or tacitly taken for granted by the author; that is to say, signs of provenance are intrinsic elements of the intentionality informing a given work or text: 'This is where we're coming from', they seem to say. It is then up to the reader to recover as much contextual information as will make the work seem optimally relevant. For some readers, contemporary historical documents may afford readings in which hidden ideological concerns are uncovered; for others, another set of features (tacit or overt literary allusion, for example) may become salient. Herrick's poem can thus be framed in different ways, according to different critical methodologies. Such methodologies are in general compatible with the relevance theory approach to communication, except where a given*

---

[1] *At the height of the structuralist phase of modern literary theory, Michael Riffaterre expounded an extreme version of this view: a potentially opaque reference is understood not by historical labour and explication but by inferring from the text as a whole what the function and sense of that allusion is; see Riffaterre,* Production du texte *(Paris: Éditions du Seuil, 1979), chs 1–2.*

*critical protocol insists on a code model of communication or seeks to eradicate a crucial component of the communicative exchange (usually, in recent times, the 'author').*

*Raphael Lyne's approach begins from within a contemporary methodology that privileges certain kinds of historical contextualization. That is a good place to start, because many readers will want to raise the questions he addresses in the course of the chapter. The resulting discussion shows how a single work may provide evidence for an 'array' of more or less specific, more or less detailed readings which may appeal to different readers at different times. Perhaps it is worth emphasizing here that the cognitive perspective adopted in this volume, and more specifically the relevance theory perspective, is in no sense 'anti-historical': it presupposes that the dynamics of communication will always be realized in terms of a given cognitive environment. 'Reverse engineering' from a specific instantiation is always a fruitful exercise, as it indeed proves to be in this reading of a seventeenth-century poem.*

# 2

# Relevance Across History

*Raphael Lyne*

## 'CORINNA'S GOING A MAYING': A POEM IN HISTORY

> Get up, get up for shame, the Blooming Morne
> Upon her wings presents the god unshorne.
> See how *Aurora* throwes her faire
> Fresh-quilted colours through the aire:
> Get up, sweet-Slug-a-bed, and see
> The Dew-bespangling Herbe and Tree.
>
> (1–6)[1]

'Corinna's going a Maying' is one of the best and best-known of the 1,400 poems in Robert Herrick's *Hesperides* (1648). The works in this collection are mostly much shorter than 'Corinna'; as its title-page announces, they span the 'Humane' and the 'Divine'. Some poems are secular, songs and epigrams and lyrics, and others are religious, carols and prayers and praises. 'Corinna's going a Maying' is one of the former, a poem in the *carpe diem* tradition trying to persuade a woman to participate in May Day celebrations and the sexual activity that tends to result.

The poem has a divine context, however. Although it starts with classical figures (Aurora and Apollo, the 'god unshorne'), it goes on to feature Christian vocabulary in various ways. This can be seen as a persuasive strategy within the *carpe diem* context: by dressing up revelry and sex in pious language, the speaker makes them more acceptable to the poem's supposed target. Such language also draws in what scholars have tended to see as a key part of the poem's work, which is its negotiation of some contemporary controversies in religious practice. Herrick was a Royalist clergyman, vicar of Dean Prior in Devon from 1629 to 1646, and he was affiliated to the Anglican project of Archbishop William Laud. This set the English Church against some of the more extreme Protestant attitudes towards popular traditions. Rather than seeing Maypoles and their associated dances, for example, as Godless deviancy, they were seen as a natural expression of a wish for the divine, and as such were something that the local priest could use to further God's work. This attitude gained the highest level of endorsement when Charles I issued *The King's Majesty's Declaration to his Subjects Concerning Lawful Sports to be Used* (known usually as

---

[1] The poem is quoted from *The Complete Poetry of Robert Herrick*, edited by Thomas Cain and Ruth Connolly (Oxford: Oxford University Press, 2013), p. 64.

*The King's Book of Sports*), printed by Robert Barker in 1633; this was a re-issue of an equivalent proclamation by James I in 1618.

A couplet later in the first stanza serves as a first illustration of the way 'Corinna' invokes the Christian context to enable specific historical resonance, while also further enriching the poem's participation in a longer-range literary tradition. Corinna is taunted with her late waking by comparison with the promptness evident in the natural world:

> Nay! not so much as out of bed?
> When all the Birds have Mattens seyd.    (9–10)

The poem puts religion into nature, and re-expresses one kind of early morning observance as another. This is by no means the first version of this readily available trope: in Edmund Spenser's 'Epithalamion', for example, there is a similar idea: 'the merry Larke hir mattins sings aloft'.[2] The birds are in pious mood on his wedding day. However, Herrick raises something familiar and readily available within the poetic tradition in a context wherein it might find new possibilities. The word 'matins' was used in the Anglican *Book of Common Prayer* but it was still redolent of the Catholic liturgical day: it could be taken as an evocation of tradition, of interconnection between modern worship in England, popular and natural festivity, and the older traditions of the Church. This then could be confrontational, demonstrating the poem's affiliation, but of course the lightness of the image means it slips away before it becomes solidly factional. In all these respects, it is not alone in the poem.

Critics disagree somewhat as to the tone of 'Corinna' in relation to these issues. Achsah Guibbory has described the *Hesperides* as 'a poetic counterpart to the Laudian church' in line with the *King's Book of Sports*.[3] Like Guibbory, Robert Deming detects an elegiac note as the poet laments the passing of a harmonious era.[4] Graham Parry sees *Hesperides* as a yet more fulsome articulation of Laud's project, in which there is 'a frictionless ease of movement between pagan antiquity, Roman Catholicism and the practices of the Laudian church', in which religion speaks to habits that are 'natural and instinctive to all times and nations'.[5] However, in *The Politics of Mirth*, while endorsing specific links between *Hesperides* and the *Book of Sports* (addressing both 1618 and 1633 versions), Leah Marcus argues for a degree of ambivalence in the way the poems portrayed the links between Church

---

[2] Quoted from *The Yale Edition of the Shorter Poems of Edmund Spenser*, edited by William A. Oram et al. (New Haven, CT: Yale University Press, 1989), 'Epithalamion', l. 79. The poem was first printed in 1595 but it was written for Spenser's wedding in 1594.

[3] Achsah Guibbory, *Ceremony and Community from Herbert to Milton: Literature, Religion and Cultural Conflict in Seventeenth-Century England* (Cambridge: Cambridge University Press, 1998), p. 88; and see pp. 79–118 on Herrick. The pioneering essay pointing in this direction was Mark L. Reed, 'Herrick among the maypoles: Dean Prior and the *Hesperides*', *Studies in English Literature, 1500–1900*, 5 (1965), 133–50.

[4] Robert H. Deming, *Ceremony and Art: Robert Herrick's Poetry* (The Hague: Mouton, 1974), pp. 47–57.

[5] Graham Parry, *The Arts of the Anglican Counter-Reformation: Glory, Laud and Honour* (Woodbridge, UK: Boydell and Brewer, 2006), p. 146.

and people: Corinna is pushed beyond the limits of sanctioned licence, and there is a gap between teachings and practices.[6]

John Creaser has issued a *caveat* against such historicist interpretations. He argues that there is insufficient evidence to date 'Corinna's going a Maying' to the aftermath of either *Book of Sports*, or indeed to Herrick's time in Dean Prior.[7] Creaser offers a counter-argument that the poem could perfectly well have been written in London, and thus it would appear as more of a generic *carpe diem* poem tapping into its readership's knowledge of a transhistorical literary pattern. By testing the feedback loop between dating and contextual interpretation, Creaser offers two kinds of challenge to a historicist tendency. The first relates to the identification of the illuminating context: this has to be correct. The second is to the privileging of the search for a specific context when a poem seems capable of multiple kinds of address, some relatively urgent, some relatively patient, but equally substantial. A poem like this rewards a careful but flexible kind of attention, alert to both its specific and its traditional qualities.

'Corinna's going a Maying' combines a potential for specific historical reference with less time-bound qualities. It has the potential for conversations within and across chronologies, with other *carpe diem* poems, and with other poems about the coming of spring and the entrance into sexuality. It is part of the pastoral tradition as well. Its speaker and the other people evoked are not shepherds, but they are rural figures whose experiences can stand for something beyond their explicit scope, which is the crucial characteristic of pastoral. Appreciating the poem requires some sort of apprehension of these different levels, these different kinds of address, and their subdivisions. In this chapter I will argue that relevance theory offers a coherent and yet flexible account of how this multiple understanding of different historical natures can work, and why readers may privilege one or the other to good effect. Such an approach may also help us reconsider some tensions in recent criticism, wherein a preference for historically oriented reading has estranged modern readers from poems they might seek to understand for and as themselves. Nevertheless, it will also be important to register the challenge posed by plural address to this particular—or any—theory of communication. A poem has multiple things to pass on, suited to multiple kinds of receiver.

## RELEVANCE AND HISTORICISM

It is fitting (given the poem in question) that one of the first to recognize relevance theory's potential for literary criticism was Alastair Fowler, known for much influential work on Renaissance genres. In a review in the *London Review of Books* he

---

[6] Leah S. Marcus, *The Politics of Mirth: Jonson, Herrick, Milton, Marvell, and the Defense of Old Holiday Pastimes* (Chicago, IL: University of Chicago Press, 1986), pp. 140–68.

[7] John Creaser, '"Times trans-shifting": chronology and the misshaping of Herrick', *English Literary Renaissance*, 39 (2009), 163–96, esp. pp. 165–7 on Marcus and the *Book of Sports*.

welcomes the alternative it offered to a pure 'code model' of communication and to the unrealistically ideal quality of Gricean maxims. He acknowledges a possible mismatch between the 'optimal relevance'/'easiest path' principle and the complexity of literature 'with its exploitation of heightened states, and even of deliberate difficulty'.[8] However, he notes that within the bounds of relevance theory 'it is possible to infer very subtle implications indeed...perhaps Sperber and Wilson's greatest triumph is to have extended pragmatics to very weak implicatures—ambiguities, implications of implications, doubtful figures—of the sort that make up the richest part of conversation'. Furthermore, he asks whether literature has 'its own special context of literary conventions, fashions, allusion, formal structuring, and confirming resonances or redundancies', which makes some of these complexities easier to reach and more compatible with 'optimal relevance'.

David Trotter also sets an approach based on relevance theory against a code-based model. In his case this arises because of the supposed or apparent undecodability of some modernist literature. He also deals, as Fowler does, with a possible tension between the cherished complexity of literature and the convergence towards a narrow final point suggested—but not obliged, as will be seen—by 'optimal relevance'. In his account, this is faced not by theoretical accommodation but by recognizing the ways in which literary works explore this tension:

> Writers frequently raise the costs of processing their 'utterances', and promise in exchange a yet richer contextual effect. They do not so much abandon as complicate the principle of relevance. They offer different kinds of relevance. They prompt us to wonder what relevance is.[9]

The test of a critical approach may not only be whether it provides problem-solving tools for readers. It may instead be whether and how the literary works themselves seem to resonate with or anticipate it, and whether and how they recognize the difficulties involved. Mansfield and Joyce 'sometimes disguise or displace the focus of a sentence, thus forcibly extending the range of inferences necessary to understand what they are talking about' (p. 14). Difficulty, then, can be an enquiry into relevance, not something that confounds or eludes it, and the potential of a cognitive pragmatics of literary criticism is revealed most when the texts themselves probe its possibilities. For Trotter, the interface between relevance as a principle and literature involves illumination on both sides:

> If the linguistic structure of an utterance 'grossly underdetermines its interpretation', then literature might be defined as a form of communication more grossly underdetermined than most by linguistic structure: the grosser the better. Literature tests to the limit not our powers of encoding and decoding, but our powers of inference. To examine the relation between linguistic form and pragmatic interpretation in a literary

---

[8] Alastair Fowler, 'A new theory of communication', *London Review of Books*, 30 March 1989, 16–17. On this question, see the Introduction to this volume, section on 'Processing Effort and Style', pp. 12–13.

[9] David Trotter, 'Analysing literary prose: the relevance of relevance theory', *Lingua*, 87 (1992), 11–27; p. 11.

text is to ask what makes literature special and to test a theory which claims to explain that relation. (pp. 11–12)[10]

Where modernist fiction may engage and test inferential processes in sentence structure, a poem like 'Corinna's going a Maying' may do so by leaving its reader productively uncertain which contexts are most relevant, and which registers and time-scales are at issue.

Fowler raises a pertinent issue in his review when he deals with the historical distance that is a part of so much literary experience. The gaps between modern readers and older authors may limit the extent to which we can muster appropriate contexts with which to understand intentions that may be more or less palpably aimed at readers or hearers other than us. Focusing on inference rather than decoding, he argues, gives grounds for optimism:

> The implications of Relevance for students of older literature are particularly signifi-
> cant. Meanings in the past are often said to be inaccessible, because of changes in the
> language code; and certainly linguistic changes often make old writing difficult,
> especially where abstract words are involved. One might deem the cipher of the past
> unbreakable, if the coding-decoding process were all. But once the fundamental role
> of inference in communication is grasped, many new interpretative resources become
> available. Interpreting past utterances need not entail decoding antique experiences
> inaccessible in their alterity: it may be enough to supply necessary associations and
> infer optimally relevant senses. True, old assumptions may be forgotten or unobvious.
> But while domains of assumption have changed in numerous ways, they have not
> changed beyond recognition.

A responsive and economic model of communication based on optimal relevance (all communication, everyday and literary) gives another way of thinking about historicist criticism. The rigour and self-denial of a code-based theory that maintains that 'meanings in the past' are 'inaccessible' are attractive. They pay respect both to the integrity of the work of art and to the value of scholarly effort. In contrast, the appeal to things being 'not changed beyond recognition', a version of common sense, appeals to general rather than specialist skills, setting aside zealous pessimism.

Relevance theorists have defined themselves against other critical movements before, and the interactions are instructive. In *Poetic Effects* Adrian Pilkington takes structuralism and post-structuralism (and, to a lesser extent, reader-response criticism) as the prevailing theoretical trends, and defines the potential of relevance theory against them.[11] Fowler takes aim in the same direction:

> Relevance theory can have little joy for structuralists and deconstructionists, both of
> whom (in opposed ways) identify communication as coding-decoding. Structuralists
> stress the power of codes so extremely as to deny the communicator any role, while

---

[10] The quotation is from Deirdre Wilson and Dan Sperber, 'Representation and relevance', in Ruth Kempson (ed.) *Mental Representations: The Interface between Language and Reality* (Cambridge: Cambridge University Press, 1988), pp. 133–53; p. 141.

[11] Adrian Pilkington, *Poetic Effects: A Relevance Theory Perspective* (Amsterdam: John Benjamins, 2000).

Derridadaists [*sic*]—and sometimes Jacques Derrida himself—stress the frailty of coding through regress of signification, and regard communication itself as enmeshed in undecidabilities.   (p. 17)

Like Pilkington, Fowler makes his case rather scornfully, but it is helpful as well as provocative to point out how differences between theoretical positions may arise from an unquestioned allegiance to a code model. A lot of literary theory gets by without acknowledging its implicit pragmatics; the same could be said of different varieties of historicism.

Fowler's view of the reachability of past literature, and more specifically of the pertinence of relevance theory in this critical territory, has not established itself among the critical mainstream. His review was written just after, and perhaps in the wake of, Stephen Greenblatt's *Shakespearean Negotiations* (1988), which is one of the landmarks of the critical practice known as New Historicism or Cultural Materialism. This did become part of the mainstream, of Shakespeare scholarship especially. While a good deal of the work in this tradition relishes the kind of inaccessibility Fowler mentions, it also includes an eloquent invocation of communication: 'I began with the desire to speak with the dead.'[12] This famous opening to *Shakespearean Negotiations* may suggest Stephen Greenblatt has faith in the possibility of communication across time, but in fact he is wary very soon after. Speaking with the dead is not a matter of receiving messages aimed at us, so it is not simply amenable to pragmatics. He portrays the process as an esoteric gleaning, requiring archaeological alertness, picking up 'traces...in the absence of life'. In this scenario, the critic is heroic and resourceful, whereas in Fowler's version, the achievements seem less dramatic. Greenblatt deems it 'paradoxical...to see the will of the living dead in fictions, in places where there was no live bodily being to begin with' (p. 1). However, literature is surely one of the most likely forms in which an individual or a culture might aspire to communicate with the future, and in that respect it seems far from paradoxical.

The particular implications of Greenblatt's 'speaking with the dead' have been discussed by Rita Felski in her book *The Limits of Critique*. Felski has a general aspiration to move criticism beyond 'the hermeneutics of suspicion' (the term is Paul Ricœur's), an all-encompassing demeanour towards literature that privileges the search for hidden details or tensions. Critical practice is adversarial: readers dig or detect, and they prize the texts that respond most sharply to their arguably paranoid attentions. One of the specific trends she identifies as part of the culture of 'critique' is a kind of historicism that sets text and reader at odds by assuming that 'speaking with the dead' through literature is only ironic or metaphorical. Felski advocates a more cooperative kind of criticism that allows 'transtemporal affinities' and 'transtemporal liveliness' without denying historical differences, that acknowledges texts as 'co-actors' capable of communicating across history as we engage positively with them and our 'co-constitution'.[13] Felski's solution is a turn to the 'Actor-Network Theory' of the sociologist Bruno Latour. Although she mentions affordances

---

[12] Stephen Greenblatt, *Shakespearean Negotiations: The Circulation of Social Energy in Renaissance England* (Berkeley, CA: University of California Press, 1988), p. 1.
[13] Rita Felski, *The Limits of Critique* (Chicago, IL: University of Chicago Press, 2015), pp. 154–6.

(pp. 164–5), she turns to the social rather than the cognitive as a field in which to situate these more productive exchanges. And although she emphasizes the import-ance of inferences (p. 178; in the context of affect), and says that reading is 'never just a matter of cognitive or analytic decoding', she does not introduce the potential for redefining the contact between reader and text that pragmatics has to offer.

Mary Crane suggests that an adversarial historicism (as part of what she calls 'symptomatic' critical practices, using Fredric Jameson's term) has an advantage over cognitive approaches to literature, because it can produce sharp, questioning readings. In comparison, interpretations tied in to the characteristics of cognition can seem to tend towards the universal or the commonplace.[14] The continuity of human cognitive resources does not strike some literary critics as remarkable. However, turning to relevance theory in cases such as 'Corinna's Going a Maying' needs to, and can, encompass diverse readings as it sets up the sort of productive dialogue desired by Felski. Furthermore, when works themselves seem to make an issue of their aspirations to future readerships in posterity in dialogue with their own temporal and cultural particularity, they give a reason to invoke the inferential processes by which modern readers, in spite of historical difference, feel able to approach them. As Trotter says, such works sometimes explore their own capacities for eliciting inferences. Literature communicates with different readers, antici-pated and unanticipated at the time of composition, but this cannot be a secret unavailable to writers themselves, and is surely a premise for any decision to write, or at least to publish.

A model of literary interpretation inspired by a relevance-based account of com-munication might tell us about things that happen normally in reading works from the past, which would be interesting in itself, but might not offer that much to criticism. Such a model might also help refine a sense of what could or should be done in that kind of reading or criticism—a way of incisively conceiving the processes that could be conducted well or badly. It is particularly promising for a poem like 'Corinna's going a Maying' because of the allowance by Sperber and Wilson for a wide array of 'weak implicatures' in an utterance. In particular, they even allow that a writer could intend readers to encounter a range of implications from which they will extract diverse and unpredictable combinations. This offers a nuanced way around a potential obstacle, the tendency in pragmatics (but not in much literary criticism) to focus on problem-solving and narrowing towards finite content. In a key passage on 'poetic effects', Sperber and Wilson develop the idea of an 'array':

> Relevance is achieved through a wide array of weak implications which are themselves weakly implicated. The speaker—or writer, since this method of achieving relevance is particularly well developed in literature—has good reason to suppose that enough of a wide array of potential implications with similar import are true or probably true,

---

[14] Mary Thomas Crane, 'Cognitive historicism: intuition in Early Modern thought', in Lisa Zunshine (ed.) *The Oxford Handbook of Cognitive Literary Studies* (Oxford: Oxford University Press, 2015), pp. 15–33, especially pp. 18–19. In the same volume, see also Natalie M. Phillips, 'Literary neuroscience and history of mind: an interdisciplinary fMRI study of attention and Jane Austen', pp. 55–83, especially pp. 63–9.

though she does not know which these are (hence they are weak implications) and is neither able to anticipate nor particularly concerned about which of them will be considered and accepted by the audience (hence they are weakly implicated).[15]

This suggests a dispersal and multiplication of possible intentions, offering an unpredictable combination of things to be inferred from a range of foreseen and unforeseen effects. Such a multiplication of voices could be complemented by a multiplication of readers: we may need to discern different readerships, and we can do so without complete self-denial. With a literary work characterized by an 'array' of intentions, its ideal reader should offer an 'array' in return.

## THE POEM AS AN ARRAY

'Corinna's going a Maying' might be taken as a paradigm of the sort of arrayed communication that I am trying to explore here. It speaks to its own historical moment, because anyone engaged in religious politics at the time knew that such celebrations were controversial. However, the poem's focus is also on a longer-range literary tradition, and a longer-range literary posterity: its pastoral vision of fleeting time and its portrayal of human beings in harmony with their natural environment (if they just let themselves) both resonate far beyond the controversies of the 1630s and 1640s.

It is convenient to see this as a double address for the purpose of this essay, though it is not a simple duality. Observing it at work requires a rather elaborate reading of some moments in the poem, with a view to the nuances of process, as much as to the outcome that a reader might take away. This method is not meant to distinguish a literary-critical mode of reading from a more routine kind of reading appropriate to poetry; nor indeed is it meant to suggest a literary kind of communication that is fundamentally different from everyday communication, although the issues involved are very much at home in literature. Rather, the point is that many of the ways in which we speak and write (metaphors, proverbs, technical language, conventional statements of consolation or exhortation) have lives that any individual utterance only briefly inhabits and fixes.

Having encouraged Corinna to wake up and participate in the Maying, the speaker of the poem invites her to observe the transformation of the familiar world into something more festive and natural:

> Come, my *Corinna*, come; and comming, marke
> How each field turns a street; each street a Parke
> Made green, and trimm'd with trees: see how
> Devotion gives each House a Bough,
> Or Branch: Each Porch, each doore, ere this,
> An Arke a Tabernacle is
> Made up of white-thorn neatly enterwove;
> As if here were those cooler shades of love.  (29–36)

---

[15] Deirdre Wilson and Dan Sperber, *Meaning and Relevance* (Cambridge: Cambridge University Press, 2012), p. 118.

Each field becomes a street because it is frequented by human revellers, and each street becomes a park because it is decorated with foliage. Herrick's elaboration builds through sacred objects ('Arke', 'Tabernacle') towards an assertion of the basic holiness of this festivity and natural harmony in unreligious terms. The 'cooler shades of love' are a gesture towards an idea of something chaste and pure that is contrasted with, as well as connected to (the force of 'As if'), the passions of Maying: the festival is again shadowed by a more holy sort of ritual.

The assertion that the whole event is fundamentally a sort of 'Devotion' is left standing in spite of the poem's *carpe diem* tendencies and obvious allusions to sexual activity. Indeed, the poem's edginess arises because of its stress on religion, rather than in spite of it. Like the idea of the birds' Matins, this might be generally evocative of a version of pastoral, or it might be specifically evocative of one or more debates in the poem's immediate religious and social environment. The processes of inference described by Sperber and Wilson match the work done by readers here, working out how multiple contexts might offer inferences that would or would not cross a threshold of activation. This poem, like so many pastorals, participates in this very process by offering multiple faces towards the future and the past. It mixes specific and general, pointed and not.

There is something similar in the next stanza. This is where the poem is most frank about the sexual nature of the Maying, for example in its reference to a 'green-gown', a dress stained by the grass during outdoor intercourse. Even here, though, it continues to build its network of religious metaphor and thus the possibility that its readers (sooner or later) will see a theological point:

> There's not a budding Boy, or Girle, this day,
> But is got up, and gone to bring in May.
> A deale of Youth, ere this, is come
> Back, and with *White-thorn* laden home.
> Some have dispatcht their Cakes and Creame,
> Before that we have left to dreame:
> And some have wept, and woo'd, and plighted Troth,
> And chose their Priest, ere we can cast off sloth:
> Many a green-gown has been given;
> Many a kisse, both odde and even:
> Many a glance too has been sent
> From out the eye, Loves Firmament:
> Many a jest told of the Keyes betraying
> This night, and Locks pickt, yet w'are not a Maying.   (43–56)

Mary Crane has noted that moments of outdoor intimacy like this 'green-gown' reference are 'usually presented in passing without special comment' in early modern literature.[16] The open air could afford a sense of privacy somewhat more than it can today. Nevertheless, even with this qualification, the stanza makes the gathering of flowers ('with White-thorn laden') and a hasty breakfast ('Cakes and Creame') sound like innuendo. It is clear enough what the speaker thinks he and

[16] Mary Thomas Crane, 'Illicit privacy and outdoor spaces in Early Modern England', *Journal for Early Modern Cultural Studies*, 9 (2009), 4–22, p. 8.

Corinna are missing. However, even here there are suggestions in a different direction: perhaps readers would have connected Herrick himself with the 'Priest', and although this sounds more like a casual and temporary clergyman, there is some continuation of the array of contexts identified already.

Near the end of the stanza the reference to 'Love's Firmament' is, in some ways, routine. Eyes are like stars sometimes, like suns at other times, and the idea of the lover's gaze as a twinkling heaven is highly congruent with the mood of the poem. The question as to what the point of this metaphor may be is more open to question. There is something standard about its presence, and its position in the line makes it seem as if its role is to fill up the metre with conventional matter. This seems to weigh against the elevation of love to some sort of spiritual level, but that whole process in the poem is handled so knowingly that it looks more like an offer to the reader to participate thoughtfully in generic interactions. Such an instance may offer a helpful way of questioning, from the perspective of a reader, where such a conventional gesture comes from. In some ways, the kinds of things a traditional poem might do seem to happen of their own accord once a framework is established, and then particular poets and speakers in their different ways let this language speak through them. They may of course adopt or inflect a particular kind of phrasing with a very strong sense of purpose. The key thing is that when dealing with the generic, the different sorts of origin and intention can all be weighed. A reader may, for example, be very aware that a poem has been set into motion according to a pattern wherein certain notable deviations or supplements carry all the sharp edges of the work's communication, even though they may be only a small part of its content.

The array of voices, readers, and contexts that may be inferred in a reading of 'Corinna's going a Maying' contributes to, and is inflected by, the larger array of the whole *Hesperides* volume. It is unclear how much design readers should see in the selection and ordering behind the collection, and how it should be read—how much its sequence and its interconnections matter, how much the occasional quality of many poems separates them from one another. The result is a plethora of patterns that could become salient, depending on dynamic intersections and the reader's own knowledge or intuitions.

Herrick prefatory poem 'The Argument of his Booke' suggests that 'Corinna' is a poem aligned with major structural themes. It mentions 'May' (line 2), 'May-poles' (3), 'Youth...Love' (5), and 'cleanly-Wantonnesse' (6) early among the things 'I sing of'. Another of the longer poems, placed much further into the collection, picks up the thread:

> Thy Wakes, thy Quintels, here thou hast,
> Thy May-poles too with Garlands grac't:
> Thy Morris-dance; thy Whitsun-ale;
> Thy Sheering-feast, which never faile.[17]

---

[17] 'The Country Life, to the Honoured M. End. Porter, Groome of the Bed-Chamber to his Maj.', ll. 52–5.

This vision of country life addressed to a courtier dwells on the kind of festivity seen in 'Corinna'. (The 'wakes' mentioned here took place on and around the parish's patron saint's day; 'quintels' were targets used in wedding games.) Although later readers have prized these two poems and made their connections closer as a result, the contribution of the nearly 500 poems in between, with varying (often minimal) shared interests, is hard to determine.

Another festive poem, a further 100 poems away, is addressed to another named woman. It too puts a speaker's search for love in the context of the ritual year:

> Come *Anthea* let us two
> Go to Feast, as others do.
> Tarts and Custards, Creams and Cakes,
> Are the Junketts still at Wakes:
> Unto which the Tribes resort,
> Where the businesse is the sport.[18]

'Junketts' here is a general term for party food—and Anthea is being invited, as Corinna is, to indulge. The reference to the 'Tribes' seems like a Biblical echo: Cain and Connolly cite Psalm 122.4, 'Whither the tribes go up, the tribes of the Lord, unto the testimony of Israel, to give thanks unto the name of the Lord.' As in 'Corinna', some sort of continuity or overlap between the Bible, the Church, and the pastimes of the country is offered. Such references are plentiful: in 'To the Lark' the speaker says his 'Mattens' 'betimes', 'because I doe / Begin to wooe' (ll. 2–4). These may be actual prayers, but the lark is then asked to be the 'Clark' (who guides the congregation in responses) who will help him know when to say 'Amen' (6–8), and later the 'High-Priest' (12).

'To the Lark' is only separated from 'Corinna' by thirty-five other poems, but there are more 'Mattens' in the 1069th, a further 850 into the collection. In this poem, 'To Julia', the context seems primarily religious, the 'Mattens' of line 2 complemented by 'Holy-water' (5) and 'Beads' (7), distinctly Catholic ways of deterring the 'Fiend' (3). The point could be erotic: private, intimate observance set against prying eyes. Julia is the target of other poems, including, for example, the 156th, also entitled 'To Julia', a love poem that (like 'Corinna') mentions a 'Tabernacle' (l. 5). Indeed, the poem right after 'Corinna' is 'On Julia's Breath', in which the speaker promises to 'deeply sweare' (l. 2) as to its wonderful aroma. The swearing may strike a religious chord; the name 'Julia' may link it to other poems to the same figure; and it participates in other threads that hold *Hesperides* together, for example in its evocation of the senses. The poem after this one is an epitaph, 'Upon a Child'; even here the request for flowers (on a grave), and the mention of the 'short Delight' (l. 2) offered by this particular life rather than life in general, offers some continuation of the mood of 'Corinna'.

At short range and long range, in ways that can seem continuous or discontinuous, *Hesperides* provides a network of possible contexts within which this poem and all its other poems can be read. This works alongside or in spite of their

---

[18] 'The Wake', 1–6.

claims to be read in the moment, on the day they are trying to seize. The kind of connectivity seen within the book shadows that beyond the book: there are elusive resonances and there are striking concatenations, and it is not easy to tell securely and definitively which is which. Herrick and his publisher have built a rich environment for inferences, wherein detail and genre and history all participate.

## SHORT- AND LONG-RANGE COMMUNICATION

Alastair Fowler suggested that genre itself could constitute the sort of 'shared domain of assumption' that enables communication to work.[19] He elaborated further in an essay on the subject:

> One may usefully think of genres as domains of association—specialized, literary equivalents of the fields of association whereby meaning is communicated in ordinary speech. As such, the genres adjust a reader's mental set and help in selecting the optimally relevant associations that amount to a meaning of the literary work.[20]

At the end of this quotation Fowler puts a footnote to Sperber and Wilson but does not explain that connection further. It is evident, though, that he recognizes the quality in relevance theory's model of communication that underlies the idea that genres provide contexts in which utterances become efficiently meaningful, and indeed possible at all.

While Fowler sees a productive link between genre and a theory of communication, it might be argued that such interactions do not require the idea of communication at all. Indeed, under the influence of Derrida and others, it has not been part of the recent critical lexicon.[21] The antipathy between Fowler's position and Derrida's has been mentioned above, and it is not only from a post-structuralist perspective that questions about literature and communication might be asked. Perhaps a direct model of communication could be tested against the indirect idea of 'overhearing', with an eye on John Stuart Mill's distinction between poetry and eloquence:

> Poetry and eloquence are both alike the expression or utterance of feeling: but, if we may be excused the antithesis, we should say that eloquence is *heard*; poetry is *overheard*. Eloquence supposes an audience. The peculiarity of poetry appears to us to lie in the poet's utter unconsciousness of a listener. Poetry is feeling confessing itself to itself in moments of solitude, and embodying itself in symbols which are the nearest possible representations of the feeling in the exact shape in which it exists in the poet's mind.[22]

---

[19] 'A New Theory of Communication', 17.

[20] Alastair Fowler, 'The formation of genres in the Renaissance and after', *New Literary History*, 34 (2003), 185–200.

[21] One key essay arguing that we should abandon the thought of a text as an intentional communication between writer and reader was Jacques Derrida's 'Signature event context', in his *Limited Inc.*, trans. Samuel Weber and Jeffrey Mehlman (Evanston, IL: Northwestern University Press, 1988).

[22] John Stuart Mill, 'Thoughts on poetry and its varieties', *The Crayon*, 7 (1860), 93–7, p. 95.

On the one hand, cognitive and pragmatic approaches have found overhearing a useful concept. It has been cited as a perspective from which to confront questions about the meaningfulness of an utterance, given that hearers are able to make sense of statements that are not spoken to or for them, wherein they have no interaction with any intention involved.[23] It has also proved useful as a framework in which to identify certain kinds of discourse where the truly important listener is, as far as explicit communication goes, not the present or intended hearer—as when a politician answers a specific question posed by an interviewer but embeds within it a sound-bite that will strike a chord with some members of later, distant audiences.[24] This might work quite well for a poem like 'Corinna's going a Maying', in which the ostensible immediate address leaves plenty for the incidental listener. However, it seems naïve to think that Herrick, with the different readerships for poetry in his time, and his awareness that he himself had read other poems like this aimed at other Corinnas, did not see such overhearers as essential hearers. 'The poet's utter unconsciousness of a listener' is a provocative but ultimately untenable thought. From another direction, cognitive readings of literature have rehabilitated some aspects of the idea of intention by seeing them as (more or less verifiable) characteristics of reading and listening. In contrast with Derrida, they claim that attention to a text always entails a posited speaker (or writer) and intention.[25]

In fact, Herrick's poem proposes its own relationship with listeners by ending with a plea to Corinna that resonates far beyond the setting. The final stanza is a call for immediate action but it is also a particularly strong intervention in the *carpe diem* tradition:

> Come, let us goe, while we are in our prime;
> And take the harmlesse follie of the time.
> > We shall grow old apace, and die
> > Before we know our liberty.
> > Our life is short; and our dayes run
> > As fast away as do's the Sunne:
> And as a vapour, or a drop of raine
> Once lost, can ne'r be found againe:
> > So when or you or I are made
> > A fable, song, or fleeting shade;
> > All love, all liking, all delight
> > Lies drown'd with us in endlesse night.
> Then while time serves, and we are but decaying;
> Come, my *Corinna*, come, let's goe a Maying.   (57–70)

[23] See Agustin Vicente and Fernando Martínez-Manrique, 'Overhearing a sentence: Recanati and the cognitive view of language', *Pragmatics and Cognition*, 12 (2004), 219–51.

[24] See Andreas H. Jucker, 'Mass media', in Jan-Ola Östman and Jef Verschueren (eds) *Pragmatics in Practice* (Amsterdam: John Benjamins, 2011), pp. 248–63; pp. 258–9.

[25] H. Porter Abbott, 'Reading intended meaning where none is intended: a cognitivist reappraisal of the implied author', *Poetics Today*, 32 (2011), 461–87, and David Herman, 'Narrative theory and the intentional stance', *Partial Answers*, 6 (2008), 233–60. See also, especially for its interesting discussion of readers as 'side-participants' in literary experience (a possible analogy with 'overhearing'), Richard J. Gerrig, *Experiencing Narrative Worlds: On the Psychological Activities of Reading* (New Haven, CT: Yale University Press, 1993), pp. 97–156.

There is not much vocabulary here to trigger contemporary associations. The most likely word of this sort is perhaps 'liberty', because it invokes a political milieu and the thought of tangible limitations on freedom. Counterbalancing this are some strikingly general similes: 'as a vapour, or a drop of rain'. Paramount among these is 'as fast away as do's the Sunne', which begs a question, to some extent, as to how speedily the sun moves. At dawn on May Day the sun is rising, not setting, and although a day is short in some respects, the moment of Maying is only part of it. It is not as if the idea is incomprehensible: the days can fly by or creep by, as and when. It is more that the sun is so temporarily recruited to the poem, performing, in passing, one of its infinite number of poetic roles. Alongside the particularity of some of the poem's images, it is striking that the final stanza should go in this direction.

One outcome of this change is that the poem ends with a compelling reach beyond its two local frameworks: the suitor's plea to Corinna and the religious politics of seventeenth-century England. Corinna—the name is classical, after all—could now be almost anyone. This remains a persuasive resource in the *carpe diem* tradition; lovers have always gestured towards the universal. Nevertheless, this final stanza has a much greater scope to its 'we'. As has already been said, this poem moves between urgency and patience, speaking in its own multiple presents but also making this scope available to later arrivals. It seems false to think of a modern reader as an overhearer of the poem. Poets cannot anticipate who will read their poems, but in the turn towards the sun and the rain in the final stanza of 'Corinna', we see how the always implicit allowance for future readers may verge on being explicit.

Like many other pastoral poets, Herrick uses tradition and posterity as screens for contemporary interests; and he uses contemporary interests as screens for tradition and posterity. Here I am using 'screen' in two overlapping senses: first, one thing may conceal the other, and second, one thing may be a surface on which the other is projected.[26] Each work will screen in different ways; some will make this interplay more evident than others. In Virgil's first Eclogue, for example, the shepherds' world is changed by the redistribution of farming land to army veterans, an immediate concern of the poet's Rome transplanted to Arcadia. The speakers of the first and later Eclogues are still possessed by their usual interests in love and nature, but their potential for addressing contemporary tensions is made explicit at an early point. Something similar may be seen to operate much closer to Herrick's time in Marvell's pastorals ('The Garden', 'The Nymph Complaining for the Death of her Faun', the Mower poems, parts of 'Upon Appleton House', and beyond). To varying extents a harsh world of conflict and political upheaval impinges on the security of the countryside; these are Civil War poems, and retreat itself evokes the origin being escaped.

Pastoral literature always has some form of double address, and often this enables a historicist approach to claim that the text's true (and perhaps only)

---

[26] For this idea in general, and specifically for the former sense, I am indebted to Simon Jarvis's essay 'Mock as screen and optic', *Critical Quarterly*, 46 (2004), 1–19.

liveliness comes in relation to its first readers and the concerns on which the text may—forlornly or not—be expected to have an effect. With the pressure from historicism on one side, and an antipathy towards invoking authorial intention on the other, it has become difficult to talk about how a poem like 'Corinna's going a Maying' is written for much later readers, and is thus communicating things to them. And yet it does not seem fanciful to say that a *carpe diem* poem cannot be innocent of its adaptability to any later *diem*. Good reading, not just good scholarly reading, can hold different time-scales in mind. The flexibility of relevance theory offers welcome relief from some of the binds that follow from thinking that a historicist approach and transhistorical reception are mutually incompatible.

One answer is to see the poem as an 'array'—the term derived from Sperber and Wilson above—of multiple possibilities, ready for a reader to infer the appropriate contexts by which to ascertain relevance. These possibilities could be called intentions, indeed authorial intentions, but that is not an essential step in the model: some could be set in motion in the writing of the poem, but they result from the life of the poem in the world and the things readers make of it. A pastoral poem may seem to have many connections with other works in the tradition, some specific and easily justified, some less so. It could be decided that only things plausibly intended by the author are admissible; or it could be decided that anything read into the poem is fair enough. Relevance theory offers a middle ground, where a poet has an array of intentions in a more open-ended way, which gives readers room to manoeuvre in making their own literary interconnections, because this type of poem evokes other examples of this type of poem, and both author and reader know they inhabit that network of possibilities in different ways. It is not limitless but it is not destined for narrow convergence.

In this model the reader may also be thought of as an array of sorts. There are forms of response taking place in the reader's present, and there are others that reconstruct the work's first appearances in the world. Different texts and different contexts of reading will adjust the balances. Although this scenario is not precisely envisaged in the work of Sperber and Wilson, which is focused on spoken communication for the most part, it only requires a small stretch to see that an utterance as complex as a poem could provide multiple contexts, and readers will dispose themselves in different ways towards those contexts. A good reading, especially within a scholarly context, will be open to the poem's shorter and longer ranges, to its urgency and its patience.

# Interlace 3

*Having considered how the shifting historical contexts of literary works can be accounted for within a relevance theory perspective, we come now to a methodological question which will remain central, in one way or another, to the remaining chapters in this book: how might the perceptual and sensorimotor effects of literary utterances be integrated into the inferential model of communication and cognition proposed by relevance theory? Guillemette Bolens begins with a classic example of a communicative exchange that depends heavily on the mutual inferential and contextual responses of the speakers. She cites the claim of relevance theorists that, as a basic ingredient of any cognitive system, inference need be neither voluntary nor conscious, and she uses that claim as the platform for an analysis of two sharply contrasted literary works in which the search for relevance is extended to specifically kinesic modes of inference.*

*What is meant by 'kinesis' is the apprehension by an observer—who may be an interlocutor or a reader[1]—of gestural and sensorimotor effects. The notion of kinesic communication evoked here rests on a widely accepted finding from neuroscience. When a salient action (chopping wood, climbing over a fence, pouring water from a kettle, getting out of a bath) is observed or even reported verbally, the corresponding part of the observer's motor system will be activated in preparatory mode. This response is felt (if it is strong enough) as an echo or reverberation of the given action: imagine what it feels like to climb over a fence, then what it feels like to climb out of a bath and you'll see the point. Such 'motor resonance' responses are apparent in collective behaviour (swarms, crowds, audiences), but they also enable reciprocal actions, whether sympathetic, defensive, or aggressive. That wider range of responses depends on typically automatic (non-reflective) inferential processes, as when tennis players project the outcome of their adversary's movements and respond with appropriate counter-movements.*

*The fact that such responses are activated in the course of verbal communication is of fundamental importance for the understanding of why literature, with its virtually limitless range of kinesic styles, can have such powerful effects. These effects operate at two main levels. The first is that of the reader's immediate encounter with the text, and is typically non-reflective (we don't keep interrupting the reading process to ask ourselves what we're feeling). The second is the higher-order, reflective mode, to which literary criticism in the broadest sense belongs. Reflective readers who are discerning about such*

---

[1] *The word 'reader' here stands in for the whole spectrum of parallel roles that includes 'listener', 'viewer', 'spectator', etc.*

*things are exercising what Bolens calls 'kinesic intelligence'.*[2] *These are not two uncon-nected levels: there is constant feedback between them.*

*Bolens's close readings of Flaubert and Cervantes demonstrate that the inferential model as elaborated by relevance theory is perfectly compatible with an analysis that focuses on kinesic effects. Indeed, whether we are speaking of the tightly tied knots on Don Quixote's home-made helmet, or Charles Bovary's apprehension of the movement of dust or the cry of a hen, the reader's attention to the insistent undercurrent of pre-reflective responses becomes the platform (the affordance) for a critical awareness that reaches across every level of the text, whether thematic, lexical, or stylistic. The percep-tual and sensory shaping of the search for relevance, in other words, saturates the whole communicative exchange.*

---

[2] *For a more detailed definition and account of 'kinesic intelligence', based on Ellen Spolsky's use of this expression, see Bolens,* The Style of Gestures, *pp. 1–5.*

# 3

# Relevance Theory and Kinesic Analysis in *Don Quixote* and *Madame Bovary*

*Guillemette Bolens*

## RELEVANCE AND KINESIS

'What can you possibly mean?' is an English sentence that belongs to a somewhat formal register of current usage. It may be used rhetorically to imply, 'What a silly idea!', or more simply, 'I don't understand your meaning.' In any case, whether intended as a way of optimizing the success of an act of communication or not, uttered with a condescending or outraged tone of voice, it exists in Modern English and is used regularly enough to be recognized as conveying a request to know—or an intention to put into question—the intended meaning of an interlocutor. The more common, 'What do you mean?' also points towards the fundamental fact that a discrepancy is expected between the words we utter or write and what we intend to convey by uttering them. He says, 'Let's go for a walk.' She opens the window and replies, 'Why not?' A moment later, they leave by the door. Relevance theory addresses the fact that they understand each other to the point of actually going for a walk. He does not launch into a tedious list of reasons why they might not do so. The central question for relevance theory is, how do they manage to communicate successfully despite the discrepancy between literal and intended meaning?[1] He makes good the discrepancy between the stated and the intended meaning of the reply by inferring supplementary information that enables him to see its relevance in context.[2]

In real-life situations, the severity of the discrepancy between literal and implied meaning is variable in an infinite number of ways, ranging from the matter-of-factly shared purpose that prompts a rapid resolution of all ambiguities, to the most sadistic power games that thrive on and require ambiguity for their effects. Mobbing (or workplace bullying) is a social instance of such a phenomenon turned

---

[1] Dan Sperber and Deirdre Wilson, *Relevance: Communication and Cognition* (Oxford: Blackwell, 2nd ed., 1995), p. 45: 'Communication is governed by a less-than-perfect heuristic. ... [F]ailures in communication are to be expected: what is mysterious and requires explanation is not failure but success.'

[2] See Deirdre Wilson and Dan Sperber, 'Relevance theory', in Laurence R. Horn and Gregory Ward (eds) *The Handbook of Pragmatics* (Oxford: Blackwell, 2004), pp. 607–32.

into a technique of mental destruction. Everything is possible between and beyond such cases. In consequence, a theory that elucidates the way relevance functions in human communication matters.

The gap between literal and intended meanings is bridged by inferential procedures geared to the search for relevance. She replies, 'Why not?' and he infers that she agrees to go for a walk. An inference 'is the production of new mental representations on the basis of previously held representations'.[3] Inference is 'a basic ingredient of any cognitive system'. It 'need not be deliberate or conscious. It is at work not only in conceptual thinking but also in perception and in motor control'.[4] In this chapter, I will focus on inferences that pertain to motor control and kinesis. By kinesis I mean the gestural, postural, and sensorimotor dimension of any interaction. He infers that she agrees to go out by the door, not the window. To analyse kinesis in literature is to focus on the way in which language is used in a work to account for the narrative space created by interpersonal gestures, for the kinaesthetic sensations experienced by characters and potentially retrieved by readers, and for the kinetic events pertaining to gravity and the physical laws governing the storyworld.[5] If she tries to leave his ninth-floor apartment by the window, she will probably never be able to go for a walk with him again—unless she is Catwoman.

Relevance in acts of communication is a focus in both Cervantes's *Don Quixote* (1605, 1615) and Flaubert's *Madame Bovary* (1856, 1857), and it operates on two levels. One level corresponds to interactions between characters in the plot, the other to readers' reception of the overarching utterance constituting the literary work. My purpose is to address both levels while linking relevance theory to kinesic analysis, in order to find ways of accounting for some of the cognitive processes activated in literary reception when we understand complex kinesic information. While relevance theory helps account for communicational inference procedures within the plot as well as in the work's literary reception, kinesic analysis addresses the specific type of inference elicited in readers by linguistic utterances referring to gestural and sensorimotor elements of the narrative (or poem, or play).

An inference process can be 'protracted',[6] for example when a narrative achieves relevance progressively, by increasing the manifestness of salient features incrementally (cf. Chapters 8 and 9 in this volume). I will concentrate on this possibility in the first section of the chapter. In *Madame Bovary*, one single kinesic verb is made gradually to appear more meaningful because of its very repetition in emotionally charged diegetic contexts. Repetition draws the reader's attention to the possibility

---

[3] Hugo Mercier and Dan Sperber, 'Why do humans reason? Arguments for an argumentative theory', *Behavioral and Brain Sciences*, 34 (2011), 57–111, p. 57.

[4] Mercier and Sperber, 'Why do humans reason?', 57.

[5] On kinesic analysis in literature and the distinction between kinesis, kinaesthesia, and kinetics, see Guillemette Bolens, *The Style of Gestures: Embodiment and Cognition in Literary Narrative* (Baltimore, MD: The Johns Hopkins University Press, 2012); and *L'Humour et le savoir des corps: Don Quichotte, Tristram Shandy et le rire du lecteur* (Rennes, France: Presses Universitaires de Rennes, 2016).

[6] Dan Sperber and Deirdre Wilson, 'Beyond speaker's meaning', *Croatian Journal of Philosophy*, 15.44 (2015), 117–49, p. 134.

of an implicature; that is, an intended implication which is not part of the encoded meaning of the words on the page, but which the reader may be encouraged to infer by stylistic features, such as reiteration.[7] A focus on one single verb will also lead me to highlight the difficulty faced by translators when they must find equivalents for a recurrent term the specific meaning of which is inflected by each new context of use. We will see that six English verbs prove necessary to translate one French verb in *Madame Bovary*. The result is that the relevance effect of reiteration is then lost, while the kinesic relevance of each English verb is satisfied.

I have selected passages from Cervantes and Flaubert which combine the two levels of relevance mentioned above. In these passages, relevance is achieved via gestures, actions, and interactions between characters in the plot, while implicatures regarding kinesis are prompted at the level of readerly reception. In *Don Quixote*, the action is that of wearing a helmet whose straps are impossible to unfasten. The cognitive process of perceptually simulating the action of trying to unfasten tight knots grounds an inference (considerable strength was used to tie the knots) that informs an unspecified yet relevant aspect in the narrative, giving rise to a humorous implicature.

Perceptual simulations are an important aspect of embodied cognition and kinesic analysis in literature. They are dynamic cognitive processes, which reactivate in the reader a type of knowledge that is sensory (derived from sight, hearing, touch, taste, or smell), motor (kinesic, kinaesthetic, proprioceptive), and introspective (pertaining to emotions and mental states).[8] Horchak and colleagues explain that 'recent years in science have been marked by accumulation of empirical and theoretical evidence to support a claim that bodily states and modality-specific simulations play important roles in processing of language' (p. 67).[9] 'There is now a wealth of evidence suggesting that sensorimotor grounding is necessary for language comprehension' (p. 77). Whether we watch a movement or read about it, the actual or mentally simulated 'perception of sequences activates motor mechanisms because they induce potential movements in relation to the attended stimuli'.[10] Indeed, 'the processing of language related to action shares the same [neuronal] resources as the corresponding motor actions' (p. 161). We understand

---

[7] Wayne Davis, 'Implicature', in *The Stanford Encyclopedia of Philosophy* (Spring 2013 edition), ed. Edward N. Zalta, http://plato.stanford.edu/archives/spr2013/entries/implicature. Laurence Horn gives the following definition: 'Implicature is a component of speaker meaning that constitutes an aspect of what is *meant* in a speaker's utterance without being part of what is *said*. What a speaker intends to communicate is characteristically far richer than what she directly expresses; linguistic meaning radically underdetermines the message conveyed and understood' ('Implicature', in Horn and Ward, *The Handbook of Pragmatics*, pp. 3–28, p. 3).

[8] Bolens, *The Style of Gestures*, pp. 11–19; see also Keith D. Markman, William M.P. Klein, and Julie A. Suhr (eds), *The Handbook of Imagination and Mental Simulation* (New York: Taylor and Francis, Psychology Press, 2009).

[9] See Oleksandr V. Horchak et al., 'From demonstration to theory in embodied language comprehension: a review', *Cognitive Systems Research*, 29–30 (2014), 66–85, http://dx.doi.org/10.1016/j.cogsys.2013.09.002 [accessed 27 June 2016]; see also Diane Pecher and Rolf A. Zwaan (eds), *Grounding Cognition: The Role of Perception and Action in Memory, Language, and Thinking* (Cambridge: Cambridge University Press, 2005).

[10] Marc Jeannerod, *Motor Cognition: What Actions Tell the Self* (Oxford: Oxford University Press, 2006), p. 142.

a kinesic verb such as *to drag* when we cognitively trigger a perceptual simulation of what it sensorily and perceptually entails to perform such an action. If we need to distinguish between the verbs *to drag, to creep*, and *to linger*, we trigger nuanced and focused perceptual simulations of the actions described by these three verbs, to cognitively enhance the kinesic variations between them. Perceptual simulations are paramount in all understanding of gestures and movements, in literary reception no less than in common verbal communications. I will claim that, while being generally pre-reflective, they may become the focus of reflective attention, especially when they feature in literary analysis.[11]

## KINESIS AND THE ART OF TRANSLATION:
## EMMA BOVARY'S GAIT

Jean Starobinski opens his essay 'L'échelle des températures: Lecture du corps dans *Madame Bovary*'[12] with the following quotation from Flaubert's novel:

> [S]he did not say a word, and neither did Charles. The draught, slipping in under the door, thrust a little dust onto the flags; he watched it creep along [*il la regardait se traîner*], and all he could hear was the inward throbbing of his head, with the cry of a hen, in the distance, laying its eggs in the yard.   (I, 3, p. 21)[13]

When I first read this quotation in Starobinski's essay, the scene struck me as strangely violent, even though it describes the least violent or frightening scene one can imagine: a silent man watching dust. A possible reason may be that in this passage the object pronoun *la* in 'il la regardait se traîner' is ambiguous: it could refer to Emma or to dust (which is feminine in French: *la poussière*). Of course, within a second we assign reference; that is, we choose and decide that, grammatically and logically, 'la' refers to dust. Yet one may conceivably need that second to perform the cognitive act of assigning the reference. Starobinski shows that the point of view in this early scene shifts from external witness to Charles's perspective.[14] Before and after the dust-watching line, Charles' attention—and ours—is on Emma. Furthermore, the verb is reflexive (*se traîner*), as if the dust were an

[11] See Guillemette Bolens, 'Les simulations perceptives et l'analyse kinésique dans le dessin et dans l'image poétique', *Textimage : Revue d'étude du dialogue texte-image*, 4 (2014), http://archive-ouverte. unige.ch/unige:74799; 'Les simulations perceptives dans la relation aux œuvres d'art littéraires', in Mireille Besson, Catherine Courtet, Françoise Lavocat, and Alain Viala (eds) *Corps en scènes* (Paris: Éditions du CNRS, 2015), pp. 115–25, http://archive-ouverte.unige.ch/unige:76393; 'Cognition et sensorimotricité, humour et timing chez Cervantès, Sterne et Proust', in Françoise Lavocat (ed.) *L'interprétation littéraire et les sciences cognitives* (Paris: Éditions Hermann, 2016), pp. 33–55, http:// archive-ouverte.unige.ch/unige:84248.

[12] Jean Starobinski, 'L'échelle des températures: Lecture du corps dans *Madame Bovary*', in Gérard Genette and Tzvetan Todorov (eds) *Travail de Flaubert* (Paris: Seuil, 1983), pp. 45–78.

[13] Gustave Flaubert, *Madame Bovary*, edited by Bernard Ajac (Paris: GF Flammarion, 1986, 2006), p. 81; the same edition is used for all quotations from this text: 'elle [Emma] ne parlait pas. Charles non plus. L'air, passant par le dessous de la porte, poussait un peu de poussière sur les dalles; il la regardait se traîner, et il entendait seulement le battement intérieur de sa tête, avec le cri d'une poule, au loin, qui pondait dans les cours' (I, 3); trans. Adam Thorpe (London: Vintage, 2011); the same translation is used for all other quotations from this text, unless otherwise specified.

[14] Starobinski, 'L'échelle des températures', pp. 45–6.

agent, dragging itself on the ground—a rather unusual lexical choice for dust in French. Thus, for a second again, this action verb is contaminating the other agent, Emma, the predominant object of Charles's attention. The potential *mis*-reading *Charles regardait Emma se traîner* is cognitively interesting, as the reader—*a* possible reader—may need a moment to decide that *la* does not refer to Emma.

Contamination also affects the sentence that follows: 'il entendait seulement le battement intérieur de sa tête, avec le cri d'une poule, au loin, qui pondait dans les cours'. A superficial translation erases the ambiguity: 'He watched it drift along, and heard nothing but the throbbing in his head and the faint clucking of a hen that had laid an egg in the yard.'[15] Adam Thorpe's translation is more to the point: 'He watched it creep along, and all he could hear was the inward throbbing of his head, with the cry of a hen, in the distance, laying its eggs in the yard' (I, 3, p. 21). My aim in the following pages is to substantiate my claim that Thorpe's translation is the more accurate and critically relevant. In this passage, it matters that dust *creeps* and hens *cry*, thus awkwardly gesturing towards potentially human agency and emotions.

When reading *Madame Bovary*, my odd assumption of violence in the passage quoted above was progressively strengthened, owing to the reiteration of the verb *(se) traîner* in the rest of the novel. For the verb *(se) traîner* occurs at expressive moments, gradually increasing its degree of manifestness.

1) Emma's voice at times 'would drawl in a singsong [*traînait des modulations*] that finished almost as a murmur' (p. 22).[16]

2) In the forest, after making love to Rodolphe for the first time, 'she heard from far and away, beyond the wood, on the opposite hills, an indistinct and protracted cry, a voice that lingered [*une voix qui se traînait*]' (p. 153).[17]

3) While Hippolyte has his leg amputated, 'Charles considered her [Emma] with the confused gaze of a drunkard, while listening, motionless, to the amputee's last screams succeeding one another in long drawn-out inflections [*en modulations traînantes*], cut off by shrill bursts' (p. 175).[18]

4) After receiving Rodolphe's catastrophic letter, Emma 'dragged herself [*se traîna*] over to the closed garret-window' (p. 194).[19]

5) During the performance of the opera *Lucie de Lammermoor*, Emma 'filled her heart with these tuneful lamentations that were drawn out [*qui se traînaient*] to the accompaniment of the double-basses, like the cries of the drowned in the storm's uproar' (p. 212).[20]

---

[15] Trans. Eleanor Marx-Aveling, The Gutenberg Project (2006, 2012), www.gutenberg.org/files/2413/2413-h/2413-h.htm [accessed 27 June 2016].

[16] '[T]raînait des modulations qui finissaient presque en murmures' (p. 82).

[17] '[E]lle entendit tout au loin, au-delà du bois, sur les autres collines, un cri vague et prolongé, une voix qui se traînait' (p. 228).

[18] 'Charles la considérait [Emma] avec le regard trouble d'un homme ivre, tout en écoutant, immobile, les derniers cris de l'amputé qui se suivaient en modulations traînantes, coupées de saccades aiguës' (p. 253).

[19] '[S]e traîna jusqu'à la mansarde close' (p. 273).

[20] 'Elle [Emma] s'emplissait le cœur de ces lamentations mélodieuses qui se traînaient à l'accompagnement des contrebasses, comme des cris de naufragés dans le tumulte d'une tempête' (p. 293).

My last example refers to the emblematic blind beggar:

6) 'Sometimes, he would appear behind Emma quite suddenly, bareheaded. She would draw back with a cry. ... His voice, feeble at first and wailing, grew shrill. It lingered [*elle se traînait*] in the night, like the indistinct lamentation of a dim distress; and, through the jingling of the harness bells, the murmur of the trees and the drone of the hollow box, it had something faraway about it that troubled Emma. Down it went into the depths of her soul like a whirlpool in an abyss, sweeping her off amid the spaces of a limitless melancholy' (p. 255).[21]

Two brief points before we grapple with *se traîner*. First of all, five of the six passages listed above refer to voices and cries. In the dust-watching scene, the *cri* is that of a hen. This domestic bird appears in this passage and reappears at the end of the novel, when Emma's father comes to visit her, unaware that she is already dead and that he is going to attend her funeral. Yet, on the road he sees three black hens in a tree and inexplicably panics.[22] Earlier in the novel, Emma is compared to a non-specific bird (p. 310); later on, she wishes she were one (p. 366). At the beginning of the novel, after meeting Charles, she thinks of passion as a great pink bird[23]—the disillusion will be long and painful. And thus, it seems that references to birds, including hens, gesture towards Emma.

My second point relates to the fact that the initial dust-watching scene shows Emma darning a white cotton stocking while her future fiancé is sitting next to her.[24] At the very end of the novel, Emma and Charles's orphan daughter Berthe is said to be raised by an aunt who, being too poor, must send her to work in a cotton mill ('une filature de coton') (p. 425). It seems retrospectively that the catastrophe is already underway when Emma, silent, is darning cotton and Charles, also silent, is watching dust creeping on the floor, sensing a throbbing in his head and hearing

---

[21] 'Quelquefois, il apparaissait tout à coup derrière Emma, tête nue. Elle se retirait avec un cri. ... Sa voix, faible d'abord et vagissante, devenait aiguë. Elle se traînait dans la nuit, comme l'indistincte lamentation d'une vague détresse; et, à travers la sonnerie des grelots, le murmure des arbres et le ronflement de la boîte creuse, elle avait quelque chose de lointain qui bouleversait Emma. Cela lui descendait au fond de l'âme comme un tourbillon dans un abîme, et l'emportait parmi les espaces d'une mélancolie sans bornes' (p. 340).

[22] 'Le jour se leva, il aperçut trois poules noires qui dormaient dans un arbre; il tressaillit, épouvanté de ce présage. Alors il promit à la sainte Vierge trois chasubles pour l'église, et qu'il irait pieds nus depuis le cimetière des Bertaux jusqu'à la chapelle de Vassonville' (p. 410) ['The day broke, he saw three black hens sleeping in a tree; he gave a start, terrified by this omen. So he promised the Holy Virgin three chasubles for the church, and that he would go barefoot from the cemetery at Les Bertaux to the chapel at Vassonville'; p. 320].

[23] 'Mais l'anxiété d'un état nouveau, ou peut-être l'irritation causée par la présence de cet homme, avait suffi à lui faire croire qu'elle possédait enfin cette passion merveilleuse qui jusqu'alors s'était tenue comme un grand oiseau au plumage rose planant dans la splendeur des ciels poétiques' (pp. 99–100) ['But the anxiety of a new state of mind, or perhaps the nervous irritation caused by the presence of this man, had sufficed to make her believe that, at last, she was in possession of that wondrous passion which up to then had remained like a great bird with rosy feathers soaring through the splendour of poetical skies'; p. 37].

[24] 'Elle se rassit et elle reprit son ouvrage, qui était un bas de coton blanc où elle faisait des reprises: elle travaillait le front baissé; elle ne parlait pas. Charles non plus' (p. 81) ['She sat down and picked up her work again, a white cotton stocking that she was darning; she worked with her head down; she did not say a word, and neither did Charles'; p. 21].

the cry of a hen. But this inference can be fully drawn only at the end of the novel. If it is viable to judge that the novel is organized in a way that induces it, then we may consider it to be an implicature. One possible implicature in *Madame Bovary* would thus be that the doom of Emma, Charles, and their future daughter is already underway in the dust-watching scene. Flaubert's novel is a tragedy for this very reason: the characters' fate is sealed from the start.

*Madame Bovary* is a tragedy on the theme of boredom. It bears on the violence of boredom and the torture of forced inaction due to socio-cultural norms and a general stupidity.[25] It is about a tremendously banal domestic cry, heard by an empty-headed man who cannot make sense of more than his own throbbing sensations, even though he keeps watching, watching but not seeing her *se traîner*. The beggar is not the only blind man in the novel.

*Une traînée* is an old-fashioned term for a prostitute or a lewd woman. This noun never appears and is not relevant in this text, even though prostitution briefly becomes an issue at the end, before being immediately discarded. An analysis of correlated passages shows that it is the verb, rather, that is relevant. 'Style arises... in the pursuit of relevance.'[26] It is through style in Flaubert's novel that the verb *se traîner* becomes relevant, as its repetition and specific use progressively call for attention.[27] Whether applied to sound and voice, or to movement and gait, this verb transmits the sensation of a vitality that is gradually drained out by meaninglessness and a slow motivational collapse. The progressive and torturing cancellation narrated in this novel is caused by repeated petty social, intellectual, and emotional limitations. It is a tragedy in the sense that it narrates the ineluctable impact of a chain of actions. Only, in this case, the actions are all marked by a mediocrity that determines the fate of a child, delivered at the end in two lines, after the meaningless life and death of her parents.

This takes us to our seventh and final instance of the verb *(se) traîner*. In the following passage, Emma is speaking to Léon: 'Is it not quite the saddest thing, to be spinning out [*traîner*], as I am doing, a useless existence?' (p. 224).[28] On reaching this passage, my assumption felt strong that the sentence 'il la regardait se traîner' in the dust-watching scene affords relevance in a particularly pregnant way that involves Emma.

In this process, perceptual simulations are instrumental. To better understand the exact way the style of *Madame Bovary* channels my attention, I may want to perceive its utterances more fully, and to perceive them more fully, I may activate

---

[25] See Jacques Neefs and Claude Mouchard, *Flaubert* (Paris: Balland 1986), pp. 154–7; Jonathan Culler, *Flaubert: The Uses of Uncertainty* (London: Paul Elek, 1974).

[26] Sperber and Wilson, *Relevance*, p. 219.

[27] Style was a constant focus of attention for Flaubert, as in this remark in a letter to Louise Colet about *Madame Bovary*: 'Ce livre, qui n'est qu'en style, a pour danger continuel le style même' ['This book, which is nothing but style, is constantly threatened by style itself'] (23 January 1854), in *Flaubert, correspondance*, edited by Bertrand Le Gendre (Paris: Editions Perrin, 2013), p. 92. On Flaubert's style in conversation with Montaigne's style, see Timothy Chesters, 'Flaubert's reading notes on Montaigne', *French Studies*, 63.4 (2009), 399–415.

[28] 'Ce qu'il y a de plus lamentable, n'est-ce pas, c'est de traîner, comme moi, une existence inutile?' (p. 306).

and increase my attention to perceptual simulations of what it means kinesically, for instance, to walk *en se traînant*, or for the modulations of a voice to *traîner*. Perceptual simulations play an important part, I wish to claim, in lexical narrowing and lexical broadening (as explained in the Introduction to this volume and discussed by Timothy Chesters in Chapter 8). Depending on whether the verb applies to a voice, to a scream, to a gait, or to Emma's life, the verb *se traîner* is narrowed or broadened into a contextually ad hoc kinesic concept. It may be that Adam Thorpe performed such cognitive acts of perceptual simulation when, for one and the same French verb, he selected six different verbs in English: *creep, draw out, linger, drag, drawl,* and *spin out*. It may be that he produced a perceptual simulation of *se traîner* situated in each specific context, each time opting for an English verb that best fitted the kinesic simulation he mentally triggered. He would then choose the English verb that was most relevant to its exact meaning in French; that is, to the way in which its use in a given context created specific inferences regarding the precise quality of the kinesic action meant by the verb.

As far as literary reception is concerned, when I engage in the text through reflective perceptual simulations, my sensorimotor memory may be impacted differently. When Flaubert uses the same verb again and again in a way that stylistically calls for attention, I may consequently be better prepared to acknowledge the lexical and kinesic correlation that is thus created between passages. In sum, perceptual simulations in literary reception may be seen as part of the cognitive process of lexical narrowing and lexical broadening, eliciting the retrospective strengthening or cancellation of assumptions regarding a type of relevance that manifests itself via stylistic choices through the text as a whole. Perceptual simulations are pre-reflective when we cognitively process and understand an action verb in a sentence. But they may become a reflective focus of attention when we try to come to terms with the reasons why we understand a narrated movement the way we do.

The bird that screams in the dust-watching scene is a hen. The violence is in the triviality. It takes a genius such as Flaubert to communicate successfully the humour of tragedy and the tragic dimension of triviality.[29] Flaubert's hen is not uttering a faint clucking, as one translator would have it, but rather the kind of louder and higher-pitched note hens produce in the middle of their clucking. Clearly, no sense of grandeur can be salvaged from a scene featuring such a sound. Meanwhile, the word *cri*, when taken out of context, is far-ranging and may suggest such emotions as distress or anger, in addition to the sound produced by a hen in a courtyard. In this instance, relevance at the level of the work as a whole resides in the choice of the word *cri*. Such a stylistic choice is relevant in the communicational acts of writing *and* of reading this novel. Lexically speaking, French has a verb for *clucking*: 'caqueter'. Flaubert did not choose it. He selected the embodied kinesic concept of *cri*, whose sensorimotor features may apply to humans. *Cri* is

---

[29] The interpretation of the verb *traîner* in the seventh quotation above is all the more interesting in that a subtle sense of irony pervades the exchange between Emma and Léon in this passage, linking triviality and banality, here as elsewhere, with tragedy and a sense of gradual cancellation.

underspecified, and this very fact makes room for inferences and a much wider range of implicatures.[30] To translate *cri* by *clucking* is to limit such potentialities in our reception. It is to remain blind (or deaf) to Flaubert's act of writing, to his literary utterance as it weaves a trivial tragedy, always and at the same time dire, ridiculous, and breathtakingly beautiful.[31] The same is true with the choice of *se traîner*. Adam Thorpe translates each occurrence of this verb very distinctly, showing an interpretive grasp of the polysemic nuances of the verb, and of the contextual and background information which affords relevance and meaning to each instance throughout the novel at large.[32] For instance, it matters that he opts for the autonomous motion verb *to creep* to translate the uncanny image of dust *se traînant* on the ground, 'dragging itself' on the ground. For the oddity of such an image in French as in English is relevant in *Madame Bovary*.

My aim in paying attention to Flaubert's use of the verb *se traîner* has been to highlight one of the ways in which relevance may arise at the level of readerly reception regarding kinesis. Through the repetition of *se traîner* (in addition to other narrative means), the novel successfully expresses what failed verbal and kinesic communication may look and feel like. Indeed, failed communication is thematically at the core of Flaubert's novel. The following quotation makes the point with ruthless eloquence:

> If Charles had wanted it, however, if he had suspected something, if his gaze, just once, had come to meet her thoughts, it seemed to her that a sudden plenteousness would have detached itself from her heart, as the fruit of an espalier falls when a hand is laid upon it. But, as the intimacy of their life pressed them closer to each other, an indifference grew inside that loosened her from him.
>
> Charles's conversation was as flat as a street pavement, and everyone's ideas paraded along it in their ordinary dress, without rousing emotion, laughter or dreams.   (p. 38)[33]

---

[30] Underdeterminacy (or underspecification) is central to relevance theory precisely because it is what triggers the inferential process; on underspecification in literary contexts, see Terence Cave, *Thinking with Literature: Towards a Cognitive Criticism* (Oxford: Oxford University Press, 2016).

[31] Flaubert writes to Louise Colet about *Madame Bovary*: 'Toute la valeur de mon livre, s'il en a une, sera d'avoir su marcher droit sur un cheveu, suspendu entre le double abîme du lyrisme et du vulgaire (que je veux fondre dans une analyse narrative). Quand je pense à ce que cela peut être, j'en ai des éblouissements. Mais lorsque je songe ensuite que tant de beauté m'est confiée, à moi, j'ai des coliques d'épouvante, à fuir me cacher n'importe où.' ['The whole value of my book, if it has any at all, will be that I managed to keep walking straight along a strand of hair suspended above the double abyss of lyricism and vulgarity (which I want to fuse in a narrative analysis). When I think of what this may come to be, it dazzles me. But then, when I realize that all this beauty is entrusted to me, to me alone, my stomach cramps with terror, and I feel like running away to hide, no matter where.'] (20 March 1852), in *Flaubert, correspondance*, edited by Le Gendre, p. 87.

[32] On this question in translation studies, see Klaus Gommlich, 'Can translators learn two representational perspectives?', in J. Danks, G.M. Shreve, S.B. Fountain, and M.K. McBeath (eds) *Cognitive Processes in Translation and Interpreting* (Thousand Oaks, CA; London; New Delhi: Sage Publications, 1997), pp. 57–76.

[33] 'Si Charles l'avait voulu, cependant, s'il s'en fût douté, si son regard, une seule fois, fût venu à la rencontre de sa pensée, il lui [Emma] semblait qu'une abondance subite se serait détachée de son cœur, comme tombe la récolte d'un espalier, quand on y porte la main. Mais à mesure que se serrait davantage l'intimité de leur vie, un détachement intérieur se faisait qui la déliait de lui.

La conversation de Charles était plate comme un trottoir de rue, et les idées de tout le monde y défilaient, dans leur costume ordinaire, sans exciter d'émotion, de rire ou de rêverie' (pp. 100–1).

In a way, Emma Bovary died because Charles was watching but would never see. Charles is guilty by perceptual, cognitive, and imaginative omission. Relevance is not only required for the speaker to make sense, it is also required for the addressee to be attentive, to acknowledge the speaker's intention to communicate, and, in the full kinesic sense, to *come to meet* his or her thoughts:[34] 'si son regard, une seule fois, fût venu à la rencontre de sa pensée, il lui semblait qu'une abondance subite se serait détachée de son cœur' ['if his gaze, just once, had come to meet her thoughts, it seemed to her that a sudden plenteousness would have detached itself from her heart, as the fruit [literally, *the harvest*] of an espalier falls when a hand is laid upon it']. This is style at work. Flaubert does not specify what this sudden plenteousness is made of, and it is eminently relevant and powerful that he does not: this type of abundance and its kinesis, expressed by a yielding movement in response to an approaching hand, has no specified object, while its express and necessary condition is the attention of another human. A perceived intention to communicate, and the act of attending to such an intention, ground the possibility of intersubjectivity and, for that very reason, the emergence of language.[35]

Relevance theory and kinesic analysis may help us pay attention to a sentence like 'il la regardait se traîner' in Flaubert's novel, and to its odd sense of violence. They may jointly shed light on important aspects of literary reception, such as pragmatic inferences and perceptual simulations. They increase our attention to some of the things we do when we read, whether the utterance is a seemingly simple exchange about going for a walk or a complex novel of social, psychological, and emotional disconnection and communicational breakdown. This form of attention to kinesic aspects and the way they achieve relevance is part of what is called kinesic intelligence in literary analysis.


## KINESIC HUMOUR IN LITERATURE: DON QUIXOTE'S HELMET AND ITS RIBBONS

In Deirdre Wilson's novel *Slave of the Passions*, we read:

> Over dinner they ran out of conversation. Grace found that being committed doesn't make it any easier to talk. Beneath the surface of her consciousness all sorts of flashes and fancies glided; she could feel them dart and slither as she bent her face to her meal. She kept reaching down with her shrimping net, but all she came up with was rusty metal. Andrew was tired and didn't help, or perhaps he was having similar problems. What we're able to fish up and formulate gives so meagre an idea of what goes on in

---

[34] This overall aspect pertains to a meta-pragmatic level that does not contradict the idea—central in relevance theory—that for optimal relevance to be achieved, an utterance must not cause wasted or gratuitous effort in the audience, so that any effort demanded by the communicator must be compensated for by some cognitive effect.

[35] See Riccardo Fusaroli, Nivedita Gangopadhyay, and Kristian Tylén, 'The dialogically extended mind: language as skilful intersubjective engagement', *Cognitive Systems Research*, 29–30 (2014), 31–9.

the depths of our minds. How to break down the dam between these rockpools, let their inhabitants flit and frolic together? How to engineer a meeting of souls?[36]

With a blend of elegance and irony, Deirdre Wilson spells out one of the greatest drives in human interaction—no matter which kinesic verbs, concepts, or metaphors are used to express it (*flit and frolic, a meeting of souls,* or *a mental shrimping net*—the half-serious, half-ironic tone of the passage makes this clear). How does communication operate when it comes to the most complex layers of our minds? One possible way of addressing this question is to narrate failure, as in *Madame Bovary*. Similarly, Cervantes's masterpiece *Don Quixote* deals throughout its plot with relevance and its opposite, communicational breakdowns. In this section, I shall begin by addressing such issues in *Don Quixote* at the level of the plot. Then I will consider the way in which the organization of the text triggers perceptual simulations of kinesic aspects, which afford implicatures regarding gestures at the level of readerly reception. Rather than the novel as a whole, I will focus on the textual organization between chapters 1 and 2 in the first volume. I will focus on the way in which we are provided with information relative to Don Quixote's helmet in chapter 2, the full grasp and humorous appreciation of which imply that we remember chapter 1 and, on its basis, derive specific kinesic inferences.

A modest land-owner of the lower nobility, Don Quixote is bored with his life and notoriously influenced by his readings of chivalric romances to the point of deciding—or believing he can decide—to live in a resuscitated world of chivalry and obey the code of knighthood he has deduced from the books in his library, such as *Amadis of Gaul*.[37] Most striking is the way in which he does succeed in making an impact on reality, albeit aberrantly, while trying with extreme determination and conviction to force it to correspond to his own system of beliefs, complete with its own system of implications. For example, as a would-be knight-errant, when he arrives in any kind of habitation, he declares that it's a castle; if two women are present, they are bound to be the ladies of the castle; if noise is made while he is eating, he is being served to the accompaniment of music. But, in volume I, chapter 2, the place is an inn, the two women are 'of the sort known as ladies of easy virtue' (p. 32)[38] (*dos mujeres mozas, destas que llaman del partido,* p. 133),[39] and the sound he hears while eating is produced by a pig-gelder arriving at the inn

[36] Deirdre Wilson, *Slave of the Passions* (London: Picador, 1991), p. 202.

[37] See Shannon M. Polchow, 'Manipulation of narrative discourse: from Amadís De Gaula to Don Quixote', *Hispania*, 88 (2005.1), 72–81; Edwin Williamson, *The Half-Way House of Fiction: Don Quixote and Arthurian Romance* (Oxford: Clarendon Press, 1984); Carlos Alvar, *Don Quijote: Letras, armas, vida* (Madrid: SIAL Ediciones, coll. Trivium de Textos y Ensayo, 2009); Augustin Redondo, *Otra manera de leer el* Quijote: *Historia, tradiciones culturales y literatura* (Madrid: Editorial Castalia, 1997); Martín de Riquer, *Para leer a Cervantes* (Barcelona: Acantilado, 2010); Anthony J. Cascardi (ed.), *The Cambridge Companion to Cervantes* (Cambridge: Cambridge University Press, 2002); Isabel Jaén and Julien Jacques Simon (eds), *Cognitive Approaches to Early Modern Spanish Literature* (Oxford: Oxford University Press, 2016).

[38] Miguel de Cervantes Saavedra, *The Ingenious Hidalgo Don Quixote de la Mancha*, trans. John Rutherford (London: Penguin Books, 2003); the same edition is used for all translations of this text.

[39] Miguel de Cervantes Saavedra, *El Ingenioso Hidalgo Don Quijote de la Mancha I & II*, edited by Manuel Fernandez Nieto (Madrid: Biblioteca Nueva, 2006); the same edition is used for all quotations from this text.

and announcing his presence with his pan-pipes (p. 35). The narrator explains how Don Quixote refuses to acknowledge the obvious discrepancy between his desires and the world as it is. Meanwhile, this fictive knight acts in accordance with his delusory belief system, leading to very concrete consequences for everyone around him.

Don Quixote's denial that his system of beliefs is at odds with reality induces acts of communication that exemplify the pragmatic impact of such epistemic discrepancies. As the two prostitutes are helping Don Quixote to take his armour off, he addresses them in verses borrowed from a Spanish chivalric ballad and, while doing so, gives his name away by referring to himself in his verses.[40] Because it is proper for an Arthurian knight to perform great feats of arms incognito before being acknowledged as the best knight in the world, Don Quixote reassuringly announces that, despite this initial chronological inversion, things will be done properly hereafter:[41]

> '[F]or although I had intended not to discover myself until the deeds done for your benefit and service should have made me known, yet the necessity to accommodate this ancient ballad of Sir Lancelot to our present purpose has been the occasion of your knowing my name ere it were meet; but a time will come when you will command and I shall obey, and when the might of this arm will manifest the desire I have to serve you.'
>
> The girls, who weren't used to such rhetorical flourishes, didn't answer, but just asked if he'd like a bite to eat.   (p. 34)[42]

The narrative presents not so much a hiatus as a gaping chasm between what is relevant to Don Quixote and what is relevant to the two women—a fact that leads to momentary silence, '*no respondían palabra*'. The two women's silence suggests the kind of interactional impasse that is induced by a complete discrepancy between worldviews—a response confirmed by their final question: would you like a bite to eat? This is equivalent to asking someone chanting rhymed verse in order to profess perfect devotion whether he'd care for a tuna sandwich—and doing so without ironic intent.

In the event, the two women offer Don Quixote not tuna but salt cod. Because the local name given to cod is *truchuela* ('troutlings') (p. 34), Don Quixote, oblivious

---

[40] See Luis Andrés Murillo, 'Lanzarote y Don Quijote', *Studies in the Literature of Spain*, 10 (New York; Brockport, NY: State University of Brockport, 1977), 55–68; Martín de Riquer, 'La technique parodique du roman médiéval dans le *Quichotte*', in *La Littérature narrative d'imagination* (Paris: PUF, 1961), pp. 55–69; Sylvia Roubaud-Bénichou, *Le Roman de chevalerie en Espagne: Entre Arthur et Don Quichotte* (Paris: Honoré Champion, 2000).

[41] See Susan Crane, *The Performance of Self: Ritual, Clothing, and Identity During the Hundred Years War* (Philadelphia, PA: University of Pennsylvania Press, 2002), chapter 4: 'Chivalric display and Incognito', pp. 107–39.

[42] '"[Q]ue, puesto que no quisiera descubrirme fasta que las fazañas fechas en vuestro servicio y pro me descubrieran, la fuerza de acomodar al propósito presente este romance viejo de Lanzarote ha sido causa que sepáis mi nombre antes de toda sazón; pero tiempo vendrá en que las vuestras señorías me manden y yo obedezca, y el valor de mi brazo descubra el deseo que tengo de serviros."

Las mozas, que no estaban hechas a oír semejantes retóricas, no respondían palabra; sólo le preguntaron si quería comer alguna cosa' (I, p. 135).

to a blatant discrepancy in tastes, thinks that he is being served young trout, and starts comparing its flesh to veal in contrast to beef, and to kid in contrast to goat. Manifesting his excessive trust in words, the knight's tirade is irrelevant in every possible respect to his interlocutors. However, it is relevant to the novel's readers, who thereby become familiar with Don Quixote's propensity to turn his desires into facts, notwithstanding the reality of taste, sound, sight, social context, and verbal exchange.

The women and the innkeeper soon adapt to Don Quixote's behavioural idio-syncrasies by finding concrete solutions to the kind of communicational problem he so obviously represents. One such problem is the fact that Don Quixote cannot take his helmet off.[43] He cannot because, to do so, he would have to cut the ribbons with which he tied the frontal pieces of the helmet to the rest of the headgear.

> Although they'd taken off his breast and back plates, they couldn't fathom how to disengage his gorget or remove his imitation visor, tied on with green ribbons that would have to be cut, since it was impossible to undo the knots; but he would by no means consent to this, and kept his helmet on all night, making the funniest and strangest figure imaginable.   (p. 34)[44]

Two aspects of this deserve our full attention: the knots tying the ribbons are too tight to be undone; Don Quixote prefers to sleep trapped in his helmet rather than cut the ribbons. Let's begin with the second aspect.

In chapter 1, Don Quixote is described refurbishing his ancestors' helmet. When he decided to become a knight-errant, 'his first step was to clean a suit of armour that had belonged to his forefathers and that, covered in rust and mould, had been standing forgotten in a corner for centuries. He scoured and mended it as best he could; yet he realized that it had one important defect' (p. 27):

> the headpiece (*celada*) was not a complete helmet but just a simple steel cap (*morrión*); he was ingenious enough, however, to overcome this problem, constructing out of cardboard something resembling a visor and face-guard which, once inserted into the steel cap, gave it the appearance of a full helmet. It's true that, to test its strength and find out whether it could safely be exposed to attack, he drew his sword and dealt it two blows, with the first of which he destroyed in a second what it had taken him a week to create. He couldn't help being concerned about the ease with which he'd

---

[43] The scene narrates the concrete consequence of eating and drinking with a full helmet on: Don Quixote must be fed by hand and he must drink by means of a hollow reed: 'Mas al darle de beber, no fue posible, ni lo fuera si el ventero no horadara una caña, y puesto el un cabo en la boca, por el otro le iba echando el vino; y todo esto lo recibía en paciencia, a trueco de no romper las cintas de la celada' (I, p. 136) ['But when they tried to give him some drink, they found this an impossible task, and he wouldn't have drunk a drop if the innkeeper hadn't bored a hole through a length of cane and put one end into his mouth and poured the wine into the other; and Don Quixote suffered it all with great patience, so as not to allow his helmet-ribbons to be cut'] (p. 35).

[44] '[L]as cuales, aunque le habían quitado el peto y el espaldar, jamás supieron ni pudieron desen-cajarle la gola, ni quitalle la contrahecha celada, que traía atada con unas cintas verdes, y era menester cortarlas, por no poderse quitar los nudos; mas él no lo quiso consentir en ninguna manera, y así, se quedó toda aquella noche con la celada puesta, que era la más graciosa y estraña figura que se pudiera pensar' (I, p. 135).

shattered it, and to guard against this danger he reconstructed it, fixing some iron bars on the inside, which reassured him about its strength; and, preferring not to carry out any further tests, he deemed and pronounced it a most excellent visored helmet.   (p. 28)[45]

The only kind of helmet or headgear Don Quixote is ready to consider when he decides to become a knight-errant is a face-covering helmet, not a simple and conquistador-like *morrión*, or steel cap. This passage suggests that the rationale behind Don Quixote's upgrading of his helmet amounts to focusing on the face-*covering* property of the headgear, to the point of not only loosening but even losing the property of effective head *protection* against real blows, usually expected from a helmet. The text elicits a fluctuating conceptualization of *helmet*. We are made to conceive of a helmet in which the *covering* of the face is a property more relevant than the *protection* of the face and head. In chapter 1, Don Quixote gives shape to the category of *helmet* that makes sense to him by fixing a cardboard visor and gorget onto his forefathers' *morrión*. But it is only in chapter 2 that we learn why, for him, to personify a knight-errant is to embody a notion of knighthood in which a knight's physical identity must ideally be concealed by means of a closed helmet. If he cannot hide his face behind his visor, he cannot accomplish great feats of arms incognito and emulate Sir Lancelot, the epitome of knight-errantry.[46] The face-covering helmet is an affordance that elicits the possibility of a certain enactment proper to heroes of knightly romances.[47] Importantly, the adaptation of the concept of *helmet* pertains to the plot as well as to its reception by the reader. To make sense of Don Quixote's action, we must think as Cervantes's hero does. This act of mind-reading is shaped by the organization of the narrative, since we must wait until chapter 2 to make sense of chapter 1 in this respect.[48] Cervantes's narrative style protracts the effects arising from relevance. The narrator does not explicate the protagonist's rationale. This rationale is an implicature the reader derives, and in two stages. In terms of literary reception, the humorous force of Cervantes's work is augmented by the cognitive involvement thus induced in readers.[49]

---

[45] 'pero vio que tenían una gran falta, y era que no tenían celada de encaje, sino morrión simple; mas a esto suplió su industria, porque de cartones hizo un modo de media celada, que, encajada con el morrión, hacían una apariencia de celada entera. Es verdad que para probar si era fuerte y podía estar al riesgo de una cuchillada, sacó su espada y le dio dos golpes, y con el primero y en un punto deshizo lo que había hecho en una semana; y no dejó de parecerle mal la facilidad con que la había hecho pedazos, y, por asegurarse deste peligro, la tornó a hacer de nuevo, poniéndole unas barras de hierro por dentro, de tal manera, que él quedó satisfecho de su fortaleza, y sin querer hacer nueva experiencia della, la diputó y tuvo por celada finísima de encaje' (I, p. 127).

[46] To emphasize this aspect in the first and second chapters of the novel is also a way to prepare for the humour of later scenes, where Don Quixote loses his helmet and opts instead for a barber's basin, which hardly covers his face, but which he conceives instead as the legendary golden helmet of invisibility that belonged to the Moorish king Mambrino.

[47] See Cave, *Thinking with Literature*, ch. 4: 'Literary affordances', pp. 46–62.

[48] See Paula Leverage, Howard Mancing, Richard Schweickert, and Jennifer Marston William (eds), *Theory of Mind and Literature* (West Lafayette, IN: Purdue University Press, 2011); also Cave, *Thinking with Literature*, pp. 110–14.

[49] On humour in Cervantes, see Anthony Close, *Cervantes and the Comic Mind of his Age* (Oxford: Oxford University Press, 2000); John T. Allen, 'Smiles and laughter in *Don Quixote*', *Comparative Literature Studies*, 43/4 (2006), 515–31; Bolens, *L'Humour et le savoir des corps*.

If we now turn to the helmet's ribbons in chapter 2, the understanding of the scene implies that readers possess the procedural knowledge and sensory memory of what it means *not* to be able to loosen and undo a knot. This cognitive act of understanding is grounded in sensory and gestural knowledge, fuelled by our embodied experience of not being able to unfasten a tight knot. We understand the information by triggering a perceptual simulation that is multimodal: it is visual, kinaesthetic, and tactile.

The ribbons within the plot function as affordance. Michael Kaschak and Arthur Glenberg explain that 'the term affordance refers to the ways in which individuals can interact with things in their environment. For instance, a person can interact with a crutch in particular ways: a crutch can be used to aid one's walking when injured; to strike something; or to push something through a long, narrow crevice'.[50] Kaschak and Glenberg use the term 'meshing' to describe a process 'that combines affordances into coherent patterns of actions; that is, actions that can actually be completed to accomplish a goal. Thus, a crutch affords poking or pushing because it can be held and jabbed'.[51] The same is not true of ribbons: a ribbon cannot be held and jabbed to push another object or a person. But it can be tied into knots, and the knots may be more or less tight. When we read a sentence, 'the affordances are meshed into what amounts to a mental simulation' and the organization of the text provides general constraints on how the mental simulation is to operate.[52]

It is by means of a haptic perceptual simulation of the way in which an extremely tight knot feels to the finger that the passage fosters an additional implicature, which is related to the tightness of the knots, and the pattern of actions associated with it. The implicature is that Don Quixote compensated for the half-admitted uselessness of his cardboard visor by tying the knots with extra strength. The use of extra strength is a kinesic inference which is based on a pattern of actions and a cause-and-effect relation between the tightness of the knots and the strength we know to be necessary to achieve a certain degree of tightness. Understanding the ribbon passage implies a type of cognitive enaction[53] that allows implicatures to be derived by means of kinesic intelligence.

At this stage of readerly reception, the humour in Don Quixote's action is intensified by our acknowledgement that the inferred extra strength the knight applied to the knots is hardly likely to make the helmet more protective, notwithstanding the iron bars he fixed to the inner side of the cardboard. The visor is still made of cardboard: tightly tied ribbons cannot make up for that fact. In other words, not cutting the ribbons is a precluded gesture that becomes humorous when it is understood via a combination of kinesic inferences based on multimodal

---

[50] Michael P. Kaschak and Arthur M. Glenberg, 'Constructing meaning: the role of affordances and grammatical constructions in sentence comprehension', *Journal of Memory and Language*, 43 (2000), 508–29 (pp. 510–11).

[51] Kaschak and Glenberg, 'Constructing meaning', p. 511.

[52] Kaschak and Glenberg, 'Constructing meaning', p. 511.

[53] See John Stewart, Olivier Gapenne, and Ezequiel A. Di Paolo (eds), *Enaction: Toward A New Paradigm for Cognitive Science* (Cambridge, MA; London: Bradford Books, MIT Press, 2010).

perceptual simulations and of implicatures grounded in mind-reading and kinesic intelligence.

Humour is notoriously difficult to explain. In the above account of the ribbon scene in *Don Quixote*, relevance theory and kinesic analysis join forces to describe the cognitive processes that may potentially trigger laughter in the reader, when the latter comes to terms with the likely reason why Don Quixote prefers to spend the night stuck in his helmet rather than undo the ribbons that tie his visor to his forefathers' *morrión*. Chapter 1 provides the narrative context for this implicature, thus grounding relevance in chapter 2. A reader who skips chapter 1 and the kinesic context it provides may overlook the humorous relevance of the ribbons in chapter 2.

*Don Quixote* and *Madame Bovary* are literary works that succeed most effectively in communicating the nature and implications of communicational breakdown. Both are about a character who forcefully rejects the boredom and meaninglessness of his or her life, no matter what it takes—including opting for fiction over reality. Meanwhile, Cervantes's and Flaubert's achievements are the least boring of artefacts. They are literary works so fascinating that other humans still peruse and discuss them centuries later. Literature makes this possible because it is not so much about events as about what can be done with language. It is about the *how* of the *what*. Even the least noteworthy events (watching dust, tying knots) can become fascinatingly expressive and meaningful when authors such as Cervantes and Flaubert turn them into acts of communication that challenge and quicken their readers' imagination, receptiveness to style, sense of humour and tragedy, and ability to think both sensorily and conceptually, one as a function of the other. In short, literature happens when language is made to mean more than any possible code, and the human mind is allowed to experience fully its embodied faculties.

# Interlace 4

*The following chapter explores another kind of synthesis between relevance theory and kinesic analysis. The example of a series of episodes in Mark Twain's* Adventures of Tom Sawyer *focuses attention on the ethical stakes involved in reading a narrative which appears to endorse at every level a reflex ('knee-jerk') response to the depiction of a stereotypical 'Indian'. Thus, at the kinesic level, the insistent pedal-note of sensori-motor actions associated with the apprehension of danger (tiptoeing, holding of breath), punctuated by moments of relief and release as the danger is averted, creates a cognitive ecology in which the figure of Injun Joe is always a threatening alien, best dealt with in the end by elimination.*

*It is easy enough to see that the beliefs of a reader who shares the attitudes that pervade this narrative are liable to be endorsed, but what of the reader whose belief-world is different? This is the problem that arises, for modern readers holding 'liberal' ethical beliefs, with R.M. Ballantyne's* Coral Island, *series such as the Biggles books of Captain W.E. Johns, or (in varying degrees) Shakespeare's* The Merchant of Venice, *the operas of Richard Wagner, and the novels of Knut Hamsun and Louis-Ferdinand Céline. A discrepancy at a crucial point in the belief system can give rise to the phenomenon of '(imaginative) resistance':[1] Neil Kenny's reference to his own 'queasiness' in response to a pejorative assumption about the criminal behaviour of Native Americans would be a case in point, but the resistance is clearly local, in the sense that he still appears to believe that the novel is worth reading. A variant of this effect is the 'default reasoning' (Pascal Boyer's phrase) that enables a reader to remain immersed in a fictional narrative which violates basic expectations about a single aspect of reality: for example, ghost stories rely on the reader's willingness to accept the supernatural agency of ghosts provided that most of the features attributable to live persons—they have bodies, they walk, they think, they speak, they wear clothes—remain in place even though ghosts violate physical laws (they are transparent or otherwise insubstantial, they pass through walls, exhibit many of the features of a corpse, and so on).[2]*

*There have been many accounts of these seemingly incompatible responses in the work of cognitive psychologists and philosophers. Kenny cites not only Boyer, but also*

---

[1] *For a helpful recent account of this question in a narratological frame of reference, see Gregory Currie,* Narratives and Narrators: A Philosophy of Stories *(Oxford: Oxford University Press, 2010), ch. 6.*

[2] *See Pascal Boyer,* Religion Explained: The Human Instincts That Fashion Gods, Spirits, and Ancestors *(London: William Heinemann, 2001), p. 85: 'The general process whereby we combine (1) a limited violation and (2) otherwise preserved inferences from a concept is a very common phenomenon in human thinking, namely default reasoning.' This remark should be read in the context of the whole of ch. 2 of Boyer's study.*

*Currie, Gerrig, Schaeffer, and others.*[3] *He assigns a key role to a distinction between understanding and believing what one is told, and to what Sperber* et al. *(2010) call 'epistemic vigilance', a capacity for assessing the reliability of the communicator and the plausibility of the communicated content, thus protecting the audience from being accidentally or intentionally misinformed.*[4] *And more broadly, he evokes relevance theory's insistence on investigating the entire communication process, from speaker to hearer, or from author to reader, and the crucial role played by inference at every stage. Fictional narratives feed on the cognitive environment of the reader, which includes the spectrum of beliefs they have acquired from that environment.*

---

[3] *One could add to Kenny's list Paul Harris's recent study* Trusting What You're Told: How Children Learn from Others *(Cambridge, MA, and London: The Belknap Press of Harvard University Press, 2012), which studies in detail the way children acquire beliefs and how those beliefs may be modified by their material and cultural environment.*

[4] *In* Thinking with Literature *(ch. 5), Terence Cave proposes a broader definition of this expression: he sees it as the pre-reflective filtering system that may be assumed to be essential to human cognition in order continuously to calibrate the value of a given thought-act in relation to empirical experience and collective norms. In other words, he extends it beyond the realm of communication as such.*

# 4

# Relevance Theory and the Effect of Literature on Beliefs

## The Example of Injun Joe in Twain's *Adventures of Tom Sawyer*

*Neil Kenny*

## INTRODUCTION

When we read novels or watch films and TV serials, are our beliefs about the world beyond those representations affected, or do those beliefs remain unchanged?[1] Perhaps the only possible answer is that it depends on the variables. One of them is the genre and character of the stimulus itself. Another variable is the addressee: for example, is my 'cognitive style' different from that of the person seated next to me in front of the television?[2] Another is the relation *between* stimulus and addressee: how often am I exposed to this kind of stimulus? How far does (what relevance theory calls) my cognitive environment overlap with that of the author of the novel I am reading?[3] Whether another variable might be the degree to which we immerse ourselves in a given fictional world is an open question, to which I return at the end.

The question of the effect of literature (in such broad senses) upon beliefs has a famous twin pedigree. On the one hand, it has provoked defences of literature as broadening the mind and fostering empathy.[4] But it has long provoked anxiety too: Plato on mimesis; Marxists on ideology; concerns about the effect of pornography and of violent video games; unease about whether racially offensive terms as

---

[1] Among those to whom I am indebted for advice are Cecilia Heyes (although her own method draws not on the models discussed here but on 'dual process' models of cognition and cultural evolutionary theory) and the late Michael Sheringham.

[2] For an application of the psychological notion of 'cognitive style' to aesthetics, see Jean-Marie Schaeffer, *L'Expérience esthétique* (Paris: Gallimard, 2015), pp. 100–12.

[3] For the notion of cognitive environments, see Dan Sperber and Deirdre Wilson, *Relevance: Communication and Cognition* [1986] (Oxford: Blackwell, 2nd ed., 1995), pp. 38–46, and the Introduction to the present volume, pp. 4, 15.

[4] For recent cognitively inflected examples, see Marco Caracciolo, 'Patterns of cognitive dissonance in readers' engagement with characters', *Enthymema*, 8 (2013), 21–37; Jèmeljan Hakemulder, *Moral Laboratory: Experiments Examining the Effects of Reading Literature on Social Perception and Moral Self-Concept* (Amsterdam; Philadelphia, PA: John Benjamins, 2000).

used in classics of western literature should be included in children's versions or even uttered in adult discussions or public readings of the works, lest such repetition subtly make racism less unacceptable. Although cognitively informed approaches cannot provide definitive answers, they can enrich such debates with improved understanding of how we process stimuli (including novels and films). Relevance theory is well placed to play a central role because it describes persuasively the whole communications circuit,[5] whereas many literary-critical approaches focus on just one of its stages, whether that of the addresser (biographical criticism; Booth's 'rhetoric of fiction'[6]), of the stimulus itself (formalism; structuralism), or of the addressee (reader-response criticism; reception theory).

Relevance theory's embracing of the whole communications circuit makes intentionality central to communication, but also gives the reader an active role. Intentionality is understood in a capacious sense, not necessarily as involving precise intentions but sometimes as merely pointing readers in a certain direction that is not even propositional. Although the illustrative examples in relevance theory tend to be of face-to-face, one-to-one communication, the theory can be extended to situations where 'addresser' and 'addressee' are, for example, a whole corporation that has created a TV series (a composite addresser) and the millions of viewers (the addressees).

By investigating whether relevance theory can help improve our understanding of the impact of literature on beliefs, this chapter also aims to contribute to discussion of the compatibility of relevance theory with other approaches that focus even more on the embodied dimension of cognition.

## *THE ADVENTURES OF TOM SAWYER* (1): COGNITIVE ENVIRONMENTS, CONTEXTUAL ASSUMPTIONS, KINESIS, AND SALIENCE

Mark Twain's novel *The Adventures of Tom Sawyer* (1876) is my chosen case study, for various reasons: it has been read by millions; its historical distance from us raises the question of diminished overlap between the cognitive environments of author and twenty-first-century reader;[7] its claim to be grounded in the childhood experiences of the author (real name Samuel Clemens) intensifies the question of its relation to beliefs about the 'real' world;[8] and the novel itself is saturated with explicit reflections on belief (as emanating from superstition, religion, children, and popular opinion). I focus on one character, who has long exerted a troubling fascination: Injun Joe.

[5] I take this famous phrase from Robert Darnton's manifesto for book history, 'What is the history of books?', *Daedalus*, 113.3 (1982), 65–83.

[6] See Wayne Booth, *The Rhetoric of Fiction* (Chicago, IL: University of Chicago Press, 1961).

[7] That question is also discussed in the contributions by Elleke Boehmer and Raphael Lyne to the present volume (Chapters 1 and 2).

[8] The author's Preface begins: 'Most of the adventures recorded in this book really occurred.' Mark Twain, *The Adventures of Tom Sawyer*, edited by Peter Stoneley (Oxford: Oxford University Press, 2008), p. [5]. Where it is clear that references are to the novel, page numbers only will be given.

I will evoke two notional clusters of assumptions about Native Americans that readers might bring to the context described by the novel—that is, to a storyworld set in the mid-nineteenth century in a fictional village in Missouri—and in particular to the character of Injun Joe. These two clusters will serve as simplifying shorthands for the endless and largely unknowable array of assumptions that readers actually do bring and have brought to the novel. Communication, in a relevance-theoretic perspective, involves the intention to make manifest a range of 'facts' (which may be about the actual world or some alternative storyworld). The addressee might adopt some of them as assumptions (or might already have done so). Communication aims at achieving 'positive cognitive effects' such as reinforcing or changing some of those assumptions.[9]

Of the two notional clusters of assumptions about Native Americans, the first will inform my whole analysis, whereas the second will be introduced near the end. The first is derived from intertextual stimuli such as dime novels (in the case of late nineteenth-century readers)[10] or Westerns (in the case of twentieth- and twenty-first-century ones). Readers who have been much exposed to these need little help from the author in having 'facts' about Injun Joe made manifest—whether or not the readers themselves share and accept them as assumptions[11]—because Injun Joe is highly stereotypical, and the relevance of stereotypes lies not just in their capacity to reinforce our existing assumptions but in the relatively small cognitive processing effort that they therefore require. So, while Twain sometimes uses explicit statements (relevance theory's 'explicatures') to set the parameters of Injun Joe's likely behaviour,[12] several of his characteristics (such as physical repulsiveness) are communicated through just a few implicatures, since the reader needs few clues

---

[9] See Sperber and Wilson, *Relevance*, pp. 39–46, 196–200, 265–6. On manifestness, see the Introduction to the present volume, p. 10.

[10] On the influence of the dime novel on Twain himself, see Gregory M. Pfitzer, '"Iron dudes and white savages in Camelot": the influence of dime-novel sensationalism on Twain's "A Connecticut Yankee in King Arthur's Court"', *American Literary Realism, 1870–1910*, 27.1 (1994), pp. 42–58, esp. 45–6.

[11] The history of the novel's reception would presumably reveal a wide spectrum in this respect. At one end would be the press, prosecutors, witnesses, and jurors whose characterization of one José Gabriel as 'Indian Joe' probably contributed to his conviction and execution for murder in San Diego County in 1893. The label was commonly used by whites, but, given that sales of the 1876 novel would soon reach two million (by 1904), Clare McKanna argues that 'the particularly close resemblance between the label and the name of Twain's infamous and well-known Indian character, "Injun Joe" helped strengthen the stereotypical drunken and savage qualities attached to José Gabriel'; C. McKanna, *The Trial of 'Indian Joe': Race and Justice in the Nineteenth-Century West* (Lincoln, NE: University of Nebraska Press, 2003), p. 107; see pp. 107–10. At the other end of the spectrum would be a man (probably of Native American and/or black descent) and his friends in Clemens's home village of Hannibal (upon which he based *Tom Sawyer*): 'Joe Douglas, good-humoredly called "Injun Joe", out at Hannibal, Mo. for one of the sinister characters in Mark Twain's book, Tom Sawyer [*sic*], resents the nickname, declaring his life has not warranted such a character as that given to Injun Joe in the book. And his friends in Hannibal indorse [*sic*] the statement'; 'Injun Joe's alibi', anonymous newspaper article in *The Grit* [*c.* 1894], reproduced in 'The characters Mark Twain used in his writings', *The Twainian*, 10.5 (Sept.–Oct. 1951), 4; quoted in Shelley Fisher Fishkin, *Lighting Out for the Territory: Reflections on Mark Twain and American Culture* (Oxford and New York: Oxford University Press, 1997), p. 44; see pp. 42–8.

[12] From the outset, Injun Joe is dubbed by Huck 'that murderin' half-breed!', even before murder is on the cards (*Tom Sawyer*, p. 65). On explicatures and implicatures, see Sperber and Wilson, *Relevance*, pp. 56–7, 69–70, 182–3, 193–202, 217–24, 235–7.

in order to make inferences along such well-trodden lines.[13] For stereotypical assumptions to be communicated, their premises—for example, that Native Americans are intrinsically inferior to the descendants of Europeans—only need to be implicated, not explicated. The novel offers readers not revision of assumptions that are derived from such premises—some readers might already assume that Injun Joe is likely to murder, disfigure, steal, deceive, and drink to excess—but rather the more limited cognitive effect of reinforcing them while providing pleasurable suspense and surprise as to exactly where, when, how, and how successfully Injun Joe will do all this. The positive cognitive effects take the form of filling in the gaps between general assumptions and less predictable specific outcomes.[14]

The suspense activates those assumptions in an embodied way. On the main occasions when Injun Joe irrupts into the plot, Twain tries to produce in readers who are psychologically immersed in the fiction a perceptual and kinesic simulation of the muscle-tensing and breath-holding that are attributed to the heroes, Tom Sawyer and Huck Finn.[15] On more than one occasion, the boys find themselves in the real or imagined proximity of Injun Joe, mostly in the dark, where they cannot always see him coming or track his current position. These moments achieve what cognitive science calls salience by progressively priming the reader, who is progressively made conceptually and indeed perceptually more alert to the features of such moments (darkness, proximity, threat) by the similarity to preceding moments.

The priming becomes more evident if one describes those moments in sequence. They do not occur only in relation to Injun Joe,[16] but also become associated through repetition with him in particular. The first occurs when the boys, concealed in the dark, see Injun Joe murder Dr Robinson (p. 65). The second occurs shortly afterwards when the boys, hiding in a tannery, hear snoring:

'Tom, s'pose it's Injun Joe!'

Tom quailed. But presently the temptation rose up strong again and the boys agreed to try, with the understanding that they would take to their heels if the snoring stopped. So they went tip-toeing stealthily down, the one behind the other. When they had got to within five steps of the snorer, Tom stepped on a stick, and it broke

---

[13] It is revealing that the only detailed description of Injun Joe's appearance comes when he has *departed* from his implicit visual stereotype by adopting a disguise (as a 'Spaniard'): 'he had bushy white whiskers; long white hair flowed from under his sombrero, and he wore green goggles' (p. 149).

[14] Since the specific outcomes in turn modify general assumptions about what Injun Joe is likely to do next, this relevance-theoretic reading is broadly compatible with the Bayesian approach to verisimilitude in literary narrative that has been developed by Karin Kukkonen: 'Bayesian narrative: probability, plot and the shape of the fictional world', *Anglia: Journal for English Philology*, 132.4 (2014), 720–39.

[15] I adopt the approach to kinesis and simulation outlined in Guillemette Bolens's contribution to the present volume (Chapter 3) and in her *The Style of Gestures: Embodiment and Cognition in Literary Narrative* (Baltimore, MD: Johns Hopkins University Press, 2012). 'Kinesis' is understood here as 'the interactional perception of movements performed by oneself or another person in relation to visuo-motor variables such as the dynamics, amplitude, extension, flow, and speed of a gesture or the relation of limbs to the rest of the body' (*The Style of Gestures*, p. 2).

[16] Indeed, several other moments of physical fear in the dark occur in Twain's *Adventures of Huckleberry Finn* (1884), from which Injun Joe is absent.

with a sharp snap. The man moaned, writhed a little, and his face came into the moonlight. It was Muff Potter. The boy's hearts had stood still, and their bodies too, when the man moved, but their fears passed away now.    (pp. 72–3)

The physical states through which the boys pass here constitute a tripartite kinesic repertoire that recurs throughout the novel:[17] first they are on tiptoes, muscles tensed, moving slowly, alert, ready to explode into movement; next they are utterly still, implicitly holding their breath; third, they implicitly relax their muscles (realizing that it is not Injun Joe but his harmless associate).

Injun Joe's next irruption into the storyworld is an exception in that it occurs in broad daylight, thereby tweaking with suspense and fear the existing assumption that Injun Joe is a threat at night-time.[18] The description of Tom's sensational testimony against Injun Joe at the murder trial follows the first two steps of that tripartite kinesic repertoire, which is now distributed across characters. First, Tom and the audience are so muscle-tensed that their breathing almost stops ('his tongue failed him. The audience listened breathless'); then, it is Injun Joe who explodes into movement ('Crash! Quick as lightning the half-breed sprang for a window, tore his way through all opposers, and was gone!', p. 138). The context is again one of close, menacing proximity, this time in the packed courthouse.

The frequency of episodes in which the boy duo is invisible to Injun Joe yet terrifyingly close to him then increases.[19] The boys recklessly decide to follow Injun Joe and his accomplice to see where they will bury their stash of money. Tom emerges from a room above a tavern and says to Huck:

'...*great Caesar's ghost!*'
'What!—what'd you see, Tom!'
'Huck, I most stepped onto Injun Joe's hand!'
'No!'
'Yes! He was laying there, sound asleep on the floor, with his old patch on his eye and his arms spread out.'
'Lordy, what did you do? Did he wake up?'
'No, never budged. Drunk, I reckon.'    (p. 158)[20]

Given the reader's assumptions about Injun Joe, the hand is the most relevant part of his anatomy that Tom could have (almost) stepped on: relevant because (unlike an elbow, for example) it gives rise to counterfactual inferences about all the grabbing, stabbing, even scalping that Injun Joe could have done with it had he woken up.[21] Moreover, although motor simulations in readers are difficult to detect through introspection (because largely inaccessible to consciousness), I myself was aware of a fleeting urge to move my own foot when first reading the passage.

---

[17] In addition to the examples outlined below, see pp. 148–50.
[18] The only other such episode to recur in daylight is in the implicated gloom of an abandoned house (pp. 148–50).
[19] See pp. 148–50.    [20] Italics in quotations are in the original unless otherwise stated.
[21] The one episode about 'Indians' that does not involve Injun Joe—one in which the boys play—makes scalping salient (pp. 105–6).

Soon afterwards, Huck, undeterred, follows Injun Joe and his accomplices a long way out of town in pitch darkness. Standing among dense sumach bushes, Huck thinks he has lost their tracks:

> But no footsteps. Heavens, was everything lost! He was about to spring with winged feet, when a man cleared his throat not four feet from him! Huck's heart shot into his throat, but he swallowed it again; and then he stood there shaking as if a dozen agues had taken charge of him at once, and so weak he thought he must surely fall to the ground.   (pp. 163–4)

The tripartite kinesic repertoire is expanded here with a fourth kind of state: that of trying to stay immobile while being shakingly unable to. When, after being in this state for the duration of two pages, Huck eventually makes his escape, it is by reverting to the more familiar state of muscle-tensed alertness, followed by the one of breath-holding muscular rigidity:

> so he held his breath and stepped gingerly back; planted his foot carefully and firmly, after balancing, one-legged in a precarious way and almost toppling over, first on one side and then on the other. He took another step back, with the same elaboration and the same risks; then another and another, and—a twig snapped under his foot! His breath stopped and he listened. There was no sound—the stillness was perfect.   (p. 165)

The reader's assumptions that Twain activates here are specific not to the context of Native Americans but to that of trying to tiptoe anywhere, in many readers' cases (such as my own) up and down stairs, also at night-time, to avoid detection, with creaking floorboards being the equivalent—bigger, but still wooden—of the snapping twig. They are embodied assumptions, stored in memory of the one-legged balancing and shifts of body weight that are necessary to pull off the trick—the kind of procedural memory that largely bypasses consciousness (as when we tie up a shoelace without thinking).[22]

The last of these close encounters occurs in the permanent darkness of the underground cave system in which Tom has been lost for days with his friend Becky, entirely alone (so it is assumed by both them and the reader). In a desperate effort to find an exit, they explore some passages:

> Tom got down on his knees and felt below, and then as far around the corner as he could reach with his hands conveniently; he made an effort to stretch yet a little further to the right, and at that moment, not twenty yards away, a human hand, holding a candle, appeared from behind a rock! Tom lifted up a glorious shout, and instantly that hand was followed by the body it belonged to—Injun Joe's! Tom was paralyzed; he could not move. He was vastly gratified the next moment, to see the 'Spaniard' [Injun Joe's earlier disguise] take to his heels and get himself out of sight. Tom wondered that Joe had not recognised his voice and come over and killed him for testifying in court. But the echoes must have disguised the voice. Without doubt, that was it, he reasoned. Tom's fright weakened every muscle in his body.   (p. 181)

---

[22] This kind of memory has been labelled 'non-declarative' by influential cognitive neuroscientists: see Brenda Milner, Larry R. Squire, and Eric R. Kandel, 'Cognitive neuroscience and the study of memory', *Neuron*, 20.3 (1988), 445–68; Larry R. Squire and Eric R. Kandel, *Memory: From Mind to Molecules* (New York: Scientific American Library, 1999), chs 2 and 3.

One positive cognitive effect is reinforcement of an assumption about Injun Joe that has been building up over the course of the novel: that he is liable to emerge at any time and place whatsoever, not just where you expect him. Readers have been primed to adopt that assumption of unpredictability by the prominence—communicated by paratactic exclamation—of the previous junctures at which Injun is recognized as irrupting into the storyworld: 'Injun Joe's!' here has been preceded by 'it's Injun Joe' (p. 65), 's'pose it's Injun Joe!' (p. 72), and 'This voice. . . . It was Injun Joe's!' (p. 149).[23] The unpredictability extends not only to where and when Injun Joe will appear but also to what he will do, notwithstanding the strength of the general assumptions about him. In the courthouse, it comes as a surprise that he chooses to jump through the window, rather than jumping on Tom. In the cave, Tom—and with him the reader—tries to mediate between the general and the particular by bringing the surprising behaviour into line with general assumptions. He does so through inferential mind-reading that takes account of the physical setting (the cave's echo effect) and that is itself made salient (by the otherwise redundant 'Without doubt that was it, he reasoned.').[24]

Most of these close encounters with Injun Joe reinforce and enrich the assumption that he will take you unawares unless your eyes and ears are on high alert and your muscles are tensed for possible flight. In other words, the assumption seems inseparable from its kinesic and perceptual as well as its conceptual and propositional dimension.[25] It could even be argued that Twain, like the authors and makers of many thrillers and horror films, activates it partly by activating what some evolutionary psychologists postulate to be an intuitive inference system (Agency Detection Device) that humans evolved to help them detect both prey and predators.[26] Twain repeatedly highlights, over the relatively slow course of successive clauses and sentences, a sequence of assessments that we are programmed to make in a split second in real life to determine whether an object is animate or inanimate, what species it belongs to, whether it is a threat, what further movement it might make, and within what range. Like their ancestors, Tom and Huck often make such assessments literally in the dark. They need to rely on partial

[23] See also the later exclamation 'it's Injun Joe!' (p. 169).

[24] On the role of salience in interpretation, see Sperber and Wilson, *Relevance*, p. 193.

[25] Although this kind of claim is not made in the main founding texts of relevance theory, it is compatible with them. Indeed, the theory's founders have argued that comprehension (a largely unconscious inferential process) is just one sub-module of our mind-reading module, with the Agency Detector and the Eye Direction Detector being further sub-modules. See Dan Sperber and Deirdre Wilson, 'Pragmatics, modularity, and mind-reading', *Mind and Language*, 17 (2002), 2–23. The fundamental insights of relevance theory seem potentially usable, at least in broad terms, by those with a wide range of views about mental architecture, including cognitive neuroscientists and psychologists for whom the activation patterns of mental representations include information from various sensory modalities. A diversity of views is found even among those proponents of 'embodied cognition': they would unpack in different ways the word 'inseparable' in my sentence in the main text above. For an overview of this diversity, see Robert A. Wilson and Lucia Foglia, 'Embodied cognition', in Edward N. Zalta (ed.) *The Stanford Encyclopedia of Philosophy* (Fall 2011 edition), http://plato.stanford.edu/archives/fall2011/entries/embodied-cognition [accessed 28 September 2015].

[26] For different versions, see for example Pascal Boyer, *Religion Explained: The Human Instincts that Fashion Gods, Spirits and Ancestors* (London: William Heinemann, 2001); Stewart Guthrie, *Faces in the Clouds: A New Theory of Religion* (Oxford; New York: Oxford University Press, 1993).

vision of the object and on sounds it makes (whether vocal or respiratory). Like some of their ancestors, they need to ascertain not just whether the object is inanimate, animal, or human, but also whether it is supernatural. When Tom and Huck are in the graveyard prior to the murder of Dr Robinson, it is devils whom they anticipate encountering (since they have gone there with a dead cat to conjure up some devils). The assessment of physical threat is inseparable from this categorizing of the nature of the creatures that are at hand, since different kinds of creature have different capabilities:

'Sh!'
'What is it, Tom?' And the two clung together with beating hearts.
'Sh! There 'tis again! Didn't you hear it?'
'I—'
'There! Now you hear it.'
'Lord, Tom, they're coming! They're coming, sure. What'll we do?'
'I dono. Think they'll see us?'
'Oh, Tom, they can see in the dark, same as cats.'   (pp. 64–5)

Then, after 'Some vague figures approached through the gloom', Huck says: 'They're *humans*! One of 'em is, anyway. One of 'em's old Muff Potter's voice' (p. 65). When it is in the 'haunted house' that the boys encounter Injun Joe, the encounter is preceded by an expectation that the only category of being that they might find there would be a ghost (p. 146). Even Tom's narration of how he almost trod on Injun Joe's hand in the room above the tavern is framed by evocation of the world of ghosts ('*great Caesar's ghost!*', p. 158).

The disambiguation of sight and sound is represented as being a potentially error-prone *process* at every real or imagined encounter that the boys have with Injun Joe in the dark. The next one—imagined, for it will turn out to be the harmless Muff Potter—starts with another category mistake,[27] before settling on the right category (human), and trying to identify the particular member of it and its precise location in space:

'Sh! What's that?' he whispered.
'Sounds like—like hogs grunting. No—it's somebody snoring, Tom.'
'That *is* it? Where 'bouts is it, Huck?'
'I bleeve it's down at t'other end. Sounds so, anyway. Pap used to sleep there, sometimes, 'long with the hogs, but, laws bless you, he just lifts things when *he* snores.'

(p. 72)

The careful sequencing of clues and inferences varies: in the 'haunted house', the boys hear voices first, then they see two figures, and only when they hear one voice at closer quarters do they realize that one of the figures is Injun Joe (p. 149); in the room above the tavern, the implicature is that Tom first sees the hand of Injun Joe, and only an instant later that he sees the whole body in a way that enables him to ascertain its state (sleeping, and more specifically in a deep sleep, if the

---

[27] And a plausible one, since the night-time soundscape in this remote spot is mainly animal: the boys have just heard a dog howling.

inference that he is drunk is correct);[28] in the pitch darkness of the sumach bushes, Huck hears first a man clearing his throat not four feet from him, and only then voices (pp. 163–4); in the cave, Tom sees first the hand and lantern (which he drastically misrecognizes as friendly) and only then 'the body it belonged to— Injun Joe's!' (p. 181).

The series of irruptions of Injun Joe into the storyworld culminates in one that I have not yet mentioned, that makes manifest an assumption familiar from dime novels or Westerns—that the only non-threatening Indian is a dead one. Tom leads the villagers to the cave, after realizing that Injun Joe will have been unintentionally trapped by the new big triple-locked door sheathed with boiler iron:

> Injun Joe lay stretched upon the ground, dead, with his face close to the crack of the door, as if his longing eyes had been fixed, to the latest moment, upon the light and the cheer of the free world outside. Tom was touched, for he knew by his own experience how this wretch had suffered. His pity was moved, but nevertheless he felt an abounding sense of relief and security, now, which revealed to him in a degree which he had not fully appreciated before how vast a weight of dread had been lying upon him since the day he lifted his voice against this bloody-minded outcast.   (p. 186)

This moment's power resides in its replacing one assumption (about the threat posed by Native Americans) with another (about dead Native Americans) via the cognitively troubling object that is a corpse—troubling because it inspires conflicting intuitions. On the one hand, it looks like a living human, rather like those 'laying there, sound asleep on the floor' encountered previously (p. 158), and it even mimics a living person by seeming to stare with longing eyes: an implicature is perhaps that the corpse's eyes are still open. On the other hand, it is inanimate and so not an appropriate object of the mind-reading and of the other mental tools that we nonetheless involuntarily direct at it.[29]

One objection to the rough model proposed so far of how Twain communicates to readers who have had much exposure to stereotype-laden stimuli might be that the novel is about one mixed-race person with Native American ancestry, not about Native Americans in general. This objection raises the question of authorial intentionality. A relevance-theoretic approach absolves readers from seeking out the precise intentions of the real Samuel Clemens (who wrote under the pen-name of Mark Twain). But it does emphasize that the communication of meaning is shaped by explicatures and implicatures from which inferences about the communicator's (or communicators') intentionality are to be made. *The Adventures of Tom Sawyer* is full of such clues. Characters and narrator alike refer to Injun Joe as a 'half-breed' at moments of menace (as we have twice seen above), implicating a link between the menace and that racial category. The very name 'Injun Joe' implicates that he is a Native American hidden in the partial appearance of a white man. Indeed, Twain gets the character himself to confess this, with reference to his murderous vengefulness: 'The Injun blood ain't in me for nothing' (p. 66). A sympathetic character called 'the Welchman', after realizing that it was Injun Joe

---

[28] 'Drunk, I reckon' (p. 158).     [29] See Boyer, *Religion Explained*, p. 376.

whose assault on Widow Douglas was averted by Huck, revises his own specific assumption about the veracity of Huck's account in the light of his general assumptions about Native Americans:

> 'When you talked about notching ears and slitting noses I judged that that was your own embellishment, because white men don't take that sort of revenge. But an Injun! That's a different matter altogether.'   (pp. 169–70)

If the first sentence here makes one feel queasy and perhaps even touch one's nose (as I found myself doing once when reading it), it is perhaps effecting a perceptual simulation based on embodied memories of cold, sharp, metallic objects cutting our flesh in sensitive places. In other words, Twain communicates not just an assumption (which we may not necessarily adopt ourselves even if we have had much exposure to it from other sources) but also an embodied experiencing of it (that is perhaps difficult *not* to experience on the level of perceptual simulation).

Here is the event that Huck will later recount to the Welchman. It is what he overhears when hiding some four feet away from Injun Joe and his accomplice in the sumach bushes in pitch darkness. Injun Joe is explaining that he intends to attack Widow Douglas because her husband, a Justice of the Peace, once had him horsewhipped for vagrancy:

> '. . . I'll take it out o[n] *her*! . . . When you want to get revenge on a woman you don't kill her—bosh! you go for her looks. You slit her nostrils—you notch her ears like a sow!'
> 'By God, that's—'
> 'Keep your opinion to yourself! It will be safest for you. I'll tie her to the bed. If she bleeds to death, is that my fault?'   (p. 164)

The description of prospective violence achieves strong relevance for various reasons: first, because it requires relatively little processing effort, since it fits in with stereotypical assumptions about Native Americans that will later be confirmed by the Welchman, and from which some readers are likely to have added inferences based on further assumptions (for example, that it was plausible for a woman in particular to be targeted for similar mutilation, since this was highlighted in period accounts of Native Americans as a routine punishment for adultery[30]); second, because it is given great salience by being the only graphic description of violence in the whole novel, and by shocking even Injun Joe's criminal accomplice.

Let me offer two small empirical pieces of evidence to support my claim about this passage's salience. The first is autobiographical (as many claims about reading inevitably are): these lines were the only ones that I found myself censoring when reading the whole novel to children over several weeks. That reaction was produced not by the text but by its interaction, as a stimulus, with my own 'cognitive style' and cognitive environment. Yet similar salience can arise from these lines' interaction with quite different cognitive styles and environments: later I learned that shortly

---

[30] E.g. Henry R. Schoolcraft, *Archives of Aboriginal Knowledge: Containing all the Original Papers Laid Before Congress Respecting the History, Antiquities, Language, Ethnology, Pictography, Rites, Superstitions, and Mythology of the Indian Tribes of the United States*, vol. i (Philadelphia, PA: J. B. Lippincott, 1860), p. 236; vol. v (Philadelphia, PA: J. B. Lippincott, 1865), pp. 684, 686.

after the novel's publication, exactly the same lines were singled out as extremely salient by a reviewer in the *New York Times*. The review concluded:

> With less, then, of Injun Joe and 'revenge', and 'slitting women's ears', and the shadow of the gallows, which throws an unnecessarily sinister tinge over the story, (if the book really is intended for boys and girls) we should have liked Tom Sawyer better.[31]

This moment in the novel—that it explicitly relates to Native Americans in general— was so salient and also so relevant for this reviewer that he or she downplayed its atypicality within the narrative. In his or her mind, it came to illustrate many other such moments; yet it would actually be difficult to pinpoint them in the novel. In another, more violent genre, the lines in question might be accompanied by many similar ones and so go barely noticed; but salience is relative to communicative context.

It is significant that this *New York Times* review did not primarily address the question posed in the present essay. The reviewer was concerned not with the epistemic question whether Twain uses a particular character to communicate an assumption about Native Americans in general, but rather with the question of the degree of fit between a character and a genre. But are those two questions connected? In other words, do some of the kinds of storyworld constructed by different narrative genres map more onto 'real-world' beliefs than others? Relevance theorists have offered a framework for exploring *that* question by distinguishing provisionally between internal and external relevance as relating respectively to the intra- and extra-diegetic worlds.[32] On this principle, Injun Joe's violent plans might be highly relevant to the context of the storyworld but not to the reader's beliefs about real Native Americans in general.

This fundamental distinction between internal and external relevance can be developed in a way that combines relevance theory with other cognitive approaches to fiction, which have examined similar questions using different terms. Putting *Tom Sawyer* to one side for the moment, let me explore how that combination might work.

## COMBINING INTERNAL AND EXTERNAL RELEVANCE WITH OTHER COGNITIVE APPROACHES

The question whether literature affects readers' beliefs has been assessed by a variety of cognitive approaches. At one end of the spectrum is the argument that the reader's pre-existing beliefs are relatively unswayed by fiction. For Jean-Marie

---

[31] Anonymous review, *New York Times* (13 January 1877), p. 3; quoted as reproduced in Stuart Hutchinson (ed.), *Mark Twain: Critical Assessments*, 4 vols (Robertsbridge, UK: Helm Information, 1993), ii, pp. 64–7 at 67. Also quoted in Twain, *The Adventures of Tom Sawyer*, edited by Stoneley, p. xix.
[32] See Deirdre Wilson, 'Relevance Theory and the Interpretation of Literary Works', in A. Yoshimura (ed.) *Observing Linguistic Phenomena: A Festschrift for Seiji Uchida* (Tokyo: Eihosha, 2012). Wilson (n. 7) credits Dan Sperber with first suggesting this distinction. Its application to the study of literature was first mooted in Dan Sperber and Deirdre Wilson, 'Presumptions of relevance', *Behavioral and Brain Sciences*, 10 (1987), 736–54 at 751. But it has been little discussed.

Schaeffer, who has investigated how readers immerse themselves psychologically in fictional narratives, even immersion does not affect the reader's 'beliefs' (by which he seems to mean basic beliefs about, for example, how their body relates to its immediate environment). In other words, the fiction does not achieve 'external relevance' in relation to those beliefs:

> It is thus important to distinguish between the state of fictional immersion and the adoption of a belief [*croyance*]. This distinction is in fact one between two levels of data-processing. Immersion accesses representations *before* they are translated into beliefs. Their translation into beliefs akin to those that would 'normally' be induced by fictionally mimicked representations is blocked at the higher cognitive level, that of conscious attention, which has been informed that the stimuli derive from mimetic self-stimulation or from shared, playful pretence. So the situation of fictional immersion involves the co-existence of pre-attentional, mimetic tricks with neutralisation of them that is achieved by blocking their effects at the level of conscious attention.[33]

Schaeffer goes on to consider two exceptions that clarify his model. One is the phenomenon where people are so immersed that they momentarily take the fictional world for reality and forget such basic beliefs (for example, lurching out of the way when a train seems to be heading out of the cinema screen towards them).[34] For Schaeffer, such moments are rare enough to be the exception that proves the rule. His second exception is when literature induces a false belief in the reader:

> If a mimeme induces false beliefs, if our conscious awareness is itself tricked, then we are no longer in a state of fictional immersion but in one of illusion in the ordinary sense of the term. But by the same token we are no longer in the domain of fiction.[35]

Schaeffer's model counters those proposed by Gregory Currie and Kendall Walton, according to which a novel does incite readers to hold an array of beliefs, but only 'pretend' ones (Currie), which are internally relevant (in relevance-theoretic terms) and distinct from readers' real-world beliefs.[36] However different from those models, Schaeffer's too relies on a fairly sharp distinction between what relevance theory calls internal and external relevance.

By contrast, the approach of Richard Gerrig, also cognitive, emphasizes more the readiness with which readers' pre-existing beliefs can be changed by immersion

---

[33] Jean-Marie Schaeffer, *Why Fiction?*, trans. Dorrit Cohn (Lincoln, NE; London: University of Nebraska Press, 2010), p. 163; translation modified. See Jean-Marie Schaeffer, *Pourquoi la fiction?* (Paris: Seuil, 1999), pp. 188–9.

[34] Schaeffer is evoking the alleged reaction of the 1895 audience to the Lumière brothers' short film of a train arriving in a station.

[35] Schaeffer, *Why Fiction?*, trans. Cohn, pp. 166–7; translation modified. See Schaeffer, *Pourquoi la fiction?*, p. 192.

[36] See Gregory Currie, *Image and Mind: Film, Philosophy and Cognitive Science* (New York: Cambridge University Press, 1995), e.g. pp. 148–51; Kendall L. Walton, *Mimesis as Make-Believe: On the Foundations of the Representational Arts* (Cambridge, MA: Harvard University Press, 1990). A more recent, co-authored paper by Currie sketches on the other hand ways in which fiction may under certain circumstances induce changes in real-world beliefs: Gregory Currie and Anna Ichino, 'Beliefs from fiction', unpublished paper, http://gregcurrie.com/images/downloads/beliefsfromfiction.pdf [accessed 4 May 2016].

in, or transportation into, fictional worlds.[37] The question is all the more complex because 'immersion' and 'transportation' have such different degrees of intensity, and because their modalities evolve with aesthetic innovation, including most recently with the rise of electronic media.[38] But even Gerrig does not explore the role of *embodied* cognition in the inflecting of pre-existing beliefs by fiction. Schaeffer, on the other hand, does allow for that role, if in an embryonic way. The distinction between what one might call internal and external relevance becomes more fluid at another point in his discussion of immersion, when he emphasizes that we learn (acquiring 'connaissances', in the sense of skills and sub-routines) through immersion in literary fiction just as we do on a massive scale through imitation (more than through precept) in the rest of our lives, while being largely unaware of all the cognitive processes activated.[39] It remains unclear, at least to me, exactly where such immersion-based learning (of what Schaeffer calls 'connaissances') stops and where our more conscious policing (of what he calls 'croyances') begins. The rarity of moments where we are so immersed that we abandon beliefs about basic physics surely does not itself prove that *all* 'real-world' beliefs are largely impervious to the influence of fiction. And Schaeffer's exclusion from the realm of fiction of cases where a narrative produces false belief ('croyance') seems somewhat arbitrary.

The fuzziness of Schaeffer's distinction between impervious 'belief' ('croyance') and conditionable learning ('connaissances') leaves it very possible, without necessarily being inevitable in the case of all readers, that the embodied dimension in particular of 'facts' (for example, about Native Americans) made manifest by literary texts might have what relevance theory calls a cognitive effect on them, by reinforcing or changing 'real-world' assumptions. Might literary texts have the potential to train the procedural or 'non-declarative' memory of the reader to react to evocations of Native Americans with perceptual and kinesic simulations of responses to physical threat? The writers of countless exemplary tales over centuries of western literature would probably have thought so. They had confidence in this belief-training and behaviour-changing power of their medium, relying as much on embodied reactions of horror and disgust as on the conceptual language of morality. But I phrase the question openly because the many variables evoked at the start of this chapter mean that perhaps only case studies within literary criticism and literary history, plus indeed experiment-based studies of real readers—of a kind that are attentive to the embodied nature of cognition—will help us move beyond assertion and hypothesis in answering it.

Pending such a programme, our thinking about the complexity of the relation of belief to literary fiction can be furthered by combining the distinction between internal and external relevance with the notion of source monitoring that has

---

[37] See Richard J. Gerrig, *Experiencing Narrative Worlds: On the Psychological Activities of Reading* (New Haven, CT; London: Yale University Press, 1993), ch. 6.

[38] See Marie-Laure Ryan, *Narrative as Virtual Reality 2: Revisiting Immersion and Interactivity in Literature and Electronic Media* (Baltimore, MD: Johns Hopkins University Press, 2015), Parts II and IV.

[39] Schaeffer, *Why Fiction?*, trans. Cohn, pp. 96–108; Schaeffer, *Pourquoi la fiction?*, pp. 118–32.

emerged in psychology in recent decades. For example, evolutionary psychologist Leda Cosmides and anthropologist John Tooby have argued that a decisive element in the success of humans relative to other animals has been the evolution of mechanisms enabling us to store information on a contingent and context-specific basis instead of simply processing all information as universally true or false; our mind has evolved ways of delimiting the scope of such information and of tagging its source to prevent it from automatically becoming accepted as a general truth. One of the mechanisms to have evolved for this purpose is that of meta-representation—the entertaining of beliefs (and other representations) as 'ones held by X'.[40]

Relevance theory too focuses on meta-representation,[41] which enables it to distinguish between (i) recognition that a speaker or writer intends to communicate something to us (recognition of the communicative intention), (ii) comprehension of that something (and thus of the informative intention), which involves entertaining certain thoughts or letting one's thoughts be steered in a certain direction, and (iii) acceptance, in other words being persuaded.[42] One can hold the meta-representation 'X believes Y and wants to communicate Y to me' without necessarily accepting Y. Yet the distinction between comprehension and acceptance is not absolute, as was argued as long ago as the seventeenth century by the philosopher Baruch Spinoza.[43] On the whole, there is a 'contract of trust' (as Terence Cave calls it; this volume, pp. 171–2) between reader and author; readers trust authors to be relevant, to write something that will reward proportionally the readers' efforts to make sense of it. That is different from trusting authors to be truthful, but the distinction may become blurred in practice, and therein lies the indeterminacy of literature's impact upon belief.

While source-monitoring models such as Cosmides and Tooby's scope syntax do not command universal scientific assent, they allow for more nuance in the relation between (what relevance theory calls) internal and external relevance than do the Schaeffer or Currie/Walton models. This is because source-monitoring models do not necessarily put internal and external relevance into a hierarchy of epistemic value. Moreover, they might subdivide both 'internal relevance' and 'external relevance' into a range of further local systems. 'Internal relevance' might be subdivided, for example, into different literary genres, which have norms such as the

---

[40] See Leda Cosmides and John Tooby, 'Consider the source: the evolution of adaptations for decoupling and metarepresentations', in Dan Sperber (ed.) *Metarepresentations: A Multidisciplinary Perspective* (Oxford: Oxford University Press, 2000), pp. 53–115. Meta-representation is closely connected to mind-reading. It is primarily in relation to mind-reading in particular that Cosmides and Tooby's work has been applied to the study of literature, notably by Lisa Zunshine in *Why We Read Fiction: Theory of Mind and the Novel* (Columbus, OH: Ohio State University Press, 2006).

[41] See Deirdre Wilson, 'Metarepresentation in linguistic communication', in D. Wilson and Dan Sperber, *Meaning and Relevance* (Cambridge: Cambridge University Press, 2012), pp. 230–58.

[42] See Sperber and Wilson, *Relevance*, pp. 29–31, 54–64, 163–72; Dan Sperber, Fabrice Clément, Christophe Heintz, Olivier Mascaro, Hugo Mercier, Gloria Origgi, and Deirdre Wilson, 'Epistemic vigilance', *Mind and Language*, 25.4 (2010), 359–93 at 364–9.

[43] See Gerrig, *Experiencing Narrative Worlds*, pp. 227–8. See also François Recanati, 'Can we believe what we do not understand?', *Mind and Language*, 12 (1997), 84–100. 'Indeed, it is generally assumed that considerations of acceptability play a crucial role in the comprehension process itself' (Sperber et al., 'Epistemic vigilance', p. 367).

ones that the *New York Times* reviewer sees transgressed if *Tom Sawyer* is defined as children's fiction; and 'external relevance' might be subdivided, for example, into the moral assumptions one holds in church and those one holds in the boardroom. Such a model seems more likely to do justice to the complexity of belief, while still allowing for some beliefs to be domain-general.[44] It also seems more able to describe phenomena such as the one identified by Margrethe Bruun Vaage whereby a legally institutionalized belief (that the crime of murder is generally more serious than that of rape) is inverted in the world of literary fiction and TV serials (where rape is often more serious than murder), especially if we interpret the 'fictional' belief not as ultimately discountable but rather as revealing an otherwise hidden dimension of our complex moral responses.[45]

A relevance-theory/Cosmides-Tooby model can also contribute to our understanding of the firewalls that a reader tries to erect between 'tagged' beliefs communicated by literary texts and that reader's other beliefs (some of which also have circumscribed scope). Relevance theorists have developed their own term for the building of such firewalls—epistemic vigilance.[46] This concept provides a powerful tool for studying literary communication so long as (i) it is not understood as intrinsically adjudicating between truth and falsehood (although it may do sometimes, and individual readers may think that is what they are doing), and (ii) a person's epistemic vigilance is emphasized to be itself always shaped by countless preceding stimuli, which might include dime novels or scholarly tomes or both: in other words, epistemic vigilance both polices literature and can itself be changed by it, for example by itself being made *less* dependent on stereotypical assumptions. Epistemic vigilance understood in these terms is different from the 'hermeneutics of suspicion' that has been common in literary-theoretic approaches since the 1970s:[47] in a relevance-theoretic perspective, the reader, even the literary critic, cannot stand in judgement entirely outside the act of communication that she is analysing. Whatever their own assumptions, readers are not just situated (as having countless assumptions of their own), but they always act as a partner—however recalcitrant—in an attempted act of communication. Even comprehension, let alone acceptance, 'involves adopting a tentative and labile stance of trust'.[48]

This returns us to the question of psychological immersion in a fiction. Is there a correlation between (i) the depth and intensity of immersion and (ii) the degree

[44] On the complexity of what might count as 'belief' in a relevance-theoretic perspective, see Dan Sperber and Deirdre Wilson, 'Beyond speaker's meaning', *Croatian Journal of Philosophy*, 15:44 (2015), 117–49.

[45] Margrethe Bruun Vaage, 'On the repulsive rapist and the difference between morality in fiction and real life', in Lisa Zunshine (ed.) *The Oxford Handbook of Cognitive Literary Studies* (Oxford; New York: Oxford University Press, 2015), pp. 421–39.

[46] See Sperber et al., 'Epistemic vigilance'.

[47] The phrase was coined by Paul Ricoeur, and the approach is epitomized by works such as Fredric Jameson's *The Political Unconscious: Narrative as a Socially Symbolic Act* (Ithaca, NY: Cornell University Press, 1981). On differences between a cognitively informed approach and the hermeneutics of suspicion, see also Mary Thomas Crane, 'Cognitive historicism: intuition in early modern thought', in Lisa Zunshine (ed.) *The Oxford Handbook of Cognitive Literary Studies* (Oxford: Oxford University Press, 2015), pp. 15–33, and the Introduction to the present volume, pp. 16–17.

[48] Sperber et al., 'Epistemic vigilance', p. 368.

of assumption-sharing between reader and author (or rather, implied author[49])? Certainly, immersion depends on many features of the narrative (ranging from style to humour[50]) other than the nature of the assumptions it is used to communicate. Yet if the assumptions made manifest by *Tom Sawyer* are inescapably perceptual and kinesic as well as conceptual (as I argue them to be), then the degree of strength with which they are activated is the same as that of the pre-attentional pull of immersion (in Schaeffer's terminology). Perhaps the best way to investigate the question would be through experiments that studied the correlation between individual readers' degree of immersion and the kinds of pre-existing assumptions they held. Such experiments would need to measure immersion and to assess someone's assumptions: it might prove impossible to do both to an adequate extent. More to prolong the question than to answer it, let me end by evoking the second notional cluster of assumptions mentioned above. What effect, if any, is it likely to have on readers' immersion in *The Adventures of Tom Sawyer*?

## *THE ADVENTURES OF TOM SAWYER* (2): FURTHER CONTEXTUAL ASSUMPTIONS

Whereas the first notional cluster of assumptions about Native Americans was derived from dime novels and/or Westerns, and others could concern, for example, the history of their displacement in North America, my second notional cluster is of assumptions we can derive specifically from Samuel Clemens's other discursive and fictional texts about Native Americans. Does reading those other texts make one bring to the novel changed assumptions about Clemens's attitude to Native Americans? Many of his writings on the topic are characterized by an enduring vitriol. This contrasts with his eventual rethinking of some of his early prejudices about blacks as well as with his opposition to imperialist oppression:[51] 'when the Red Man declares war, the first intimation his friend the white man whom he supped with at twilight has of it, is when the war-whoop rings in his ears and tomahawk sinks into his brain'.[52] The assumption of Native American duplicity is here imbued, as in *Tom Sawyer*, with an embodied sense of proximate threat.

But rather different assumptions about Native Americans can also be derived from the writings and dictated notes that comprise *Mark Twain's Autobiography*. One such assumption is that Twain consciously gave the fictional Injun Joe certain

---

[49] Wayne Booth's concept of an implied author (in *The Rhetoric of Fiction*), while focusing mainly on just one stage of the communications circuit, seems broadly compatible with a relevance-theoretic view of communication.

[50] Twain periodically uses humour to leaven suspense fleetingly, using, for example, a towel in the tavern-room episode and a cat in the courtroom one (pp. 138, 158).

[51] See Harry J. Brown, *Injun Joe's Ghost: The Indian Mixed-Blood in American Writing* (Columbia, MO; London: University of Missouri Press, 2004), pp. 13–16; Greg Camfield, *The Oxford Companion to Mark Twain* (Oxford: Oxford University Press, 2003), pp. 289–91; Shelley Fisher Fishkin, *A Historical Guide to Mark Twain* (Oxford: Oxford University Press, 2002), pp. 127–62.

[52] Mark Twain, 'The noble red man', *The Galaxy: A Magazine of Entertaining Reading* (September 1870), pp. 426–9 at 428.

characteristics and experiences with a view to maximizing the novel's cognitive effects on the reader rather than remaining as true as possible to what he saw as historical reality.[53] Another is that Twain's attitude towards the main model for Injun Joe was emotionally complex: he claims that the death of a real man who was known as Injun Joe unleashed in him a torrent of guilt (concerning his own bad life rather than the circumstances of the death, it seems). Readers who adopt that assumption of emotional and moral complexity are more likely to attribute stronger relevance to the only passage in *Tom Sawyer* to question the dime-novel stereotypes that surround Injun Joe. It occurs immediately after Injun Joe's death (its start was quoted above), when the narrator expresses great pity for him. This questioning does not last long: the narrator then pulls back from that pity in order to lambast villagers who had wanted to pardon him when he was alive (p. 187). Biographical assumptions we make about Twain do not necessarily reveal what he 'really' felt, but they do recalibrate the relevance and salience of certain passages as we read the novel.

Do they also recalibrate immersion? Do they intensify the meta-representing that the reader does ('This is what the author believes and wants me to believe')? And, if so, might that increase any psychological resistance to immersion (less 'Ouch, eek, yuk!' and more 'I can't lose myself in this novel by an author who wants to make me assume that Native Americans are very likely to be vengeful mutilators of innocent white women')? These are not 'either/or' questions. They ask about the degree of correlation, or inverse correlation, between two frequently co-existing reactions. Relevance theory can help in the search for answers because it sees communication as involving partial and shifting overlaps between vast arrays of assumptions held by addresser and addressee, and because it is compatible with approaches that explore the embodied dimension of those assumptions in the immersive context of literary fiction.

---

[53] Twain refers to one real man whom he and his childhood friends called Injun Joe: 'I think that in Tom Sawyer I starved Injun Joe to death in the cave. But that may have been to meet the exigencies of romantic literature. I can't remember now whether the real Injun Joe died in the cave or out of it.' More implicitly, Twain's description of this real man fosters, by its parallel with the process of literary creation, an assumption that Twain the writer's overriding concern in fashioning Injun Joe was with the impact he would have on the reader. Of his own childhood, Twain reminisced: 'Injun Joe, drunk, was interesting and a benefaction to us, but Injun Joe, sober, was a dreary spectacle.' Both quotations from Mark Twain, *Mark Twain's Autobiography*, with an Introduction by Albert Bigeloe Paine, 2 vols (New York and London: Harper and Brothers, 1924), ii, p. 175 (dictated on 8 March 1906). It seems likely that Twain knew at least two men who were labelled Injun Joe in Hannibal. The other was Joe Douglas (mentioned in footnote 11 above), who outlived Twain.

# Interlace 5

*Like Bolens and Kenny, Sellevold chooses her case study from a fictional storyworld. Like them, too, she focuses on features that seem to provoke the reader not only to realize that world for themselves, to furnish and complete it, but also to embark on a continuing process of recalibration. The responses triggered by Quixote's curious helmet, for example, or at a quite different level by the alarming implicatures arising from the depiction of Injun Joe as a stereotypical character, invite inferential work that needs to be tested and readjusted as the narrative unfolds. In this instance, a single counter-intuitive remark in the opening episode of Edith Wharton's* The House of Mirth *offers a point of leverage for reflection on some of the major issues raised by this volume. When Wharton writes, '[Lily Bart] still had the art of blushing at the right time', the effect is disconcerting: no one believes that blushing is voluntary, or that it can be faked at will. But we trust Wharton enough to ask ourselves what a relevant reading would be here. Sellevold's analysis raises questions about the status of blushing in communicative models that place heavy reliance on a distinction between ostensive and non-ostensive acts. We might simply remark, by way of introduction to her reading, that the assumption that blushing is an art is only problematic in a discourse of maximal correspondence to common belief. Wharton's remark itself, in the context of the novel, makes perfect sense—a sense that is the more perfect, indeed, because it is surprising.*

*As for kinesis, it is helpful to insist once again (see Interlace 3) on a distinction between kinesis in the fictional event and the reader's (and author's) kinesic intelligence. A scene such as the chance encounter between Lily Bart and Percy Gryce on the train certainly calls for a higher-order kinesic intelligence on the part of the reader. But what about the characters? Lily herself is apparently only a superficial reader (she carries a copy of Edward FitzGerald's* The Rubaiyat of Omar Khayyam *around with her in her bag as a sign of her cultural capital);*[1] *Selden is a book collector. But they don't need to be readers. The kinesic intelligence they rely on is a social art, one that would have been familiar to the world of La Bruyère's characters. They read minds and bodies avidly, intelligently, although in the end always imperfectly; but then kinesic intelligence never was a perfect art, as Bolens has shown.*

*This chapter, then, raises the question of how far non-verbal, and largely non-ostensive, expressions of emotion (on a spectrum from blushes via tears to shudders and smiles) can be exploited in the course of ostensive communication. In exploring that question, it introduces the notion of 'emotional vigilance', a term recently coined by analogy with*

[1] *See Edith Wharton,* The House of Mirth, *edited by Martha Banta (Oxford: Oxford University Press, The World's Classics, 1994), p. 65.*

*the more familiar 'epistemic vigilance' mentioned by Neil Kenny. At the same time, it demonstrates a linguistically based technique for micro-analysis, referring, for example, to the scalar term 'almost', which, on the margins of the reader's awareness, directs and redirects the inferential process. It thus puts into effect one of the key contentions of this book, namely that relevance theory and related cognitive approaches can provide an integrated set of instruments for literary analysis at every level of the text.*

# 5

# On the Borders of the Ostensive
## Blushing in Edith Wharton's *The House of Mirth*

*Kirsti Sellevold*

## THE ART OF BLUSHING AT THE RIGHT TIME

Blushing is a phenomenon of which we are all painfully aware. Yet the impression that emerges from the recent literature on blushing is that it is still a poorly understood phenomenon.[1] It is unclear what distinguishes blushing from other types of temporary changes of skin colour, provoked, say, by anger, alcohol, or physical exertion, or the feeling of being flustered. Nor is there any consensus regarding the types of emotions or mental states that elicit the blush, although embarrassment is a prime candidate, shame a good second, closely followed by modesty, shyness, pride, and guilt. Whether blushing is a form of self-expression,[2] whether it can be explained exclusively in terms of self-attention, has a communicative function, or plays a role in evolution, are also thorny issues.[3] The one thing that seems indisputable, by contrast, is the view that blushing is uncontrollable, that it is a bodily reaction impossible to fake.[4] It thus comes as something of a surprise when Edith Wharton, in the opening pages of *The House of Mirth* (1905), endows her leading character, Lily Bart, with a capacity for timing her blushes, or so it seems: 'she still had the art of blushing at the right time'.[5] As the word 'art' suggests, blushing appears here as a skill which Lily has acquired over time, cultivated, and refined

---

[1] The blurb of a recent interdisciplinary anthology on blushing states, for instance, that 'the blush is a ubiquitous yet little understood phenomenon'; see W. Ray Crozier and Peter J. de Jong (eds), *The Psychological Significance of the Blush* (Cambridge: Cambridge University Press, 2013).

[2] Mitchell Green excludes blushing as a form of self-expression but keeps the question open in his study *Self-Expression* (Oxford: Oxford University Press, 2007), p. 27.

[3] Darwin proposed the first scientific (and still widely referred to) account of blushing; see Charles Darwin, *The Expression of the Emotions in Man and Animals*, edited by Paul Ekman (New York: Oxford University Press, 1998), ch. 13. Current research may be characterized broadly speaking in terms of three partly overlapping, partly competing theories: (i) remedial theory: the blush functions as a signal of apology or appeasement; (ii) undesired social attention theory: the blush is triggered by conspicuousness, whether negative, positive, or neutral; (iii) exposure theory: the blush is triggered by exposure of the private self.

[4] This was first remarked by Seneca: see 'On the blush of modesty', Letter XI, http://thriceholy.net/Texts/Letters/Letter11.html.

[5] Edith Wharton, *The House of Mirth*, edited by Martha Banta (Oxford: Oxford University Press, Oxford World's Classics, 2008), p. 8. All page references in the text refer to this edition.

into an art; although, as the word 'still' gives away, the nature of this art is elusive and ephemeral.

Is this just a cruel trick played by Edith Wharton, displaying her power as author to equip her character with a counter-intuitive, even counterfactual, skill, the ability to turn on a blush whenever she fancies it, only to strip it away from her as the novel develops? Not quite: for although she is still fairly young, Lily has considerable experience of handling her social environment, including members of the opposite sex. Her art, if art it is, consists in the ability to continue to react like a young innocent girl, and to exploit the blush to enhance her charm, to turn it to her advantage. There is no indication either that she blushes more as she grows older (the time span of the story is in fact only two years); it is rather that she blushes at the wrong time, thus laying herself open to exploitation by others. It is in any case unlikely that Edith Wharton would have arbitrarily defied the conditions of the real world. If her novels have retained their power, it is because they are psychologically plausible. I would rather suggest that her use of blushing as a narrative device in her novels and short stories prefigures some of the knowledge that is currently emerging about the role of bodily reactions in communication. I will argue, more specifically, that blushing, although clearly unintentional, carries information that gets picked up and exploited in communication.

Before setting out this argument in more detail, we need to take a closer look at the passage where Lily displays her art of blushing:

> [Selden] paused a moment. 'Come up and see,' he suggested. 'I can give you a cup of tea in no time—and you won't meet any bores.'
>
> [Lily's] colour deepened—she still had the art of blushing at the right time—but she took the suggestion as lightly as it was made.
>
> 'Why not? It's too tempting—I'll take the risk,' she declared.   (p. 8)

In this opening sequence of the novel, Selden invites Lily on the spur of the moment up to his apartment for a cup of tea. He has come across her at the railway station in New York on his way home from work, and taken her out for a stroll in the heat while she is waiting for the next train. The invitation prompts in Lily an instant bodily reaction that precedes her verbal reply. The reaction betrays a sensitivity to the potentially transgressive aspect of the invitation: by accepting it, she risks compromising her reputation. There is presumably also an element of erotic attraction here. As my use of the word 'betray' indicates, these inferences operate at Lily's sub-attentive or pre-reflective level (while of course remaining open to the reader).[6] The ensuing aside ('she still had the art of blushing at the right time') suggests, as I have argued above, that Lily is still in possession of a certain innocence, enough for her body accidentally to betray her attraction to Selden, but also that she is able to take advantage of it.

---

[6] That humans can run 'unconscious' or pre-reflective inferences was first proposed by the nineteenth-century polymath Hermann von Helmholz; see Chris Frith, *Making up the Mind: How the Brain Creates our Mental World* (Oxford: Blackwell Publishing, 2007), pp. 40–1.

Even if the blush is beyond her conscious control, she no doubt still welcomes it, as it allows her to enhance her charm.

## OSTENSIVE AND NON-OSTENSIVE COMMUNICATION

Edith Wharton here pinpoints one of the main topics of this volume: to what extent can non-ostensive, non-verbal, or bodily responses feature in a cognitive pragmatics of communication? Relevance theory of course acknowledges the importance of non-verbal communication,[7] although mainly when used ostensively:[8] non-ostensive or involuntary responses are not part of what the theory sets out to explain.[9] Such responses, especially as regards emotional forms of expression, have also been difficult to explain in evolutionary terms. They do not, for example, invariably guarantee the honesty of communication—some of them can be faked, although not easily—and they might be detrimental to the sender insofar as they reveal emotions such as fear, embarrassment, and shame.[10] Recently, however, evolutionary pragmatics (which builds on relevance theory) has proposed an account of non-ostensive, involuntary uses of emotional expressions,[11] where such expressions are seen to contribute to the stability of communication. According to this account, humans display an extreme sensitivity to emotional expressions;[12] more specifically, they are endowed with a capacity for emotional vigilance that enables them to evaluate emotional signals and modulate their responses accordingly. Although functionally similar to epistemic vigilance (see Introduction; also Chapter 4 in this volume), emotional vigilance is seen less as a defence against misleading emotional signals than as a means of figuring out when it is beneficial to respond to them. To borrow an example from Dezecache and colleagues: 'A child's extreme anger display when she is told that she cannot have a second serving of ice cream should not elicit submission; a raised eyebrow by a mafia Don may.'[13]

The fact that such expressions elicit different reactions in different contexts suggests that the reactions are not automatic or reflex-like,[14] although indeed involuntary,

---

[7] See Deirdre Wilson and Tim Wharton, 'Relevance and prosody', *Journal of Pragmatics*, 38.10 (2006), 1559–79; Tim Wharton, *Pragmatics and Non-Verbal Communication* (Cambridge: Cambridge University Press, 2009).

[8] To succeed in ostensive communication, a speaker must not only inform her audience of something but also make manifest her intention to do so; see Dan Sperber and Deirdre Wilson, *Relevance: Communication and Cognition* (Oxford: Blackwell, 2nd ed., 1995), ch. 1.

[9] They provide information for an observer, but do not manifest an intention to do so. See the distinction between sign and signal presented in the publications referred to in note 7.

[10] The standard explanation, however, is still that because emotional expressions cannot be easily faked, they secure the honesty of communication, and thus benefit both sender and receiver.

[11] Guillaume Dezecache, Hugo Mercier, and Thomas C. Scott-Phillips, 'An evolutionary approach to emotional communication', *Journal of Pragmatics*, 59.B (December 2013), 221–33; p. 222.

[12] The claim is supported by experiments showing that subtle expressions of emotion are picked up, even at second hand. See G. Dezecache, L. Conty, M. Chadwick, L. Philip, R. Soussignan et al., 'Evidence for unintentional emotional contagion beyond dyads', *PLoS ONE*, 8(6): e67371 (2013), doi:10.1371/journal.pone.0067371.

[13] See Dezecache et al., 'An evolutionary approach to emotional communication', 226.

[14] Except perhaps in the very general sense that they automatically trigger inferences.

but source- and context-sensitive. This does not mean that it is easy to infer which emotional state has triggered a blush (for example), or even that the inferential process to this end is necessarily conscious.[15] As we shall see, Darcy's blush in *Pride and Prejudice* is triggered by an emotional state which is different from Percy Gryce's in Wharton's novel, yet both involve motor resonance or kinesic reactions.[16]

Edith Wharton's use of these non-ostensive means of communication is of course itself ostensive, but that does not change the fact that on the level of the narrative they are non-ostensive. What is interesting here above all is the interplay between these levels. The way Wharton draws on readers' capacity for emotional vigilance and motor resonance reactions, for instance, clearly increases the propensity of the reader to become immersed. Her art of writing does not, however, consist only in drawing on emotional expressions to trigger the reader's inferences. I shall show how she makes such expressions interact in subtle—often almost unnoticeable—ways with linguistic expressions that similarly trigger inferences, this time on the ostensive level. We have already encountered the adverb 'still', which made us infer that Lily's ability to control her blushing is not likely to last. The modal adverb *perhaps* and the complex expression *as if* will also play a role, but my prime example is the scalar expression *almost*, the function of which is to trigger implicatures (intended inferences) which may be set aside if they prove to be irrelevant.[17] Such expressions afford counterfactual thinking, and thus contribute to the suspense of the story: they induce readers to entertain alternative outcomes.

## REFLECTIVE AND PRE-REFLECTIVE INFERENCES

Let us now return to Lily's opening blush in this perspective. Since Selden first laid eyes on her at the railway station, he has taken in every aspect of her appearance— her long lashes, the smoothness of her still youthful skin, the purity of her tint, her graceful line—and it seems beyond doubt that the blush has an effect on him. It is equally clear that the blush is brought on by the situation: Lily would not have blushed had Selden not risked inviting her to his apartment. In addition to being context-sensitive in these ways, her blush—even if she takes the invitation as 'lightly' as it is made—points to an undercurrent of unstated (or unrecognized) feelings between them which will set the conversation on an unforeseen and risky track.

---

[15] Although it might be, as when parents try to figure out why their baby is crying.

[16] For the notions of kinesis and motor resonance, see the Introduction and Interlace 3; also Chapter 3 in this volume.

[17] On scalar expressions, see Jean-Claude Anscombre and Oswald Ducrot, *L'Argumentation dans la langue* (Liège: Pierre Mardaga, 2nd ed., 1988), p. 167; Robyn Carston, 'Informativeness, relevance and scalar implicature', in Robyn Carston and Seiji Uchida (eds) *Relevance Theory: Applications and Implications* (Amsterdam: John Benjamins, 1998), pp. 179–236; Jay David Atlas, 'Intuition, the paradigm case argument, and the two dogmas of Kant'otelianism', in Klaus Petrus and Uli Sauerland (eds) *Meaning and Analysis: New Essays on Grice* (London: Palgrave MacMillan, 2010), pp. 47–75.

That is exactly what happens when Lily provokes Selden to disclose his reasons for not visiting her:

> 'Why don't you come oftener?'
> 'When I do come, it's not to look at Mrs. Peniston's [Lily's aunt's] furniture.'
> 'Nonsense,' she said. 'You don't come at all—and yet we get on so well when we meet.'
> 'Perhaps that's the reason,' he answered promptly. (pp. 9–10)

Neither intended seriously nor taken so, the reply makes Lily ponder further why Selden does not visit her. As he does not seem to dislike her, yet surely does not expect to marry her (both of course know that his financial situation excludes him as a marriage prospect), she simply cannot figure him out, so she presses him once more: 'Well then,—?' Selden, amused and unable to resist the challenge of her provocative tone, pursues the line the conversation has taken:

> 'Well then,' he said with a plunge, 'Perhaps *that's* the reason.'
> 'What?'
> 'The fact that you don't want to marry me. Perhaps I don't regard it as such a strong inducement to go and see you.' He felt a slight shiver down his spine as he ventured this, but her laugh reassured him. (p. 10)

Although the words are exactly the same as in his first reply to her query, and are qualified again by the modal adverb 'perhaps', which gives both replies a tentative character, the stress on 'that' in the second shows that it is proffered involuntarily (this is doubly underlined by the italics and the use of the word 'plunge'). Unable to stop himself, Selden has literally plunged into an unplanned line of conversation of which he cannot foresee the consequences. That this is the case is further confirmed by his bodily reaction, the sudden shiver that runs down his spine, which is not just a momentary anxiety that he might have misjudged the situation and that Lily will take him seriously, but also a measure of the danger of the situation, his fear that he may accidentally have let slip his feelings for her.

Despite this, and although Lily's laugh instantly reassures him, he is nonetheless tempted to pursue this line, although now in an imaginative, counterfactual world: 'if they had been in her aunt's drawing-room, he might almost have tried to disprove her deduction' (p. 10). As the qualifying expressions show ('if they had been', 'might', 'almost'), his temptation is extremely tentative and constrained, and the scalar expression *almost* (which prompts the implicature 'but not quite') suggests that even in a counterfactual scenario, he will not go all the way. The modal expression *perhaps* which introduces both replies points in this direction too. And yet, these expressions also open up the possibility of more than one outcome. In that light, it is as if the qualifying expressions conspired with the blush to make Selden risk more than he intended, prompted him in fact to tell the truth. The blush, one might say, triggers his capacity for emotional vigilance: he takes it to be more honest than her words. And, as the scalar and modal expressions show, he moves in this early part of the novel on a threshold where things can still go in different directions.

## ALMOST BUT NOT QUITE: THE DOMAIN
## OF THE SCALAR

Among the books that Lily picks out from Selden's bookshelves during her subsequent visit to his flat is a copy of La Bruyère's *Caractères*. That only this particular work is mentioned while all the others remain anonymous is clearly not only echoic (in the sense defined elsewhere in this volume; see Introduction, section on 'Echoic utterances and irony', and Chapter 9), but also an integral feature of the narrative design, since the memory of exactly this gesture is what will first come to Lily's mind when she unexpectedly turns up on Selden's doorstep for their last encounter at the end of the novel. Wharton must have been thoroughly familiar with the seventeenth-century French writer whose work thus frames the narrative of *The House of Mirth*.[18] Famous for his satirical portraits of members of the French court, he depicted a close-knit society which strongly echoes the societal pressures of 'Old New York' that Lily moves in and that Wharton knew intimately herself. Both consisted in relatively small groups where everybody knew (and gossiped about) each other, both displayed immense wealth, and both had strict rules of social conduct. But what Wharton perhaps most crucially picked up from La Bruyère's work is the ability to observe (and communicate in writing) the fine nuances of non-verbal communication in a rule-bound universe where one is on constant display.[19] Like La Bruyère's 'characters', Lily moves in a society where success, even survival, depends on the ability to track other people's emotions (and potentially exploit them for personal advantage) while hiding one's own. Lily is an extremely skilled practitioner of this art, trained by her mother to fit into the environment in ways that maximally benefit her. As we have already seen, however, the blush is a sign of the costs of maintaining her façade.

Wharton is of course not indebted solely to La Bruyère's ability to put on display and satirize the involuntary effects of non-verbal communication. As is well known, Jane Austen and other exponents of the eighteenth- and nineteenth-century English novel used blushing not only to display their characters' emotional states but also as an effective narrative device.[20] As in pragmatics, in literature too

---

[18] Wharton spent long summers in France in her youth and settled there from her mid-forties; see Hermione Lee, *Edith Wharton* (London: Pimlico, 2013 [2007]).

[19] Louis van Delft calls it 'un univers fait pour l'œil' ('a universe designed for the eye'); see van Delft, *La Bruyère moraliste: Quatre études sur les Caractères* (Geneva: Droz, 1971), p. 75.

[20] Blushing in the nineteenth-century English novel is extensively discussed by Mary Ann O'Farrell, *Telling Complexions: The Nineteenth-Century English Novel and the Blush* (Durham, NC: Duke University Press, 1997); see also Katie Halsey, 'The blush of modesty or the blush of shame? Reading Jane Austen's blushes', *Forum for Modern Language Studies*, 42.3 (2006), 226–39. The social scientist W. Ray Crozier also uses literary examples of blushing in his work; see, for instance, his 'Blushing and the private self', in W.R. Crozier and P.J. de Jong (eds) *The Psychological Significance of the Blush* (Cambridge: Cambridge University Press, 2013), ch. 11, pp. 222–42; also 'The blush: literary and psychological perspectives', *Journal for the Theory of Social Behaviour*, 46.4 (2016), 502–16. More specifically pertinent to the concerns of this chapter is Ruth Rosaler's study *Conspicuous Silences: Implicature and Fictionality in the Victorian Novel* (Oxford: Oxford University Press, 2016), since it uses the notion of implicature as a primary instrument of narrative analysis, while touching on blushing at various points in the analysis of nineteenth-century English novels; for Rosaler's concluding point on this theme, see pp. 171–2.

the phenomenon seems to resist easy categorization and to acquire a somewhat ambivalent status. While George Eliot, for instance, airs an explicitly negative attitude to blushing in *Daniel Deronda*,[21] and the narrator of *Middlemarch* claims that Dorothea is not prone to blushing, critics have counted more than several dozen cases of Dorothea blushing.[22] Like La Bruyère, Wharton satirizes the involuntary effects of non-verbal communication, but for her they are not only an object of ridicule: she also draws on them to display conflicting emotions in her characters. In her sometimes ironic echoing of the canonic English novel, she takes this ambivalence one step further.

Lily's encounter with young Percy Gryce, just after she has left Selden and taken the train for Bellomont, the country estate of her friends the Trenors, provides an example where Lily skilfully exploits Gryce's non-ostensive reactions in order to reach her goal of marrying him. At the age of twenty-nine and having over the years thrown away several marriage opportunities, she is painfully aware that this might be her last chance. While on the train, she spots young Gryce and decides to make a move to catch this inexperienced marriage prospect:

> As she passed Mr Gryce, the train gave a lurch, and he was aware of a slender hand gripping the back of his chair. He rose with a start, his ingenuous face looking as though it had been dipped in crimson: even the reddish tint in his beard seemed to deepen.
> The train swayed again, almost flinging Miss Bart into his arms.  (p. 19)

The scene echoes in ironic mode the moment in *Pride and Prejudice* when Elizabeth and Darcy unexpectedly meet at Darcy's country estate Pemberley.[23] As Guillemette Bolens has persuasively shown, Darcy's strong emotions when seeing Elizabeth, indeed the whole drama of the scene, are conveyed through two standard items from the lexicon, the adverb 'absolutely' and the verb 'started'.[24] The first conveys the extreme character of the situation, the implausibility of the two meeting at that place and at that moment; the second transmits Darcy's strong, almost electrified, bodily reaction, prompted by his surprise and shock on seeing Elizabeth. Highly relevant for our purposes is also the fact that, when Elizabeth and Darcy recognize each other, they both blush, leaving no doubt that the motor resonance reaction is reciprocal.

There is a superficial resemblance between the two couples. Lily, like Elizabeth, is of good family, but poor and with meagre marriage prospects, and Gryce, like Darcy, is rich; it is perhaps not accidental, too, that his first name echoes Darcy's family name. However, the irony does not arise primarily from character description,

---

[21] See George Eliot, *Daniel Deronda*, edited by Terence Cave (London: Penguin Classics, 1995), p. 420: 'a blush is no language: only a dubious flag-signal which may mean either of two contradictories'.

[22] See O'Farrell, *Telling Complexions*, pp. 119, 120.

[23] On irony as echoic, see Deirdre Wilson and Dan Sperber, *Meaning and Relevance* (Cambridge: Cambridge University Press, 2012), ch. 6 ('Explaining irony'), pp. 123–47; see also this volume, Introduction (pp. 11–12), Chapter 6 (pp. 113, 120, 124), and Chapter 9 (pp. 172–9).

[24] See Guillemette Bolens, *The Style of Gestures: Embodiment and Cognition in Literary Narrative* (Baltimore, MD: The Johns Hopkins University Press, 2012), pp. 28–33.

but through the identical kinesic reactions of the two male characters, more specifically through the fact that these identical reactions are triggered by different emotions. Just as Darcy does, Gryce blushes and starts, although not when he sees Lily but as she grips his seat in the train, thus provoking an encounter which, as the absence of the adverb 'absolutely' indicates, is less unexpected than the one in *Pride and Prejudice* (that Lily and Gryce should meet on the way to a place they have both been invited to is not all that surprising). And unlike Darcy's, Gryce's reactions are not prompted by his surprise on seeing Lily—if he hides behind his newspaper, it is precisely because he *has* seen her, as Lily has indeed figured out— but by his inability to handle her physical proximity. Having received a large inheritance after his father's death and recently arrived in New York with his mother, young Gryce has none of Darcy's self-assurance and arrogance. He exhibits on the contrary all the qualities of a prototypical blusher: extreme shyness, lack of emotional experience, fair skin; his reddish hair and beard do not exactly dampen the impression either. One could speculate that if he had stayed in his seat and not stood up, he might have been able to handle the situation better;[25] he might even have managed to blush less, if not to avoid doing so altogether. As it is, his inability to control his bodily reactions makes it impossible to hide the impression Lily makes on him.

To understand and enjoy the encounter between Lily and Gryce, one of course does not need to know (or remember) the encounter at Pemberley. And yet it is astonishing to what extent the two encounters asymmetrically echo one another. Precisely because it recalls the mutual blush at Pemberley, so striking in the Jane Austen version and so evidently revealing mutual feelings between Elizabeth and Darcy, the one-sided blush in the train drives home much more strongly the absence of such feelings between Lily and Gryce. It also removes any thought that Gryce might have blushed as a result of his nascent feelings for Lily. If he blushes, it is exclusively because he is shy, liable to blush in awkward situations, unaccustomed as he is to being in the proximity of a beautiful woman who takes an interest in him. Whereas the mutual blush of the encounter at Pemberley is a proleptic sign of the happy union to come, the one-sided blush of the train scene becomes rather a sign (or an authorial signal) of the reverse.

Wharton also ironically echoes Austen's use of distance to convey her characters' emotions. While Darcy and Elizabeth's strong reactions when spotting each other at a distance are a sign of their intense feelings for each other, a sort of inverted forecast of their future emotional closeness, in Wharton the characters are brought much closer, yet without quite touching each other: Gryce's haptic contact with Lily's hand is conveyed indirectly through the chair. This situation of almost-but-not-quite touching intensifies the emotional distance between Lily and Gryce. Wharton in fact exploits this moment just before the two characters touch by means of the scalar *almost*. As previously indicated, scalar expressions prompt conversational

---

[25] W. Ray Crozier discusses an example from *The Mill on the Floss* (1860) where a change in movement brings a shift in consciousness in one of the characters (Maggie), which again triggers a blush; see 'Blushing and the private self', pp. 224–5.

implicatures; if Lily is flung *almost but not quite* into Gryce's arms, it inevitably triggers the impression that the two will not end up as husband and wife. However, the nature of the implicature, the fact that it *can* be cancelled in context, leaves the outcome of the situation open at this early point in the novel. The kinesic verb 'fling', for instance, which signals the violence and speed with which Lily gravitates towards Gryce, makes salient the possibility of an opposite situation where the implicature is cancelled and Lily will in fact marry Gryce. But that gravitational impetus might just reflect Lily's desperation at having to, but not wanting to, catch a rich husband. It is also noticeable that it is not Lily herself but the train that performs the flinging, as if the train stands in for the societal pressure forcing her to marry against her feelings. One might even say that it is ironically significant that what stays the movement, prevents Lily from ending up in Gryce's arms, is not her own agency but the scalar *almost*.

Relevance theory defines irony as a type of 'echoic' utterance in which the speaker expresses a mocking, scornful, or contemptuous attitude to a thought (or utterance) she attributes to someone else (see Introduction, p. 11). Wharton's brilliant allusion to Austen's Pemberley scene, which, as we have seen, is a repetition of structure rather than of content,[26] voices an attitude to Austen's marriage plot that is perhaps more humorous than contemptuous. It performs a subtle satire of that novel's depiction of feelings and its eventual happy ending. To grasp the full scope of the irony, however, the reader needs to draw on her own kinesic intelligence: she needs to feel an echo of the bodily reactions of both Darcy and Gryce. Without that kinesic echo, the suspense of the story, opened up by the scalar *almost*, would be less powerful, less painful. The scalar expression anticipates not only an unhappy outcome, but also the way Lily becomes immobilized in the in-between situation of neither giving in to societal pressure nor following her feelings.

As a remake of the Pemberley scene from a totally different perspective and with a totally different outcome, then, the train scene in *The House of Mirth* is both an ironic echo of Austen's marriage plots and a brief but painful anticipatory glimpse of what will become the lot of Wharton's female character. As such, it acquires a type of external relevance it would not have had if read without the kinesic echo from the Pemberley scene.[27]

## COUNTERFACTUAL IMAGININGS AND ASYNCHRONOUS BLUSHING

If Percy Gryce is the agent and victim of the most embarrassing blush in *The House of Mirth*, he is by no means the only male blusher. Lawrence Selden also blushes at various points in the story, although more discreetly than Gryce. That said, Lily is

---

[26] See Oswald Ducrot, *Les Mots du discours* (Paris: Seuil, 1980), pp. 211–12.

[27] For the notion of external relevance, see Deirdre Wilson, 'Relevance and the interpretation of literary works', in A. Yoshimura (ed.) *Observing Linguistic Phenomena: A Festschrift for Seiji Uchida* (Tokyo: Eihosha, 2012), pp. 3–19; also published in *UCL Working Papers in Linguistics* (2011).

the one who (perhaps unsurprisingly) blushes most, and often at key moments. One such moment occurs the day after her arrival at Bellomont in the early stages of the story. When Lily is helping the hostess Judy Trenor with invitation cards, the conversation turns to Lawrence Selden. Having heard that Bertha, the rich George Dorset's spoilt wife, with whom Selden has previously had an affair, is still after him (although the affair is over as far as he is concerned), Mrs Trenor has invited Selden to Bellomont. He has declined the invitation, however, and now she is worried that Bertha will blame her and take her revenge; 'I believe I'll call up Lawrence on the telephone', she exclaims, 'and tell him he simply *must* come?' The exclamation is framed as a question, indicating that she will only do it with Lily's approval, but she does not get the reply she expects:

> 'Oh don't,' said Lily with a quick suffusion of colour. The blush surprised her almost as much as it did her hostess, who, though not commonly observant of facial changes, sat staring at her with puzzled eyes.   (p. 45)

The first thing to note is that the non-ostensive blush here does not appear on its own, but mixed with another type of communication, namely the semi-linguistic interjection 'oh'. Interplay between ostensive and non-ostensive elements is in fact extremely common in everyday communication, and its effect on the way utterances are interpreted has recently become a focus of interest in linguistics.[28] The interplay between the ostensive 'oh' and the non-ostensive blush captures brilliantly Lily's strong and totally unexpected emotional reaction to Mrs Trenor's exclamation, the intensity of which is measured by the emotion it triggers in return—not just Mrs Trenor's surprise, but also Lily's own.

Still, as the scalar *almost* indicates, Lily is not as surprised by her emotional outburst as her friend is. Until this moment she has not been wholly aware of her conflicting feelings for Selden: as we have seen, she cannot quite understand why he keeps her at a distance. Now, by contrast, she will have difficulties with interpreting her reaction as something other than a signal of her own feelings for Selden. And indeed, from now on Lily will see Selden in a different light. In this case, then, the blush seems to act as an affordance for switching Lily's view of Selden; he has changed from an agreeable but insignificant presence in the background to a major factor in her life (and her imagination). That Lily should have warm feelings for Selden is, however, so inconsistent with Mrs Trenor's background knowledge of Lily—it is Gryce, not Selden, that she has in her sights—that she totally misinterprets the reaction: 'Good gracious, Lily, how handsome you are!— Why? Do you dislike him so much?' Despite this, Lily must have sensed in her puzzled stare the danger of such disclosure, for she plays the one card she knows will divert Judy's attention, namely her growing intimacy with Gryce. The worry seems justified, however: despite Judy's inexperience with interpreting facial changes, she seems to have tracked something in the blush other than what her verbal reaction implies—after all, she knows as well as anyone that Lily's interest in Gryce is purely economic. It is telling

---

[28] See Tim Wharton, *Pragmatics and Non-Verbal Communication*; Dezecache et al., 'An evolutionary approach'.

that, at the end of the conversation, she returns to her question, leaving a little residue of doubt: "'You're quite sure...that you wouldn't like me to telephone for Lawrence Selden?' 'Quite sure,' said Lily' (p. 46).

What this conversation—and a fortiori the scalar expression—exposes is Lily's divided self. She struggles with several inclinations: on the one hand, her attraction to Selden, whether she should follow her feelings and be free, although poor; or, on the other, give in not only to the societal pressure of having to marry for money but also to her own taste for luxury. How difficult it is to handle that conflict is revealed through a series of blushes a couple of chapters later (chapter VI). Unable again to resist Selden's invitation (he has after all turned up at Bellomont), this time for an afternoon walk up on the hills, she gets Gryce—to whom she has promised the same—out of the way by sending him off on a trip with the other guests, on the pretext of a headache. Initially only intending to 'taste the rare joys of mental vagrancy', Lily on the ascent up the hill in fact leaves one of her selves behind her 'gasping for air in a prison-house of fears' (p. 64) and lets her 'free spirit [quiver] for flight'. This feeling of being free, of metaphorically flying as it were, makes her seize instantly what Selden means by personal freedom (his definition of success), a kind of ticket into the 'republic of the spirit':

> She leaned forward with a responsive flash. 'I know—I know—it's strange; but that's just what I've been feeling today.'
> He met her eyes with the latent sweetness of his. 'Is the feeling so rare with you?' he said.
> She blushed a little under his gaze.   (p. 68)

Again, it is not what she says but that momentary surfacing of half-submerged feelings, provoked by his gaze, that catches his attention, triggers his emotional vigilance. The blush reveals to him (and the reader) that she is not unaffected by his view of her, and that hint of emotional weakness which previously, as he reflects, 'he would have been almost sorry to detect in her'[29] now makes him see her differently. Unable as he is, however, to fulfil her aims, he instead makes her visualize how her life would be if they were to be realized:

> 'Then the best you can say for me is, that after struggling to get [the things I like] I probably shan't like them?' She drew a deep breath. 'What a miserable future you foresee for me!'
> 'Well—have you never foreseen it for yourself?'
> The slow colour rose to her cheek, not a blush of excitement but drawn from the deep wells of feeling; it was as if the effort of her spirit had produced it.   (p. 71)

The visualization of what Lily's ambitions might have in store for her should she succeed brings on a second blush; not a fleeting one of excitement this time but slowly developing, revealing that Selden has touched on a truth. His provocation has in fact got her free spirit up flying, her regular cautious self no longer controlling it, and put it in a position to elicit the blush voluntarily as it were. Couched

---

[29] And, as the implicature triggered by the scalar 'almost' shows, Selden is still, despite what he tells himself, open to 'sentimental experiments'.

in an *as if* construction, that voluntary control of body response happens of course only on a counterfactual or hypothetical level, but it all the same makes one think that if not the conscious Lily, some pre-reflective part of her *has* wanted to show that she is aware of what the realization of her ambitions would imply. She is clever enough not to deny that she has foreseen the scenario Selden draws up for her— '"Often and often," she said', but her qualification ('But it looks so much darker when you show it to me!') cannot hide the fact that out in the open, it sounds even more grim than in her imagination. The contrast (prefigured by the *as if* construction) between the real world, where Selden has 'nothing to give her instead', and the hypothetical one where he has ('if I had, it should be yours, you know'), makes her weep. As such, the construction—deliberately or ostensively put there by the author—underlines the extent to which the blush sets loose a train of pre-reflective or unconscious inferences in Lily.[30] Not just in her, but also in Selden: 'He himself did not know why he had led their talk along such lines', and deflects the conversation onto unknown, uncontrollable terrain: 'it was one of those moments when neither seemed to speak deliberately, when an indwelling voice in each called to the other across unsounded depths of feeling' (pp. 71–2). Far from being automatic or reflex-like, although of course involuntary, Lily's non-ostensive blush creates a space where they can test or explore their real feelings, and where their wavering intentions can go either way.

The communication of those undeliberate voices, stripped as they are of their usual jesting tone, is highly fragile though, and if Selden is moved by Lily's emotional outburst, he quickly checks the impulse when he notices not only how brief her weeping is, but also that she exploits it to her advantage: 'she turned on him a face softened but not disfigured by emotion, and he said to himself, somewhat cruelly, that even her weeping was an art' (p. 72). That Lily has the art of crying within her power (whether reflectively or pre-reflectively) is not so surprising, however, for, as opposed to blushing, tears can be brought on voluntarily.[31] Along with smiles and shudders, they are located at the other end of the spectrum of emotional expressions that can be exploited in communication. It is thus not unlikely that crying at the right time is part of Lily's repertory of devices for charming a susceptible male, as indeed Selden seems to think. Despite this, Lily's emotions still have an effect on him. Her crying seems at least to have softened him enough to lead the conversation onto a track where they probe the possibility of imagining a life together, and this time not in a jesting but a serious mode.[32] It is not until the sound of a vehicle calls them abruptly back to the real world that the spell of that counterfactual world is broken. Selden's dry reaction to Lily's impatience when she realizes

---

[30] As Terence Cave puts it in an unpublished paper, ' "as if" often specifies a tense or counterintuitive relation between appearance and reality: the appearance is strange, hard to believe, but it looks *as if* it might not be an illusion'.

[31] See Dezecache et al., 'An evolutionary approach'.

[32] pp. 72–3. The whole of this extraordinarily rich and complex episode (Book I, ch. vi) would repay detailed analysis in the perspective of relevance-oriented mind-reading (the use of modalizing and scalar expressions, counterfactuals, epistemic and emotional vigilance).

how late it is, pointing out that the vehicle is not the one returning with Gryce, provokes a third blush:

> 'I know—I know—' She paused, and he saw her redden through the twilight. 'But I told them I was not well—that I should not go out. Let us go down!' she murmured.   (p. 74)

The pause, set in relief by the double dash, allows the blush to develop into a colouring that is probably stronger than the first 'little' blush and the slowly developing second, visible as this one is even through the twilight. It adds a double layer of meaning to the 'I know—I know', indicating not only that Lily knows that the vehicle is not the one returning with Gryce, but also that she knows that Selden knows that his presence has in no way deflected her from her intentions with regard to Gryce (as she pretended in the beginning). It is significant that she blushes *before* making it clear that all along she had no intention of giving up her plans of marrying Gryce. In that pause during which the blush develops, Lily reads—kinesically as it were, in his tone of voice, its dryness—the way he mind-reads her, and consequently how quickly he regains his usual view of her. More than her own reaction to the sound of the vehicle, it is that kinesic reading that provokes the blush. It thus becomes the pivotal element that determines the next stage of verbal communication. It removes the expectation built up in the course of the chapter that the two might actually become a couple.

This almost-but-not-quite happy-ending scenario between the two would-be lovers is also reflected in how Wharton exploits the combination of the scalar *almost* and the blush to make the reader gauge the temperature of the fleeting and rapidly shifting feelings between the two. As we have seen, Lily's first blush prompted Selden to explore Lily's emotional weakness, a weakness he was almost (but in fact not) sorry to notice in her. It is also striking that Lily is not completely impatient to get back when she realizes how late it is ('"I had no idea it was so late! ...," she said, *almost* impatiently'; p. 73). The ability of the scalar to trigger implicatures that are open to cancellation matches, as such, the fluid non-verbal implications of the blush itself. Edith Wharton's skilful combination of the scalar and the non-verbal blush thus sets the pattern of the love story. Lily and Selden will at various intervals almost but not quite succeed in overcoming their internalized societal expectations. However, whereas the cognitive gap that the scalar allows for, that space where they might still choose each other, will increase in Lily's case, it will gradually shrink in Selden's. For although later he seems once more to be at the point of declaring his love for her ('"The only way I can help you is by loving you," Selden said', p. 135), his 'almost puerile wish to let his companion see that, their flight over, he had landed on his feet' (p. 74), in other words his need to regain control before returning from the walk, is a clear indicator that the gap is closing.

In Lily's case, by contrast, it is increasing. In light of her rapidly deteriorating situation, having become the object of gossip in her circle (thanks largely to the vengeful Mrs Dorset), it is somewhat surprising that she will set personal freedom over luxury. Nowhere, however, is this more evident than when she is given the opportunity to buy Bertha Dorset's letters to Selden (carelessly thrown away by Selden and intercepted by a servant). With this weapon Lily could easily destroy

Bertha, clear her own name of links to married men such as Dorset and Trenor, and regain her place in society. If disgust prevails in the end, it is because '[h]er strongest sense was one of personal contamination' (p. 103). Echoing kinesically the spreading power of such an action (as involuntary as the blush), its ability to infect everything, the word 'contamination' conveys Lily's fear rather than her moral aversion, her fear of becoming like her enemies. The moral superiority of her reaction comes through, however, and all the more ironically, in comparison with her aunt Mrs Peniston. In disinheriting Lily because 'she is talked about' (regardless of whether the gossip is true), the aunt not only becomes Lily's perfect antithesis, she also embodies Wharton's scathing critique of the material values of Lily's set: 'Mrs. Peniston felt as if there had been a contagious illness in the house, and she was doomed to sit shivering among her contaminated *furniture*' (p. 125, my emphasis).

Lily is hardly a moral heroine in the Rochefoucauldian sense, according to which the only truly heroic deed is one without witnesses.[33] In buying the letters, she protects Selden's name, but she also acquires a sense of security, the thought that she might or could use them. However, when it becomes clear that both George Dorset (Bertha's husband) and the social climber Simon Rosedale (both exceedingly rich and Lily's suitors at various points in the story) know about them, the sense of security disappears. As an instrument of extreme temptation as well as the very item that prevents her from taking revenge and rehabilitating herself, the letters reify the suspense of the story into an almost-but-not-quite structure, showing with palpable clarity to what extent Lily remains trapped, and totally disarmed, in a limbo state between following her feelings and complying with societal pressures.

Lily's handling of the letters is heroic, however, in the sense that the most important witness, the only one that counts, is incapable of witnessing her action even when it is placed plainly before his eyes. This becomes clear in the final encounter between Lily and Selden, which, like the very first, takes place in his apartment. Having finally decided to trade back the letters to Bertha, so as to get her off her back, on her way she happens to pass by Selden's apartment and cannot help going up, this time uninvited. If to her '[t]he scene was unchanged' (p. 296), everything else is changed, and perhaps most conspicuously by the fact that she remembers Selden taking down La Bruyère's *Caractères* from the bookshelves, while in fact it was she herself who not only took it down but also replaced it.[34] The irony of this gender reversal echoes La Bruyère's satirical portraits of his contemporaries, in which he made women and men alike move around like puppets on a floodlit stage by the strings of societal pressures, an image also used by Wharton in describing Lily's set.[35]

---

[33] See Duc de La Rochefoucauld, *Maximes*, edited by Jacques Truchet (Paris: Garnier, 1967), p. 55, maxim 216: 'La parfaite valeur est de faire sans témoins ce qu'on serait capable de faire devant tout le monde' ('Perfect valour is doing without witnesses what one would be capable of doing in public').

[34] 'It was so pleasant sitting there looking up at her, as she lifted now one book then another from the shelves...and as she replaced his first edition of La Bruyère...' (p. 13).

[35] '[The Wetheralls] belonged to the vast group of human automats who go through life without neglecting to perform a single one of the gestures executed by the surrounding puppets' (p. 53).

As such, the *Caractères* becomes the sign that prefigures Lily's unsuccessful attempt to dissolve the cloud of misunderstanding between Selden and herself. Her explanation that she has managed to save 'herself whole from the seeming ruin of her life' (p. 299) is of course clear enough, but even accompanied by tears that this time unambiguously are not contrived, it only elicits embarrassment on Selden's part. Neither can she control the rush of colour triggered by her accidental touching of the letters when retrieving her handkerchief. If Selden had known about the letters, he might have paid less attention to what she is saying at that moment. As it is, he misinterprets her blushing as a sign of embarrassment at her plans to get back into society: 'You have something to tell me—do you mean to marry?' (p. 300). Lily, on her part, is too puzzled by this question to pick up his emotional turbulence ('The blood had risen strongly under Selden's dark skin'). Had he had fairer skin, like her other suitors, Lily might have picked up his emotion more easily.[36] As it is, she is as unable as he is to connect his bodily reaction to his words, cognitively dissonant as they are. As opposed to the mutual blush between Darcy and Elizabeth, the nearly but not quite synchronized mutual blush between Lily and Selden hammers in with ruthless precision their failure to recognize their mutual feelings, and hence the tragedy of this almost-but-not-quite-fulfilled love story.[37] So it is not surprising that Selden hardly notices that Lily throws something into the fire, or indeed what that in fact is. But if their love for each other could not surface at the level of explicatures, be expressed verbally as it were, it has been communicated all along and very strongly on the level of implicatures and implications, through the non-verbal blush and the scalar expression *almost*. The emotions this implicit communication triggers are what makes it so painful for the reader to know that only in the silence of death could 'the word which made all clear' pass between them (p. 320).

## CONCLUSION

If Edith Wharton's novels are widely regarded as highly sophisticated, that is no doubt because of her ability to create complex ironic narratives. Newland's laughter in Wharton's most famous novel, *The Age of Innocence* (1927), when he realizes he has been tricked into acting against his own feelings, is a striking example;[38] and one might, perhaps even plausibly, consider Lily's ability to blush at her own will as a case of authorial irony. What counts against such a reading, however, is that Lily is only credited with this power at the outset of the novel, when she still

---

[36] It was already noted by Darwin that dark-skinned people blush as much as fair-skinned people, only less visibly (at least for the exclusively white observers cited by Darwin); see *The Expression of the Emotions*, ch. 13, pp. 315–19.

[37] Cf. the case of Emma Bovary, analysed by Bolens in Chapter 3 of this volume.

[38] See Svetlana Rukhelman, 'The laughter of gods and devils: Edith Wharton and the Coen Brothers on deception, disappointment, and cosmic irony', in David Gallagher (ed.) *Comedy in Comparative Literature: Essays on Dante, Hoffman, Nietzsche, Wharton, Borges, and Cabrera Infante* (Lewiston, NY: Edwin Mellen Press, 2010), ch. 3.

believes that she is in control of her life. I hope my analysis of Lily's blushing has shown that, far from being a simple case of authorial irony, it is a complex and nuanced case of real-life blushing. One might even argue that Lily's ability to exploit reflectively her pre-reflective reactions displays the feedback loop between these two processes. What is ironic, by contrast, is the asymmetric echoing of Elizabeth and Darcy's blushes. Unlike the synchronic blush in Austen's *Pride and Prejudice*, which displays the simultaneous surfacing of mutual feelings, Lily and Selden never blush at the same time. The tragedy of their love story lies precisely in the non-synchronic motor resonance reactions between them, in the fact that their feelings for each other come to consciousness either at the wrong moment or too late. Their incapacity to pick up at the right time the implications of the other's emotional expressions, be they verbal or non-verbal, is ultimately the reason why Selden's declaration of his love for Lily can only take place posthumously.

The argument of this chapter relies on the hypothesis that humans are equipped with emotional vigilance mechanisms, that we possess an ability to track and evaluate, consciously or unconsciously, other people's emotional expressions. Such expressions modify the chain of communication as well as the flow of the narrative, either by slightly shifting its course or even reversing it. What blushing communicates is not always very clear, but Wharton was aware of precisely this uncertainty and knew how to exploit it. Lily herself blushes some thirty times, and there are nearly as many occurrences of the scalar *almost* in *The House of Mirth*. In many cases these instances of bodily reactions and scalar expressions follow each other closely, thus creating a web of implications and implicatures which not only give substance to the emotional life of the characters but also keep the reader in a state of immersive suspense. Contributing to the continuous feedback loop between reflective and pre-reflective levels of cognition, they make the novel into a privileged domain in which to conduct an exploration of human imagination, of the emotions, and indeed of life itself.

# Interlace 6

*After a group of three essays devoted to narrative fiction, we return to lyric poetry, with three case studies that focus on poems by Seamus Heaney (Chapter 6), Mary Oliver (Chapter 7), and Emily Dickinson (Chapter 8). Wes Williams uses the rich weave of Heaney's verse to explore a topic addressed in one way or another in all of the preceding essays, namely the kinds of literary allusion that are still widely known as 'intertextual' (on this term, see Introduction, section on 'Relevance and Literary Theory', and Chapter 9 of this volume, section on 'Passing Echoes'). In this chapter, such effects are explored via metaphors such as 'invisible guests', the 'echoing' of voices, and other expressions designed to capture the proliferating human agencies at work in poetic affiliations and canons. What is at stake here is the sense in which intertextual allusion implies or indeed creates shared contexts of the kind relevance theory presupposes.*

*That topic in turn is shown in this chapter to be deeply connected with the question of the kinds of truth for which poetry is, or can be, the vehicle. Paul Grice's pragmatics of conversation proposes as a 'supermaxim' the injunction, 'Try to make your contribution one that is true'; relevance theory suggests that, for an ostensive act to be relevant, it must at least imply something true. In most communicative contexts, truth-value judgements are made on a practical rather than a metaphysical basis, constrained by the limits of time, access to information, and the pull of individual desires and preferences.[1] This essay, however, invites us to accept that the pragmatic is inseparable in the end from the ethical and even the metaphysical. The relevance-guided heuristic, from that angle, becomes the launch-pad for a blue-skies notion of the truth that poetic communication, as a paradigm of communication itself, might be able to achieve.*

*This chapter, then, of all the contributions to the book, exhibits the least 'instrumental' use of concepts and analytic procedures from relevance theory. Chapters 7 and 8 (and the opening of Chapter 9) are primarily concerned with micro-analysis, and with the specific ways in which metaphors and other figures function within a relevance theory perspective. Chapter 6, by contrast, suggests ways in which reading 'beyond the code'—the inferential, context-rich dynamic that is fundamental to relevance theory— can help to answer the perennial question of why we read poetry at all, and why it is widely acknowledged to be a uniquely powerful mode of human communication.*

---

[1] *On practical (subjective) versus metaphysical (objective) notions of truth, see Sperber* and *Wilson,* Relevance: Communication and Cognition *(Oxford: Blackwell, 2nd ed., 1995), pp. 263–6.*

# 6

## 'Invisible Guests'
### Shared Contexts, Inference, and Poetic Truth in Heaney's 'Album V'

*Wes Williams*

### 'OUR HOUSE IS OPEN': INTERTEXTUALITY AND THE POETICS OF RELEVANCE

In the very essence of poetry there is something indecent:
a thing is brought forth which we didn't know we had in us,
so we blink our eyes, as if a tiger had sprung out
and stood in the light, lashing his tail.

...

The purpose of poetry is to remind us
how difficult it is to remain just one person,
for our house is open, there are no keys in the doors,
and invisible guests come in and out at will.

One of the central insights of relevance theory is that 'literature tests to the limit not our powers of encoding and decoding, but our powers of inference'.[1] Inference is a richly complex process, and the informative 'powers' it affords to readers of literature are distributed unevenly, being in large measure a function of such salience as can be derived from the relation of specific cues to broader, shared contexts. Some readers, for instance, might reasonably infer from the first and last elements in the title of this chapter that the two stanzas quoted above are taken from the Heaney poem here invoked: the 'invisible guests' seem to come from Heaney's 'Album V'.[2] Other readers, however, inferring different import from the same cues, might reach the opposite conclusion. Informed either by a general familiarity with Heaney's tone and voice, or by a more specific memory of how 'Album V' reads as the last in a brief sequence of photographic memories found in the poet's (as it turned out) final collection, *Human Chain*, this second group of

---

[1] David Trotter, 'Analysing literary prose: the relevance of relevance theory', *Lingua*, 87 (1992), 11–27, p. 12; for more discussion of Trotter's claim, see Chapter 2 in this volume.
[2] Seamus Heaney, 'Album V', from *Human Chain* (London: Faber and Faber, 2010), p. 8; reprinted by permission of Farrar, Straus and Giroux LLC for rights in the United States of America.

readers would correctly infer that the lines which serve to open this discussion are not originally by Heaney at all: they just don't *sound* like him.

They constitute, in fact, the second and eighth stanzas of Czesław Miłosz's 'Ars Poetica?', translated by Lilian Vallee and Miłosz himself from the original Polish.[3] But, for anyone who first encountered Miłosz's poem in the last movement of a lecture given by Heaney about the work of Sylvia Plath, subsequently published as part of the collection *The Government of the Tongue*, these lines will always resonate in ways tempered by the Irish poet's reading voice.[4] The distinctly somatic force of the 'indecent' image of the tiger's lashing tail in the one stanza, and the haunting presence of the invisible guests in the other, do not, then, *belong* to 'Album V'; but they both inform and prove powerfully salient to the exploration of Heaney's poem which I offer in what follows. And if I draw attention to these specific 'visitations', it is in order to argue a more general case about intertextuality, inferential reading, and the determining force of shared contexts in the comprehension of poetic communication. Those moments within Heaney's poems where readers are encouraged to lend particular significance to physicalized memory and a shared grasp of kinesic intelligence will be explored here in an effort to explicate the crucial work of inference which structures our understanding of the rhythms, the sounds, and the senses of poetry caught in print on the page.[5] By the same token, paying close attention to Heaney's translation, quotation, and discussion of fellow poets and their work in his critical writing should allow us to attend more clearly to the *literary* salience of what Wilson and Sperber refer to as 'mutual predictability' and 'mutual adjustment': to acknowledge the lingering presence of Miłosz's 'invisible guests' is to comprehend the force of mutually manifest contexts, and in so doing to grasp something of how it is that readers and writers collectively construe poetic truth.[6]

Poets—in this respect, close kin to relevance theorists—have both a firm grasp of the urgency of the human need to communicate, and a clear recognition that our tongues are governed by a wide range of contexts and constraints. Like Sperber and Wilson, poets understand that rather than being governed by a *convention* which might attach itself to paraphrasable meaning, our tongues are governed by varying *expectations* of truthfulness. These may be either weakly or strongly invoked or inferred in any given instance, but there is (no more in poetry than in

---

[3] Czesław Miłosz, 'Ars Poetica?' [1968], in *Selected and Last Poems*, 1931–2004 (London: Penguin, 2014), pp. 92–3; this edition is prefaced with a foreword by Heaney. Excerpts of twelve lines from 'Ars Poetica' from *Selected and Last Poems: 1931–2004* by Czesław Milosz. Copyright © 1988, 1991, 1995, 2001, 2004, 2006 by The Czeslaw Milosz Estate. Reprinted by permission of HarperCollins Publishers.

[4] 'The indefatigable hoof-taps: Sylvia Plath', in *The Government of the Tongue: The 1986 T.S. Eliot Memorial Lectures and Other Critical Writings* (London: Faber and Faber, 1988), pp. 148–70; pp. 166–7.

[5] For more on kinesic intelligence, see the contributions by Banks, Bolens, Cave, and Chesters in this volume; for a differently accented set of approaches to embodied reading, see Michael Burke and Emily T. Troscianko (eds), *Cognitive Literary Science: Dialogues between Literature and Cognition* (Oxford: Oxford University Press, 2017).

[6] For more on the key terms here, see 'Truthfulness and relevance', chapter 4 of Deirdre Wilson and Dan Sperber, *Meaning and Relevance* (Cambridge: Cambridge University Press, 2012).

conversation) no reasonable expectation that the truths we communicate to each other 'should be literally or conventionally expressed, as opposed to being explicated or implicated'.[7] Poetic intention, in other words, need not be construed only with reference to psychological or rhetorical claims concerning this or that individual writer's talent, originality, or success in conveying a specific message, adopting a certain stance, or even creating a distinctive voice. Poets' words both echo and enrich each other across languages and traditions, even as readers make their way along 'the infinitely calibrated gradient of plausible construal'.[8] And literature in turn sustains and transforms itself by way of both inference and transference, the carrying across of a wide array of intentional information, embedded and embodied in shapes and sounds which create richly contextual implications: 'conclusions deducible from input and context together, but from neither input nor context alone'.[9]

One of several affordances which both enable and constrain readers' comprehension of a poem's import, intertextuality has a particular role in enriching the array of implicatures operative in a given context.[10] When, for instance, Virgil has Aeneas reach out, three times, to embrace the shade of his dead father, he does so knowing that some readers will not only recall his hero's earlier unsuccessful attempt to embrace Dido, his wife, repeated verbatim in the text, but also recognize in the very repetition of this gesture a relaying of moves already enacted in Homer's *Odyssey*; and when in 'Album V' Heaney folds this failed embrace into his own characteristic tercets—three times four, a couplet short of a sonnet—he gestures in turn towards (his reader's knowledge of) those precursors and contemporaries who have made of this trope common poetic property.[11]

Heaney's work suggests, then, that poets who encourage their readers to recognize that their own voices respond to and echo the prompting call of otherwise invisible guests need surrender none of their own agency or poetic individuality in so doing. He reminds us that it is important not to think of intertextuality as a purely exclusionary device, nor yet to fall into the trap set by those who would appropriate Virgil (for instance) for themselves alone, claiming that he—and Homer, and others of their kind—*belong* to elite culture. *Human Chain* gives the

---

[7] Wilson and Sperber, *Meaning and Relevance*, p. 83; see also Robyn Carston, 'Truth-conditional content and conversational implicature', in C. Bianchi (ed.) *The Semantics/Pragmatics Distinction* (Stanford, CA: CSLI, 2004), pp. 65–100.

[8] Timothy Chesters, Chapter 8 of this volume, p. 153.

[9] Deirdre Wilson and Dan Sperber, 'Relevance theory', in L. Horn and G. Ward (eds) *The Handbook of Pragmatics* (Oxford: Blackwell, 2004), pp. 607–32; p. 608.

[10] For more on 'literary affordances', see Terence Cave, *Thinking with Literature* (Oxford: Oxford University Press, 2016), ch. 4.

[11] For a clear account of Virgil's reworking of the Homeric trope, see Elizabeth Belfiore, '"Ter frustra comprensa": embraces in the "Aeneid"', *Phoenix*, 38.1 (1984), 19–30; for two very differently emblematic reworkings of this trope, see Pierre de Ronsard's *Prosopopée de Louis de Ronsard* (his dead father) and *Discours à Loys des Masures* (where he encounters his dead friend and fellow-poet Joachim Du Bellay), in Pierre de Ronsard, *Œuvres complètes*, edited by Jean Céard, Daniel Ménager, and Jean Céard ([Paris]: Gallimard, Bibliothèque de la Pléiade, 1994), vol. 2, pp. 785–7 and 1017–20, respectively; and Bernard O'Donoghue's evocation of the unspoken love between siblings on an Irish farm, 'Ter conatus', in *Here nor There* (London: Chatto and Windus, 1999), p. 52.

lie to both of these notions, countering as it does by both precept and practice that poetry makes best sense when grasped as the communication of common, shared knowledge. For the gestures with and through which such poetry works are, like overheard conversations between family members, the stuff of daily life; so too are imagined dialogues both with oneself and with the dead. Miłosz and Heaney, like others both before and after them, stress that poetry's 'house is open', reminding us as they do so that none of us is ever 'just one person', and that the 'stuff' of an individual life hangs by a common thread:

> ter conatus ibi collo dare bracchia circum;
> ter frustra comprensa manus effugit imago,
> par levibus ventis volucrique simillima somno.
>
> Three times he tried to reach arms round that neck.
> Three times the form, reached for in vain, escaped
> Like a breeze between his hands, a dream on wings.[12]

## 'HOW DIFFICULT IT IS': POETIC EFFECTS AND COGNITIVE MUTUALITY

It is not immediately obvious that lyric poetry and relevance theory share either a common 'essence' or a common 'purpose'; but Miłosz's keenly felt sense of the difficulty of poetic communication is something relevance theorists would both recognize and share. Commonality, and the establishment, through imagery, metaphor, and rhythm, of a shared grasp of the mutual cognitive environment is a recurrent theme in relevance-theoretic discussion of lyric function and form; and with good reason. Some early studies in this field drew productively on Heaney's work, both because of its canonical status and because of the poet's distinctive use of metaphor, taken to exemplify 'poetic effects'.[13] The term derives from Sperber and Wilson, who argue that 'poetic effects create common impressions *rather than* common knowledge'. Glossing this distinction, Sperber and Wilson further explain that while poetic effects bring about changes in 'the mutual cognitive environment of speaker and hearer', the 'mutuality' established in poetic communication is 'apparently affective *rather than* cognitive'.[14] Pilkington develops this theme to explore the affective mutuality created by these 'impressions', and the ways in which some poets generate an unusually strong 'feeling of intimacy' in their readers, skilfully invoking 'mutually manifest contextual information'.[15] Heaney's work

---

[12] Virgil, *Aeneid*, 2. 792–4; 6. 700–2; Seamus Heaney, *Aeneid Book VI* (London: Faber and Faber, 2016), p. 38.

[13] Adrian Pilkington, *Poetic Effects: A Relevance Theory Perspective* (Amsterdam: John Benjamins, 2000) includes an extended focus on Heaney's 'Digging'; Anne Furlong, 'A modest proposal: linguistics and literary studies', *Canadian Journal of Applied Linguistics*, 10.3 (2007), 325–47, incorporates brief discussion of 'Mid-term Break'; both poems were originally published in Heaney's *Death of a Naturalist* (London: Faber and Faber, 1966).

[14] Dan Sperber and Deirdre Wilson, *Relevance: Communication and Cognition* (Oxford: Blackwell, 2nd ed., 1995), p. 224 (emphasis added). I return to this repeated turn of evaluative phrase below.

[15] Pilkington, *Poetic Effects*, pp. 165–8.

lends itself to such analysis, not least since the poet is peculiarly careful to offer his readers enough cues to be able to infer a rich set of contextual assumptions about any individual poem:

> It took a grandson to do it properly,
> To rush him in the armchair
> With a snatch raid on his neck.[16]

The three opening lines of 'Album V' here quoted suggest that complex gestures, inferences, and conversations can be both powerfully and successfully communicated not only *about*, but also *within* the compass of a poem, even as the reader progresses in line with its measured beat. Concentration on the poem's opening moves shows how this process works by way of unfolding inferential construal, in response to a series of never-quite-answered questions. The grandson's rush (towards his grandfather? how do we *know* it is 'him'?) is designated from the outset as a form of success: something done 'properly'. And yet it is no less unsettling for that. For the child's 'rush' (but how do we *know* he is a child?) seems oddly aggressive in intent. Indeed, the boy's unexpected taking hold of the grandfather's neck represents a kind of at once affective and cognitive reinforcement to this import: a sensorimotor cue to the reader to *feel* the shock of being grabbed from behind. A relevance-theoretic reading might characterize this move as bringing about a determining change in the mutual cognitive environment: like the grandfather, the reader experiences a measure of surprise. But there are differences, too, between the old man's position in the (*for him*) comforting armchair, and that of readers in theirs: for we have been encouraged from the outset to *infer* the threat of violent action, even in this domestically determined context. As a consequence, we *feel* the impact of the 'snatch raid on his neck' at once 'with' him and against him: unlike the reader, the grandfather didn't see it coming...

The grandson himself, of course, need not be construed as having *intended* to threaten anyone at all. It is, rather, precisely the disjuncture between the assumption that a grandson's actions in a domestically determined location will prove to be affectionate, and the escalating threat enacted in the poet's words, that constitutes the poetic, unsettling effect: 'do it properly / rush him / with the snatch raid / on his neck.' At this early stage in the poem's gradual unfolding, the poet's careful recalibration of just how much is mutually manifest in the prevailing cognitive environment means that even as readers register the increasingly dark implications of the words used to describe the grandson's physical gesture, we also find ourselves beset with further questions. Raised initially by that 'properly' at the end of the opening line, the questions are further compounded by the kinesically sensed strangeness of the formulation 'snatch raid': so who has tried before? How many

---

[16] First stanza of 'Album V'; the twelve-line poem, with four unrhymed tercets, a form which Heaney discovered in his first 'ghostly' collection *Seeing Things* (London: Faber and Faber, 1991), is one which he returns to insistently in *Human Chain*, although it is largely absent from the intervening collections; see Peter McDonald, '"Weird brightness" and the riverbank: Seamus Heaney, Virgil, and the need for translation' (forthcoming); I am grateful to him for allowing me to read this chapter in manuscript.

times, and to what bodged effect? Whatever the grandson's initial intentions, is the old man now, finally, 'properly' done for: dead?

'*To do it properly*': success, when it comes to inferential construal, is hard to define or measure, and should never be taken for granted. Indeed, as Sperber and Wilson have memorably argued, 'communication is governed by a less-than perfect heuristic…what is mysterious and requires explanation is not failure but success'.[17] Through the loosely woven skein of Heaney's tercets failure runs like a thread; it is also, I think, made sharply manifest in Miłosz's lines, quoted above in opening. In their distinctively different ways, both poets argue that when they communicate, they do so *not only* by way of the sustained translation of the words and works of others, *but also* by means of the imperfect recording of the many tongues and voices which constitute their own several selves. And in so doing, they recall to their readers a truth that we often forget in the busy-ness of work or home, and in the automaticity of routine; a truth that becomes all the clearer when we *not only* read, *but also* re-read: the 'mysterious[ness]' of even partially successful communication.

Returning to Heaney's opening tercet, we realize that once we have been dislodged from the comfort of the 'armchair', the cognitive effort of establishing the coordinates of relevance—of thinking and feeling our way through the minefield of potential implicatures—is not inconsiderable: isn't a snatch raid something done by paramilitaries, for example when freeing a hostage? Like the Israelis in that raid on Entebbe? Or has this a more specifically Irish set of resonances to it? To do, say, with the young hero of the Cattle-Raid of Cooley (*Táin Bó Cúalnge*) during the central epic of the Ulster cycle or, perhaps more recently, with the Troubles? And is this a further sign that Heaney's poems increasingly acknowledge the haunting presence of the Troubles during the last decades of his life…? As the poem progresses, the poet asks us to recalibrate our sense of his grandson's initial gesture, weakly specified but strongly embodied as it is. In so doing, we not only follow the sensorimotor cues of the characters *within* the poem, but also follow, shadow, or even mirror the poet's attempts to grasp the significance of a wide range of at once intimate and distant contexts, as they move from being manifest in only the weakest sense, to taking on the shape of something like shared, or even common, knowledge.

Some of what we think of as mutually manifest context is, then, generated within the compass of an individual poem; but we have already seen that much of it derives either from a consideration of a poet's work as a consistent set of themes, or from the broader, socio-historical *situatedness* of the work within a life. In Heaney's case, this situatedness is at once domestic and public, as the coordinates of his exemplary life were powerfully communicated in lectures, critical works, and published interviews. He was one of a long line of writers stretching from Montaigne to Miłosz and beyond who made the most of the genre of the anecdote to make manifest both an intense concern with the meticulous resurrection of a particular

---

[17] Sperber and Wilson, *Relevance*, p. 45. This passage is also quoted by Bolens, Chapter 3 in this volume; I share her theoretical interest in literature's obsession with both sensorimotor embodiment and failures in communication.

moment now past, and with longer-term communicative intentions: imagining, if not quite determining, how he himself might be recalled, read, or resurrected by way of print, long after his death.[18] A relevance-theoretic understanding of this tradition might suggest that such anecdotes, drawn from writers' exemplary lives, can usefully be thought of as creating a species of 'poetic effect'.

The ostensible subjects of the lectures which Heaney published as *The Government of the Tongue* are the American/Anglophone poets Auden, Lowell, and Plath; but it is the (variously) Eastern European Swir, Mandelstam, Herbert, and Miłosz who set the tone of the discussion throughout. The lives (and works) of these initially invisible guests powerfully argue poetry's cause in these lectures, as they seem to Heaney to share a collective understanding of its 'essence' and 'purpose', as of the imagination's function and force. Eastern European poets clearly held a particular place in the Irish poet's Pantheon as exemplary modern figures, and their searching investigation of what it means to be truthful in contemporary poetry animates his work from the early seventies to the end of his life. Witness the strongly experiential account of 'The Impact of Translation', which begins with an anecdotal recollection of the revelatory force that a reading of one of Miłosz's poems had on Heaney's younger poetic self:

> My first experience of these lines, spoken in the upstairs study of a silent house, empty that afternoon except for ourselves, was altogether thrilling. ... *Nothing was being dramatized*: the speaker in the poem *seemed* to be irrefutably one with the voice of the poet; he *seemed*, moreover, to know exactly what he wanted to say before he began to say it, and indeed the poem *aspired* to deliver what we had once long ago been assured it was not any poem's business to deliver: a message. It proclaimed in argent speech truths we had assumed to be previous to poetry, so richly established outside its formal citadel that they could never be admitted *undisguised* or untransmuted through the eye of the lyric needle. Now here they were in a modern poem—big, pulpit-worthy affirmations.[19]

The words and phrases here italicized show that even in the critical essay Heaney frames his recollection as a form of dramatic monologue—a quasi-Wordsworthian narrative dramatizing of the young poet's growth in the philosophical understanding of his craft. Listening hard, he moves in stages from wonder through enquiry to the revelation of a collectively determined truth. At first, he stands amazed at the seemingly 'untransmuted' and 'undisguised' clarity of the lines he has just heard. The Biblical tenor of his own critical coinage—*the eye of the lyric needle*—corresponds to the *pulpit-worthy* truthfulness communicated by—it seemed—both speaker and poet, fused into one prophetic voice. But the repeated *seemed* (along with other similar cues, such as *aspire*, and the epistemically vigilant

---

[18] See Cave in Chapter 9 in this volume, and Lyne's argument (Chapter 2), that poets often work with a double-address system, representing both 'short and long-term communicative intentions'. For more on this theme, see Colin Burrow, 'You've listened long enough', review of *Aeneid: Book VI*, trans. Seamus Heaney, *London Review of Books*, 38(8) (2016), 13–14.

[19] 'The impact of translation', in *The Government of the Tongue*, pp. 36–7; emphasis added.

prefix 'un' attached to key poetic terms) primes the reader for the recalibration that is to follow:

> *What was going on?* The crucial point was, of course, the title, 'Incantation'. This is a spell, uttered to bring about a desirable state of affairs, *rather than* a declaration that such a state of affairs truly exists. . . . What gives the poem its ultimate force is, *therefore*, the intense loss we recognise behind its proclamation of trust.[20]

Moving on from apparent recollection, the poet's *rather than*, like his later *therefore*, responds to the self-directed question which begins this paragraph. Through these carefully plotted moves, Heaney prepares for the transformation of Miłosz's 'message', from one which decried a loss of trust in poets' capacity to generate 'truths', to one which both clarifies and redeems the worth of poetic communication. Taking into account not only the resources of genre (the poem's title), but also the Polish-Lithuanian poet's 'lifetime of exile and self-scrutiny', Heaney suggests that Miłosz's work:

> elicits the admiration of English-speaking readers partly because of this extra-literary consideration. It is *therefore* typical of the work by many other poets, particularly in the Soviet Republics and the Warsaw Pact countries, whose poetry *not only* witnesses the poet's refusal to lose his or her cultural memory, *but also* testifies thereby to the continuing efficacy of poetry itself as a necessary and fundamental human act.[21]

The second and clinching *therefore* in this argument allows for a *not only . . . but also* to replace the earlier *rather than*: what underscores this is a strong presumption of external relevance, and more specifically of that form of external relevance that is a poet's exemplary life. Heaney is of course not wrong to invoke such matters, but it is not quite right to call such reference to a poet's life an 'extra-literary consideration'. For it is precisely this kind of gesture that serves within Heaney's work to create a form of 'poetic effect', making manifest a range of assumptions whose specific gravity the reader is encouraged to investigate further. Conceiving of the worth and work of poetry as *not only* witnessing, *but also* testifying, we gain a clearer sense of a poet's directional set. Poetic effects are, Heaney's critical writings here suggest, at once enabled and constrained by specifically charged cultural moments on the one hand, and on the other by the long evolutionary history of human cognition. This dually inflected context is—as we shall see in more detail below—made mutually, and powerfully, manifest in Heaney's final collection: *Human Chain*.

Even to talk of this collection as 'final' is to acknowledge the degree to which Heaney's genius lay in making the movement from intensely personal anecdote to general reflection seem like a natural part of an exemplary poetic life. But his sense of his own 'exemplarity' is contentious, not least since he so often perpetuates a specifically gendered account of poetic labour and the canon; this remains as true in several of the poems in *Human Chain* as it is in 'Digging', the poem with which

---

[20] 'The impact of translation', p. 37; emphasis added.
[21] 'The impact of translation', p. 38; emphasis added.

he made his name.[22] By the same token, Heaney's sense of Miłosz's 'typicality', and the larger claim that Soviet and Warsaw Pact poets were to be admired for their shared common purpose in respect of poetry's claim on our alienated western imaginations, has not gone uncontested. Even before the geo-political transformations of the last two decades made the landscape of this vision itself appear nostalgic, Heaney's characterization of Miłosz's work and his invocation of other Eastern European comrades in arms doing poetic battle with 'the professionalized literary milieu of the West' was subject to cogent critique.[23] Indeed, it became something of a commonplace for a time to criticize the Irish poet, if not for engaging in such a crude presumption of external relevance, then at very least for being in this respect a lumper rather than a splitter: overly—and as it were orientalizingly— keen to see connections and similarities amongst poets to whom difference mattered very much.[24]

These are fair criticisms. But I want nonetheless, in the final section of this chapter, to try to recover something of the energy of Heaney's polemical claim in *The Government of the Tongue* that 'poetry itself is a necessary and fundamental human act', and to do so by way of close attention to certain moments in 'Album V'. For what becomes salient to a reading of this poem informed by the concerns of relevance theory conjugated with those of embodied cognition is, in the first instance, the *government* of the poetic tongue, the *therefore*s and *rather than*s which the constraints of political, confessional, and otherwise culturally determined contexts impose. In Miłosz's *Ars poetica*, as we saw in opening, a tiger's tail and certain invisible guests serve as emblems of different kinds of contextual claim; invisible guests further haunt 'Album V', even as Heaney both invokes and enacts the sensorimotor effects (if not of tiger's tails, then) of necks, hands, and 'very arms'. And as the reader progresses, recalibrating for relevance at each stage, both the guests and the gestures stake their compelling, at once intertextual and kinesic claims. What emerges, over the course of the poem's four tightly woven stanzas, is the degree to which Heaney engages his readers in the inferential work of 'mutual parallel adjustment': a process of reading on the fly, in which we grasp *not only* the crucial significance of 'warranted' inference in respect of the unfolding construal of a particular poem, *but also* a distinctly embodied sense of poetic truthfulness and proof.[25]

---

[22] For a richly insightful and pioneering critique of 'Digging', see Patricia Coughlan, '"Bog Queens": the representation of women in the poetry of John Montague and Seamus Heaney' [1991], republished in Claire Connolly (ed.), *Theorizing Ireland* (Basingstoke, UK: Palgrave, 2003), pp. 41–60.

[23] 'The impact of translation', p. 38; for a finely judged conspectus and critique of this trend (including, but not specific to Heaney), see Chris Miller, 'The Mandelstam syndrome and the "Old Heroic Bang"', *PN Review*, 162(31.4) (March–April 2005).

[24] See Justin Quinn, 'Heaney and Eastern Europe', in Bernard O'Donoghue (ed.), *The Cambridge Companion to Seamus Heaney* (Cambridge: Cambridge University Press, 2009), pp. 92–105; and for two differently accented studies, Magdalena Kay, *In Gratitude for All the Gifts: Seamus Heaney and Eastern Europe* (Toronto: University of Toronto Press, 2012), and Carmen Bugan, *Seamus Heaney and East European Poetry in Translation: Poetics of Exile* (Oxford: Legenda, 2013).

[25] For more on the key terms here quoted, see Dan Sperber and Deirdre Wilson, 'The mapping between the mental and the public lexicon', in P. Carruthers and J. Boucher (eds) *Language and Thought: Interdisciplinary Themes* (Cambridge: Cambridge University Press, 1998), pp. 184–200.

# '*THREE TRIES*': HEANEY, VIRGIL, AND RETROACTIVE CONSTRUAL

> What reasonable man would like to be a city of demons,
> who behave as if they were at home, speak in many tongues,
> and who, not satisfied with stealing his lips or hand,
> work at changing his destiny for their convenience?[26]

Poets, over time, have conducted a collective experimental inquiry into the changing conditions of communicable proof, at once enabled and constrained by an understanding of the barely graspable shades of love and poetic intention. They also insistently ask their readers (and themselves) how it is that we find ourselves compelled to share what we think, feel, and sometimes *know* to be true. From Virgil's late-ish Latin through Miłosz's several tongues to Heaney's distinctly accented Hiberno-English, the experiments in inference which poets find themselves 'bringing forth' constitute a sustained, if sometimes daemonic, inquiry into the limits of mutuality made manifest, across languages, genres, and generations. And of course poetry knows about failed communication, too; indeed, much poetry, concerned as it is with our repeated efforts at inferring the intentions of others, comes with the memorable relevance-theoretic health-warning attached: 'Failures in communication are to be expected.'[27]

If Virgil's *Aeneid* offers, as Heaney tells us, 'images and symbols adequate to our predicament', these include, very specifically, the 'predicament' of repeated failure.[28] While the acts of piety, remembrance, and translation which structure the *Aeneid* clearly served as a rich resource for the poet as he worked both within and beyond the conflicted political landscape of Ireland, the failure of such gestures to achieve the desired communicative effects develops into a recurrent theme, as Heaney's recently published translation of *Book VI* bears posthumous witness. That this particular book, a constant presence for years, had become a preoccupation, if not a kind of daemonic possession, becomes retrospectively all the clearer in *Human Chain*, resonating with Virgilian echoes throughout: 'Route 110' is a re-imagining of Aeneas's descent into the underworld tracked against significant moments in Heaney's own life; 'The Riverbank Field', beginning with the injunction 'Ask me to translate', moves through a characterization of the poet as if on the banks of the River Styx, 'waiting, watching, / Needy and ever needier for translation', before signing itself off as '*after* Aeneid, VI, 704–15, 748–51'.[29]

The five 'Album' poems not only anticipate both of these later Virgilian sequences in the *Human Chain*, they also connect to other metapoetic moments from the

---

[26] Miłosz, 'Ars Poetica?', stanza four.

[27] Sperber and Wilson, *Relevance*, p. 45.

[28] Seamus Heaney, *Preoccupations: Selected Prose, 1968–1978* (Faber and Faber: London, 1980), p. 56.

[29] For an account of the significance of translation in this poem, in relation to its several poetic and geographically determined contexts, see Peter McDonald's 'Weird brightness', referred to in footnote 16 above.

history of (Heaney's own) poetry, as the title of the sequence as originally published further suggests: 'Lapse of Time'.[30] Retroactively, these critical moments can be construed as part of a potentially salient context, and consequently as having import relevant to the present moment. One such is the lecture on Plath published in *The Government of the Tongue*, discussed above, where Heaney's largely uncommented quotation of Miłosz's *Ars Poetica?* is preceded by his frankly allegorical reading of a famous passage in Wordsworth's autobiographical poem, the *Prelude*: 'There was a boy, ye knew him well.' The sequence begins as the older Wordsworth recalls (a version of) his childhood self, calling through his fingers to the owls in the hope of eliciting a response, and Heaney moves from this initial recollection to infer from Wordsworth's poem an argument concerning a three-part process of poetic maturation. In the first instance, Heaney suggests, what matters is acquiring the technical skill required to 'get the whistle right': this 'original act of making' serves, in other words, as a figure for the onset of poetic vocation.[31]

This first stage of 'getting it right' finds itself transposed in 'Album V' into the grandson's 'snatch raid': carefully prepared, expertly executed, and 'properly' embodied. Re-reading the opening stanza with both Virgil and Wordsworth as part of a context made mutually manifest allows us to see just how the grandson's estranging physicalization of a fairly settled trope achieves its intended effects: demonstrable proof of the human capacity for both mimicry and life-affirming delight. Much as the boy in the *Prelude* creates human hoots which echo across the valley and in so doing 'awaken the owl-life in *us*', so, too, the opening kinesic gesture in 'Album V' emblematizes the second stage of poetic maturation. Heaney's grandson moves, then, in concert with both Virgil's Aeneas and Wordsworth's boy, 'beyond the primary sounding forth of one's presence into the poetry of relation, of ripple-and-wave effect upon audience'.[32]

V

It took a grandson to do it properly,
To rush him in the armchair
With a snatch raid on his neck,

Proving him thus vulnerable to delight,
Coming as great proofs often come
Of a sudden, one-off, then the steady dawning

Of whatever *erat demonstrandum*.
Just as a moment back a son's three tries
At an embrace in Elysium

---

[30] 'Lapse of Time' was originally published in *The Poetry Ireland Review*, 98 (2009), 6–8.
[31] 'The indefatigable hoof-taps', p. 153; the 'Boy of Winander' passage is in the *Prelude*, Book V, lines 389–449 (see *William Wordsworth: A Critical Edition of the Major Works*, edited by Stephen Gill (Oxford: Oxford University Press, 1984), pp. 444–5). Recent theories of situated simulation and the ecology of human cognition might further allow us to construe the young poet's call to the owls as not merely *analogous* to animal behaviour, but rather continuous with our animal being.
[32] 'The indefatigable hoof-taps', pp. 154–9.

> Swam up into my very arms, and in and out
> Of the Latin stem itself, the phantom
> *Verus* that has slipped from 'very'.

The specific effects of the 'poetry of relation' are here clearly and carefully plotted, not in the contextual expanse of the *Prelude*'s lakes and mountains, nor yet on the banks of the River Styx, but rather in the domestic interior of a living room; and they are further constrained by the distribution of construable sense across and between the poem's four short stanzas.

The potential aggression noted in our earlier discussion of the opening lines is, like the contextual shadow of dimly, anxiously implied violence that hangs over the entire first stanza, carried over into the opening line of the second. The threat holds all the way through to 'vulnerable to', before being in the very last beats of the line displaced by the dawning of the light of understanding: 'de/light'. Say it aloud and you somehow hear the light, even as you also imagine the sound of the grandfather's hoots of laughter, which accompany the mock wrestling match conducted from within in the compass of the 'armchair': a noisy response to the grandson's initial grappling call. But the peculiarity of this human drama, its *difference* from the Wordsworthian fable, and its closer relation to Virgil, is the space it creates for readers to hear the poet's own silence, and to feel the weight of its force. The 'waiting, watching, / Needy and ever needier' son finds himself transposing the act of successful communication between the generations-but-one into a memory of his own failure to connect in this way: in other words, to 'do it properly'. The grandson and the grandfather's noisily non-verbal call and response contrasts sharply with the poet's all-too-wordy reticence. The weak implicature of the poem's opening line also adumbrates, then, the poet's effective incapacity: his failure *properly* to embrace his own, embodied father, before he became a species of poetic effect, a Virgilian shade.

And yet, of course, this failure is also success of a kind. For even as Heaney here finds himself inhabited by the voices of the invisible guests who seem to ghost-write the words which pass for his own, it is the narration of precisely this experience that works to extend the conversation further, as the poet turns to address his readers. Attention, furthermore, to the domestically charged sounds in the room itself reminds us that as well as being a sequence of images, one of a number of photographs within a family 'Album', this poem is also a conversation of sorts, overheard by the poet himself, and in virtue of the 'ripple-and-wave effect' of poetic communication, by his audience as well: it awakens the family life in *us*.

At first, Heaney seems to care little for this more public dimension to his domestic drama, or indeed for any generally communicable sense of intimacy. The airily dismissive first line of the third stanza affects to set proverbial, commonly graspable proof aside, drawing down the curtain on the 'scene' just represented with a clod-hopping rhyme to complement the poem's first full-stop: *proofs often come; demonstrandum.* From this point on, however, as we move into the poem's second half, it is far less clear what is going on. The language of experiment and proof gives way to a watery indeterminacy, and lapses in time, as of the tongue, become the substance of the drama. *Just as*: the poem's only simile (barely one at all) inaugurates a process whereby sequence, duration, and location all take on more complex shapes, and prepositions point in all sorts of directions: *back, up into, and in and out*. Gestures swim, words are lent ghostly agency, and even truth itself seems to slip its moorings in the closing tercet's last two lines. The imperfectly rendered Latin proverb sets off, in other words, a chain of richly determined poetic effects. The lines shade into something like *terza rima* at precisely the point at which things start to get, syntactically speaking, distinctly more complex, while the ostensively marked acoustic patterning encourages the reader to persevere with the effort of making semantic links in a chain of unlikely associations across languages, cultures, and times.

Pointing forwards as well as backwards, then, *demonstrandum* serves not only to echo 'proofs often come', but also to make salient the beat and hum of both *Elysium* and *the phantom*. Indeed, it is precisely the contextual noise generated by this potentially reassuring rhythm that encourages us to read for relevance and for sense. By asking ourselves where we have heard these sounds before, we find ourselves able to follow the cue of the key directional qualifier: *a moment back*. For this is *a moment back* best grasped by way of three inferential 'tries', the first of which is the most directly manifest: 'back', that is, to *the Latin stem*, back, by way of *Elysium* and *the phantom*, to the *Aeneid*'s staging of the ancient trope of the three-fold failed embrace.

The temporality of this move may seem, initially, less than straightforward: the *Aeneid* was, we might think, hardly 'a moment back'. But to argue that Virgil is too temporally and linguistically distant to be salient is not only to overspecify the original 'moment' of a poem's emergence, it is also, crucially, to underestimate poetry's capacity to extend our cognitive grasp of both sequence and duration: poems take place (in) time, and time again. *Human Chain* insists, as we have seen, on acknowledging the determining *presence* of sometimes invisible guests, and Virgil is as much of a reality for the poet as the old man in the armchair, not least because of Heaney's frequent recollection of his own childhood initiation into the tongue which proved central to the development of his poetic vocation, even as it took him away from his taciturn and seemingly inexpressive father...

This biographically charged context is made at once more manifest and more salient to the interpretation of this particular poem by the second of the three inferential tries the poem calls forth, pointing as it does in an opposite temporal direction: back, that is, to the contemporary, the local, and to Heaney's specifically inflected tongue. For it is in the voicing of the *v* which connects Virgil's corpus to Heaney's body, the one poet's *Verus* to the other's *very arms*, that we can detect the sound of both consciously crafted poetic diction and a confessional shibboleth. Heaney, with his school-satchel barely off his back, recalls the fact that Protestant grammars, with their determination of the pronunciation of *w*erus, worked to distinguish between properly learned Latin and the fleshy tongue commonly spoken by followers of the Catholic Church. In so doing they trained their boys in the art of cultural distinction: an art, and a politics, not of shared and mutually manifest contexts, but of the determinedly *un*common; and they still do.

The third and final try is differently accented again: *a moment back*, understood now not in relation to intertextual or contextual relations, but rather to the temporal unfolding of Heaney's poetic collection. More specifically, it relates to Heaney's carefully plotted sequencing of the five 'Album' poems, since the directional phrase also gestures, I think, to a series of gestures, moves, and sounds which are found in the previous poem in the collection, 'Album IV'. This is not (only) a temporal move. For in urging the reader to turn the page *back*, and to return to the previous poem, in asking us, then, to *re-read*, the poet is not seeking to turn back time. In Elleke Boehmer's words, Heaney is, rather, asking us, now, as Yeats does in his time, to 'reflect (back) *in the moment of reading* upon the cognitive processes that are both generated and simulated in literary reception'.[33] This process led to the 'steady dawning' of delight in the first half of the poem, and Heaney now urges us to recognize this poem and the one we might have read a moment back as being *not only* sequentially, *but also* inferentially relevant each to the other.


## CONCLUSION

*Just as*: Wordsworth's *Prelude* serves Heaney as an allegorical grid against which to track the distinctive arc of a poetic life, so here I have tried to show that we can infer from the poet's commentary on the work of others the enabling—and con-straining—contexts of his own writing. In that same densely populated lecture on (Miłosz and Wordsworth and) Plath which has ghosted this reading of 'Album V', Heaney also calls on one further poet's work to exemplify the last of the three stages of poetic, communicative achievement. The poem he invokes has particular salience in the context of the essays in this, our own collectively determined volume concerning relevance in literature:

> we feel the poem as a gift arising or descending beyond the poet's control, where direct contact is established with the image-cellar, the dream-bank, the word-hoard, the truth-cave—whatever place a poem like Yeats's 'Long-Legged Fly' emerges from.[34]

I want by way of conclusion to suggest that a third try at construing Heaney's *a moment back* would enact this third stage of poetic maturation, engaging readers in what the poet calls an echoic 'interweaving of imaginative constants from different parts of the *oeuvre*'.[35] Were we to follow his directional signal here and (re)turn to 'Album IV', we would see how the poem's first two stanzas move through modal verbs and indistinct counterfactual tenses towards an initial failed embrace with 'him':

---

[33] Boehmer, Chapter 1 in this volume, pp. 30–1.

[34] 'The indefatigable hoof-taps', p. 163. On Yeats's poem, see Chapter 1 above.

[35] He is talking about Plath: 'The indefatigable hoof-taps', p. 162; for an exquisite account of how such echoing works in relation to the gift that is 'A Kite for Aibhín', the closing poem of *Human Chain*, see Maria Johnston's review, www.towerpoetry.org.uk/poetry-matters/reviews/reviews-archive/434-maria-johnston-reviews-human-chain-by-seamus-heaney.

That should have been the first, but it didn't happen.

The second did, at New Ferry one night
When he was very drunk and needed help
To do up trouser buttons. And the third [...]    (lines 6–9)

The third stanza is still more painfully domestic in its detail, but at the poem's close, we are called on to witness the poet's 'right arm / Taking the webby weight of his underarm': an embrace of sorts takes place. Heaney does not, in this earlier poem in the sequence, position himself as the over-watching speaker, the point of tensioned triangulation between the cardinal characters of grandfather and grandson. The geometry of generational affection is here altogether more simply plotted than in 'Album V': the (grand)father is never named as such, nor is the *Aeneid* directly invoked. 'Album IV' is not a staging of the failure to connect, and it does not, in *its initial moment*, hum to the rhythm or tune of Virgil's *Verus*. No invisible guests are invoked in this scene, nor, it seems, are any needed: the poet's own right arm is support enough for the needful old man, and the weight of *his* underarm is proof great enough.

But then again: even as he lingers over the last few of the pictures in his family album, Heaney asks us to think again about those invisible guests, about the shared contexts they serve to remind us of, and about the sequence of inferential tries by which we make sense of poems, of others, and of ourselves. *A moment back*, Heaney acknowledges, his right arm was in truth already not only supporting the webby weight of the one father, but also gesturing *back, up into, and in and out of* the web of allusiveness, to the poetic father that Virgil here represents, and through him, to the rich array of poetic effects by which generations of readers and poets-as-readers communicate and contest with each with other, across languages, cultures, and time. Poetry need not, then, be thought of as beyond contemporary reach, nor yet as a confessional and class-marked shibboleth, whose utterance serves only to determine the speaker as being possessed of a crudely grafted tongue.[36] The first two tries at construing the sense of the closing moves of 'Album V' need, in other words, to be supplemented by a third: one in which we comprehend poetry's capacity to accede, by interweaving betwixt and between different scales of contextual implication, to the state whereby the idiosyncratic becomes communicable: 'the poet's art has found ways by which individual distinctively personal subjects and emotional necessities can be made a common possession of the reader's'.[37] Poetic truth, if grasped inferentially by way of repeated and renewed tries, can be re-imagined as polemically common property, a necessary and fundamental human act, and one of the links which make up the *Human Chain*.

---

[36] I borrow this last turn of phrase from Patricia Palmer, *The Severed Head and the Grafted Tongue: Literature, Translation and Violence in Early Modern Ireland* (Cambridge: Cambridge University Press, 2014). I am enormously grateful to her for richly inflected discussions of Heaney's (and others') poems.
[37] Heaney, 'The indefatigable hoof-taps', p. 159.

# Interlace 7

*Figurative utterances raise an abiding question not only for literary study, but also for philosophy and linguistics. This chapter and the following one open a pathway into that question offered by the notion of a 'cognitive criticism' for which relevance theory provides a valuable frame of reference. Once again, what makes the difference above all is the insistence on a broadly inferential model rather than a code model of communication. Literary analysis needs to attend to stylistic and poetic effects that are often tenuous, nuances that may seem virtually intangible, reverberations that shift with the act of reading and re-reading. Relevance theorists approach such effects in terms of a notion of 'weak implicature', and often characterize the type of communication involved as 'vague'. Literary specialists are liable to see these as pejorative terms, but for relevance theorists they carry no such connotation. They belong to the spectrum of implicatures which, at one extreme, take the form of propositions that the communicator unarguably intended to convey, and at the other involve no more than hints or pointers, for which the evidence that they were intended by the communicator is typically less than conclusive. The spectrum itself, including the 'wide array of weak implicatures' generated by some very common kinds of utterance, is straightforwardly analysable within a relevance theory perspective, but presents a challenge to purely formal or code-based accounts of communication.*

*It is time, perhaps, for literary study to become attentive once more to these effects, which demonstrate what language is capable of where communication is tested to its uttermost. Programmatic or ideological modes of reading are liable to set them aside as non-essential, or purely 'aesthetic', but this book takes the opposite view. We (the contributors to this volume) share the belief that the massively rich implicatures characteristic of literary language have an ecological wildness that can only be tamed at a heavy cost: they bespeak human capacities which, in an increasingly instrumentalized world, risk being marginalized, and potentially even stunted or etiolated.*

*Kathryn Banks focuses primarily on the so-called 'emergent properties' that arise from the convergence or superimposition of figurative and sensorimotor elements in the poetry of Mary Oliver. As Banks explains, what is meant by 'emergent' here is that such properties take shape as the poetic utterance develops without being reducible to the sum of its parts. This way of thinking about processes has been deployed across the disciplinary spectrum, for example to characterize the way in which biological 'life' might emerge (or might have emerged) from a series of chemical reactions. It imposes an essentially dynamic conception of cognitive process, and thus lends itself well to the analysis of how utterances unfold themselves progressively along a temporal axis: in this respect, it is not unlike the 'array of implicatures' or the 'spreading activation patterns' that characterize the cognitive afterlife of a given utterance.*

*Banks uses the poetry of Mary Oliver to show how poetic uses of language can invite the reader to participate in an experience which may well be sensory, or sensorimotor, and which cannot be fully captured in terms of a finite propositional description. Her discussion thus touches on the somewhat controversial notion of 'qualia', the distinctive feelings that are familiar in life yet are hard to communicate in language: what it 'feels like' to drink a glass of cold water when you're thirsty, or catch the scent of new-mown grass, or realize that you've lost your wallet.[1] Seen in terms of relevance theory, such effects are a special case of a generalization which holds for all communicative acts: utterances are offered as evidence of what the speaker feels or thinks.*

[1] *See Adrian Pilkington*, Poetic Effects: A Relevance Theory Perspective *(Amsterdam: John Benjamins, 2000). For an extended philosophical account of 'experience' as an aesthetic phenomenon, see Jean-Marie Schaeffer,* L'Expérience esthétique *(Paris: Gallimard, 2015). This issue is arguably intrinsic to the discussion elsewhere in this volume of sensorimotor effects, kinesis, etc.*

# 7

# 'Look Again', 'Listen, Listen', 'Keep Looking'
## Emergent Properties and Sensorimotor Imagining in Mary Oliver's Poetry

*Kathryn Banks*

## INTRODUCTION

Relevance theory articulates what happens when we communicate not only meanings but also 'vague' impressions and emotions.[1] Therefore it offers literary studies a framework for analysing the imprecise and the elusive; and it challenges us to reflect more on what is at stake if we say a literary text or author 'means' something, and on how else we might talk about what texts and authors and readers do. Furthermore, because relevance theory scrutinizes acts of communication which 'show' as much as they mean, it allows for a consideration of how texts engage our bodies, and for a dialogue with approaches to literature grounded in kinesic analysis or embodied cognition. However, as a number of contributions to this volume make clear, there is more thinking to do in relevance theory about the role played by the sensorimotor imagination, and investigating literature might offer distinctive insights. In this chapter, I examine how sensorimotor responses to poetic images can make something emerge which goes beyond what a code model of communication would predict that the words on the page might produce. I will work with the notion linguists have termed 'emergent properties', but extend it to engage with the multiple sensorimotor responses that poetic images can invite.

The images are taken from the work of Mary Oliver (b. 1935), a US 'latter-day Romantic' and 'ecopoet' who foregrounds embodied experience of the natural world.[2]

[1] I am indebted to the late Andrea Noble for her insightful responses to a draft of this chapter. The chapter began as a paper presented at the Oslo Centre for the Study of Mind in Nature, at a conference on 'Metaphor, Imagery, and Communication', and I am grateful for the invitation to speak about a literary example in English, which gave me the opportunity to think more about Oliver. I would like to thank the Leverhulme Trust for a Philip Leverhulme Prize which is funding my current research into literature and the cognitive sciences; this chapter forms part of that research.

[2] On Oliver's 'latter-day Romanticism', see Mark Johnson, '"Keep looking": Mary Oliver's Emersonian Project', *The Massachusetts Review*, 46.1 (2005), 78–98 (pp. 78, 88). Oliver has also been described as 'Romantic' or 'post-Romantic'. On Oliver as 'ecopoet' or her poetry as 'ecological', see John Elder, *Imagining the Earth: Poetry and the Vision of Nature* (Athens, GA; London: University of Georgia Press, 2nd ed., 1996), pp. 216–28; J. Scott Bryson, *The West Side of any Mountain: Place, Space, and Ecopoetry* (Iowa City, IA: University of Iowa Press, 2005), pp. 75–97; Kirstin Hotelling Zona,

Oliver's poetry arguably communicates impressions as much as meanings; it shows as much as it means. Therefore relevance theory might enable us to articulate better how her poetry works. A new theoretical approach seems particularly desirable for poets like Oliver, at least if we want to take seriously poets' and readers' claims to experience and emotion. Although Oliver is a prolific and popular prizewinning poet, her work has received little critical attention, and this has been plausibly attributed to contemporary critical models ill-suited to considering what is arguably the crux of her poetry, namely her profound interest in 'merging' with the world, or in a concomitant merging and individuation.[3] Furthermore, where postmodern literary theory has been marshalled to tackle her poetry, this has not, in my view, done much to account for likely experiences of reading it. In this chapter, in addition to advancing the relevance theory account of how emergent properties can stem from sensorimotor responses to images, I aim to use this enhanced account to explain how Oliver's readers might get a sense of her concomitant merging and individuation. Then, towards the end of the essay, I turn to a painting which dialogues with Oliver's poetry. This enables me to explore how we might flesh out the relevance theory account of communicative showing, and articulate differences between artistic genres and media within the model of human communication and cognition which it provides.

## SHOWING, VAGUENESS, AND SENSORIMOTOR RESPONSES

Relevance theory draws attention to effects of human communication which are 'vague'. While vague communication includes what is conveyed by use of verbal forms, Sperber and Wilson focus at the outset on the example of Mary who—on a visit to the seaside with Peter—looks out of the window and sniffs ostensively and appreciatively.[4] What Mary does is to show something to Peter; that is, invite him to engage his senses, to look and sniff as she does. For relevance theory, such showing is on a continuum with meaning: its account of communication is intended to work across the full range of human communicative acts, which to varying degrees show and/or mean.

Mary Oliver also does a great deal of showing. While her poems include reflective or abstract statements and questions, they frequently offer concrete and detailed observations of individual aspects of nature, such as an animal or bird or flower or weather phenomenon or part of a landscape. Oliver evokes her own looking, listening,

---

'"An attitude of noticing": Mary Oliver's ecological ethic', *Interdisciplinary Studies in Literature and Environment*, 18.1 (2011), 123–42; Laird Christensen, 'The pragmatic mysticism of Mary Oliver', in J. Scott Bryson (ed.) *Ecopoetry: A Critical Introduction* (Salt Lake City, UT: The University of Utah Press, 2002), pp. 135–52.

  [3]  Zona, 'An attitude of noticing'; Todd F. Davis and Kenneth Womack, *Postmodern Humanism in Contemporary Literature and Culture* (Basingstoke, UK; New York: Palgrave Macmillan, 2006), pp. 37–49; Johnson, 'Oliver's Emersonian project'; Bryson, *The West Side*.

  [4]  *Relevance*, pp. 54–60.

touching, smelling, and tasting, as well as her walks through nature. She invites her readers both to look at nature literally (Oliver has commented that readers unfamiliar with nature cannot really 'feel' nature poems[5]) and also to engage with the images of nature which she paints for them. This invitation takes the form of both explicit instruction (imperatives like the examples in my chapter title appear frequently) and also various more indirect means, such as offering concrete descriptions or metaphorical images, questioning whether her addressees have observed a particular natural phenomenon or commenting on the likelihood that they have done so, emphasizing the importance of sensory perception, and using the present tense and deictics to encourage readers to engage with what her poetry depicts. So, like the Mary of relevance theory fame, albeit verbally, Mary Oliver 'shows' her addressees what she sees and invites them to 'look' in turn.

So, what happens in showing or, more generally, in 'vague' communication? Sperber and Wilson note that while Mary can expect to steer Peter's thoughts in a certain direction, she cannot have precise expectations about the exact conclusions he will draw. Or, in the vocabulary of relevance theory, any communicator has in mind a representation of the *array* of assumptions which she intends to make manifest (perceptible or inferable) or more manifest, but not necessarily of *each* assumption in the array, and, in the vaguest forms of communication, she represents none of them individually. The communication of an impression is described as producing a noticeable change in one's cognitive environment; that is, relatively small alterations in the manifestness of many assumptions. Peter might notice that the air smells fresh, that it reminds him of their previous holidays, that he can smell seaweed, and so on; he is reasonably safe in assuming that Mary must have intended him to notice at least some of these things. However, she may not have intended to draw his attention to any one of them in particular. So, in vague communication, at least part of the communicator's intention can be fulfilled in several roughly similar but not identical ways, with roughly similar import, and the addressee takes a greater responsibility for the resulting interpretation than in cases where the speaker makes a small number of assumptions strongly manifest.[6]

As Raphael Lyne suggests in Chapter 2 of this volume, this analysis of vague communication allows us to articulate a middle ground situated between, on the one hand, judging that 'anything read into the poem is fair enough' and, on the other hand, understanding authorial intention narrowly as the communication of a specific determinate meaning. If we read in accordance with what relevance theory calls a communicator's 'informative intention', then our readings can (and do and should) radically exceed what is encoded, yet at the same time they are constrained by our human cognitive predisposition to consider intentions and agency, and by the shared understanding of communication which results from that predisposition.[7] Where authors offer 'vaguely' communicated impressions, readers (like Peter at the

---

[5] *Rules for the Dance: A Handbook for Writing and Reading Metrical Verse* (Boston, MA: Houghton Mifflin, 1998), p. 73.

[6] *Relevance*, pp. 55–60.

[7] Beyond this continuum—beyond the 'middle ground' that Lyne describes—are readings an author could not recognize (or have recognized) as fulfilling their intention, readings against the grain,

seaside) take a large degree of responsibility in constructing their interpretations, so that the responsibility is shared (to different degrees) between author and reader. In other words, there is an array of possible readings which an author could, in theory, recognize as fulfilling her intention, without her having intended them in the sense of having represented them to herself in the forms in which readers might verbalize them. While this might seem unsurprising, I think it does invite us to reflect on how we articulate what authors and texts and readers do, and on when and whether we can talk about 'competing' interpretations or 'the meaning' of a text. In Oliver's poetry, sometimes particular thoughts are communicated quite explicitly, but often what she shows us, as the case of Mary and Peter might suggest, invites a wide array of possible responses. The images I analyse might be read differently—and there exists neither critical consensus concerning their interpretation nor much evidence of how Oliver's many readers respond to them[8]—but my readings are intended to be situated in the 'middle ground' of responding to authorial intention conceived broadly and following the relevance theory model of informative intention.

Oliver's mode of 'showing' of course differs from that of relevance theory's Mary not only because it is expressed in language but also insofar as it promises different kinds of insights and thus invites a different intensity of 'looking'. It is a central claim of relevance theory that the effort devoted to processing a communicative act is in proportion to the cognitive benefits we expect to accrue from doing so.[9] For Peter at the seaside, the fact that he can satisfy Mary's intention in various ways means that he does not need to invest much time weighing up the different possibilities. By contrast, Oliver is writing poetry, which, in her words, is 'sacred',[10] and, in those of Cave and Wilson in the Introduction to this volume, 'is an ostensive act which raises expectations of relevance'. Cave and Wilson observe that the distinctiveness of many literary texts (and religious ones) as communicative acts might be captured in terms of an overt linguistic or logical difficulty which rewards interpretive effort and invites sustained processing. Oliver's poems are not usually difficult in this obvious sense. Instead, sustained 'processing' is provoked by repeated suggestions that close and slow attention—which Oliver models for readers—might offer some

---

intended, for example, to expose ideologies, but which are distinct from those which fit somewhere along the continuum of fulfilling an author's intention.

[8] Adrian Pilkington, Barbara MacMahon, and Billy Clark have argued that an approach to literature based on relevance theory should consist in explaining 'existing readings in cognitive pragmatic terms'; 'Looking for an argument: a response to Green', *Language and Literature*, 6.2 (1997), 139–48 (p. 141). However, even where there is a dominant 'existing reading' to work with, it is difficult to distinguish absolutely between explaining readings and performing them, insofar as accounts of what readers and authors do cannot be divorced from 'reading' the texts they use to do it.

[9] Our cognitive system is automatically geared to picking out objects and inferences that seem likely to meet the requirements of an optimal 'cost-benefit analysis', producing the greatest cognitive effects (the benefits) for the available processing effort; see *Relevance*, pp. 123–32, and the Introduction to this volume, pp. 12–13.

[10] www.onbeing.org/program/mary-oliver-listening-to-the-world/transcript/8051#main_content.

special experience of the world, so that, as Oliver has put it, by reading nature poems we 'begin or deepen our own journey into the leaves and the sky'.[11]

But how can reading poetry make this happen? A postmodern approach, grounded in the code model of linguistic communication, seems to come up short in answering this question. Laird Christensen argues that 'only a poor caricature of the experience can be rendered in the clumsy building blocks of language', which 'necessarily diminishes presences', but that Oliver's repeated leaps from concrete observations to metaphysical speculations alert the reader to moments of presence experienced by the poet in the gaps between the two.[12] While Oliver's shifts between observations and speculations are undoubtedly crucial, this analysis does not tell us anything about the role of the observations themselves—of the sensory imagining in which they invite the reader to engage—except to suggest, implausibly to my mind, that they have little effect. By contrast, approaching the reader's experience using relevance theory allows us to consider how authors and readers do something with language, so that authors might make readers feel something—not, to be sure, as literary theories have demonstrated in various ways, a reproduction of the author's own experience, but nonetheless something which bears some similarity to it, and which can be communicated and felt rather than only borne witness to in the 'gaps' of language. Relevance theory offers a way of going beyond the postmodernist obser-vation that words do not in themselves achieve as much as we might think, and of getting at what Christensen calls 'the constellation of emotions and implications that accrue to those words and flicker through the spaces between them' (p. 139). More specifically, I will argue in this chapter that employing and expanding the notion of 'emergent properties' within a relevance theory framework can enable us to grasp how sensorimotor imagining makes something 'emerge' for Oliver's readers.

## EMERGENT PROPERTIES AND POETIC IMAGES

Emergent properties, or features, most often stem from metaphors. In that case, they are properties which are attributed to the metaphor topic but are not stored as part of our representation of the metaphor vehicle. For example, the expression 'my surgeon is a butcher' is used to communicate that the surgeon is incompetent and does not care for his patients, although incompetence and lack of caring are not properties associated with butchers. Emergent properties have also been found in the comprehension of intuitively literal language; for example, experiments indicate that, in understanding 'Oxford graduate factory worker' or 'rugby player who knits', people typically produce properties such as 'failure' and 'confused' respectively, which are not usually associated with any of the terms in the compound.[13]

---

[11] 'Foreword', in *Poetry Comes Up Where It Can: An Anthology*, edited by Brian Swann (Salt Lake City, UT: The University of Utah Press, 2000), p. xiv.

[12] 'The pragmatic mysticism', pp. 139–42.

[13] James Hampton, 'Emergent attributes in combined concepts', in T. Ward, S. Smith, and J. Vaid (eds) *Creative Thought: An Investigation of Conceptual Structures and Processes* (Washington, DC: American Psychological Association, 1997), pp. 83–110.

The term 'emergent properties' is not specific to relevance theory, and linguists of different persuasions (for example, conceptual metaphor theorists) have sought to explain the existence of this phenomenon; however, explanations articulated within a relevance theory framework seem to me both plausible and promising for the analysis of poetic images.

In a relevance theory perspective, emergent properties are derived inferentially, shaped by the context of the metaphor or conceptual combination in question.[14] Wilson and Carston also note that premises for inference might be provided by sensory and kinaesthetic representations. In the case of a metaphorical butcher, we might—in the context of talking about surgeons, who cut bodies—imagine how a butcher cuts animal bodies, slicing swiftly through whole lumps of flesh and bone. A surgeon who cut bodies in such a manner would be grossly incompetent and at best indifferent to his patients' wellbeing, and thus we infer these properties in the surgeon.[15] In the clichéd case of the surgeon-butcher, sensorimotor engagement with the image is probably fairly cursory. According to relevance theory, this metaphor is processed using so-called 'ad hoc' concepts: the encoded concept BUTCHER is replaced by the ad hoc concept BUTCHER*, meaning somebody who cuts bodies in a particular way, and this ad hoc concept then forms part of the explicit content of the utterance. However, Carston has suggested that novel or extended metaphors can be processed using not ad hoc concepts but rather 'a slower, more global appraisal of the literal meaning of the whole', involving a more sustained sensorimotor engagement.[16] Carston comments that this sensorimotor imagining might be responsible for emergent properties, citing Zoë Heller's description in her novel *The Believers* of depression as 'a toad that squatted wetly on your head until it finally gathered the energy to slither off'. This image, in Carston's analysis, gives rise to the emergent property of 'the (not fully verbalizable) feeling of heavy hopelessness and inertia that is typical of depression but is not a component of our encyclopaedic (conceptual) knowledge about (squatting) toads'.[17]

It seems to me that Carston's insight points to a way of thinking about what 'emerges' in poetry when sensorimotor responses are prompted. However, some poetry also demands that we reflect more on the sensorimotor responses that images can invite, and on the ways in which they can produce emergent properties. While we easily infer that the butcher-surgeon is incompetent, and feel confident about this inference, more creative poetic images require a more extensive gloss to

---

[14] Deirdre Wilson and Robyn Carston, 'Metaphor, relevance and the "emergent property" issue', *Mind & Language*, 21.3 (2006), 404–33; Deirdre Wilson and Robyn Carston, 'Metaphor and the "emergent property" problem: a relevance-theoretic treatment', *The Baltic International Yearbook of Cognition, Logic and Communication*, 3 (2008): *A Figure of Speech*, 1–40; Rosa E. Vega Moreno, *Creativity and Convention: The Pragmatics of Everyday Figurative Speech* (Amsterdam; Philadelphia, PA: John Benjamins, 2007), pp. 101–12; Vega Moreno, 'Metaphor interpretation and emergence', *UCL Working Papers in Linguistics*, 16 (2004), 297–322.

[15] 'Metaphor, relevance' (2006), 423 and n. 11.

[16] 'Metaphor: ad hoc concepts, literal meaning and mental images', *Proceedings of the Aristotelian Society*, 110.3 (2010), 295–321 (p. 297). See also Robyn Carston and Catherine Wearing, 'Metaphor, hyperbole and simile: a pragmatic approach', *Language and Cognition*, 3.2 (2011), 283–312. On ad hoc concepts, see the Introduction and Chapter 8 in this volume.

[17] 'Metaphor: ad hoc concepts', 307, 314.

capture what emerges and how it does so. Although the metaphors analysed by Carston are more complex than the clichéd butcher-surgeon, she focuses on (more or less) extended metaphors, such as Macbeth's claim that 'Life's but a walking shadow, a poor player / That struts and frets his hour upon the stage', and she has in mind a metaphor with a literal level understood as single and coherent, so that 'a coherent set of conceptual representations is formed' (p. 310). By contrast, my discussion of poetry aims to move the notion of emergent properties away not only from obviously inferred properties like those of the surgeon-butcher, but also from images conceived as single and coherent; that is, away from the model of a metaphor which imagines 'one thing through another'. Instead, I will examine images which can produce multiple sensorimotor responses and hence a particularly 'vague' nexus of feelings and ideas, a particularly complex set of 'emergent properties'. Some of the images in question are literal description, others metaphorical; often it is difficult to say—which, as we shall see, in Oliver's case is often very much part of the point.

## 'AS I STOOD LIKE THAT, RIPPLING'

Oliver's poem 'Wings' exemplifies her characteristic dual emphasis on both individual consciousness and merging or identifying with nature, and recalls Christensen's definition of a 'typical Oliver poem' as beginning 'with a narrow perceptual focus that frames an animal, a plant, or a portion of landscape' before moving towards 'revelation' and a sense of identity 'expanded' by its connection with the world.[18]

> I saw the heron
>     poise
>         like a branch of white petals
>             in the swamp,
>
> in the mud that lies
>     like a glaze,
>         in the water
>             that swirls its pale panels
>
> of reflected clouds;
>     I saw the heron shaking
>         its damp wings—
>             and then I felt
>
> an explosion—
>     a pain—
>         also a happiness
>             I can hardly mention

---

[18] 'The pragmatic mysticism', pp. 140, 144.

as I slid free—
   as I saw the world
      through those yellow eyes—
         as I stood like that, rippling,

under the mottled sky
   of the evening
      that was beginning to throw
         its dense shadows.

No! said my heart, and drew back.
   But my bones knew something wonderful
      about the darkness—
         and they thrashed in their cords,

they fought, they wanted
   to lie down in that silky mash
      of the swamp, the sooner
         to fly.[19]

I focus on line 20, '[a]s I stood like that, rippling'. The poet has just described her own 'explosion', 'pain', and 'happiness' (ll. 13–15), so standing 'like that, rippling' suggests the shaking of a person experiencing intense joy or pain, a person who has just undergone an 'explosion'. But another possible implication is that the poet stands like the heron. Indeed, there are clues earlier in the poem that the poet resembles the heron she observes. Her experience of 'rippling' was prompted by seeing a heron 'poise' then 'shak[e]' its wings (ll. 2, 10–11). The verb 'poise' implies a posture of balance, and also readiness or expectation;[20] with reference to herons, it indicates their statuesque stillness which can last for some time before it is broken by movement, and during which they often observe the water intently. For a reader familiar with Oliver's work, this is likely to recall the poet who stands intently observing until the sudden advent of epiphanic experience. Thus the expansive movement of a heron's huge wings—outwards from the centred stillness of the balanced or 'poised' heron—makes sense as a metaphor or comparator for the observer who 'explodes' in ecstasy. The poet describes herself responding to the 'shaking' of the wings by seeing through the heron's eyes and 'standing like that': one meaning of 'like that', then, is 'as the heron stands when he shakes his wings'. Yet, 'rippling' is, of course, most often used to describe the light undulation of water into small waves, and we have been primed to think of water by the water in which the heron stands and which is on its 'damp wings' (l. 11). So we may also imagine the poet's 'rippling' movement as resembling that of gently undulating water. Finally, since the line is followed by a reference to a 'mottled sky' (l. 21), with 'mottled' placed

[19] 'Wings' from *House of Light* by Mary Oliver (Beacon Press Boston, Copyright © 1990 by Mary Oliver; reprinted by permission of The Charlotte Sheedy Literary Agency Inc.).
[20] www.oed.com/view/Entry/146666?rskey=G3sldR&result=3#eid [accessed 27 August 2016].

just three words after 'rippling', the two words may become associated so that the 'rippling' seems to be of light and darkness as well as of water.

So readers (or listeners[21]) might imagine movements made by the human body in explosive ecstasy; by enormous expansive heron wings interrupting the bird's poise; by undulating waves of water; and perhaps by ripples of light in the sky. The combination of these sensorimotor imaginings gives some indication of what Oliver's experience might be like, of what it might feel like to 'slid[e] free' (l. 17), to merge with nature. Taken together, the imagined movements suggest to me expansive suddenness combined with a softer repeated movement, and violence combined with gentleness.[22] This cluster of ideas is not, of course, a priori associated with standing or with rippling. 'Rippling' certainly indicates some kind of movement but nothing like the complex or contradictory one suggested by combining the sensorimotor simulations I have outlined. So the cluster of ideas around movement, violence, and gentleness could be described as an emergent property. However, it rather extends the purview of this category.

Unlike the incompetence of the butcher-like surgeon, the cluster in question is not strongly communicated by Oliver's images—it is part of her intention only in the extended sense of authorial intention that I articulated earlier. Moreover, it stems not from *comparing* sensorimotor simulations focused on a metaphor topic and vehicle—for example, how a butcher cuts with how a surgeon cuts—but rather from *combining* multiple sensorimotor responses to an image. Nor, by contrast with the hopeless inertia suggested by Heller's metaphorical toad in Carston's analysis, does it emerge from simply imagining 'one thing through another', exploring a single scenario from a single perspective to extract a 'coherent set of conceptual representations'. Instead the emergence of 'properties' results from engaging in a range of imaginary sensorimotor experiences, undertaken from multiple perspectives or focused on different entities (some of which may or may not be metaphorical).

What does this suggest about how Oliver's readers can get a sense of 'merging' with nature? Arguably the emergent property described is suggestive of what 'merging' feels like not only because this is the poem's theme but also because it arises from 'merging' experiences focused on different entities (the observer, the heron, the landscape): the reader experiences or *knows* this sensorimotor merging in an embodied way. This assertion is very different from suggesting that metaphor indicates similarity or that it 'blends' X and Y, not only because the heron is not necessarily metaphorical but also because it is important that what 'merges' are embodied experiences rather than simply the entities X and Y. Therefore Oliver's images suggesting multiple embodied experiences are particularly suited to her

---

[21] Sensory effects of poetry might, of course, include not only those produced by its images—the subject of this chapter—but also hearing (or imagining hearing) the poet's voice. On metre and sensory images, see G. Gabrielle Starr, 'Multisensory imagery', in Lisa Zunshine (ed.) *Introduction to Cognitive Cultural Studies* (Baltimore, MD: The Johns Hopkins University Press, 2010), pp. 275–91.

[22] The final lines of the poem reinforce this conjoined violence and gentleness, through references to 'darkness' and 'thrashing' of the 'bones' together with lying down 'in that silky mash'.

distinctive 'Romantic' theme of merging, as well as particularly apt for demonstrating how emergent properties can arise.

## 'THE SOFT ANIMAL OF YOUR BODY'

I take my next example from Oliver's well-known poem 'Wild Geese', which is not about ecstatic 'merging' with the world but does concern, among other things, our relationship to nature. I focus on the expression 'the soft animal of your body' (l. 4), which is likely to provoke not only thoughts about what it means for human beings to be animals but, especially for readers who heed Oliver's calls to slowness and thinking with the body, also sensorimotor responses:

> You do not have to be good.
> You do not have to walk on your knees
> for a hundred miles through the desert, repenting.
> You only have to let the soft animal of your body
>     love what it loves.
> Tell me about despair, yours, and I will tell you mine.
> Meanwhile the world goes on.
> Meanwhile the sun and the clear pebbles of the rain
> are moving across the landscapes,
> over the prairies and the deep trees,
> the mountains and the rivers.
> Meanwhile the wild geese, high in the clean blue air,
> are heading home again.
> Whoever you are, no matter how lonely,
> the world offers itself to your imagination,
> calls to you like the wild geese, harsh and exciting—
> over and over announcing your place
> in the family of things.[23]

Readers might imagine touching soft skin; indeed, the enactive account of perception suggests that imagining something soft activates the sense of touch.[24] This may involve animal skin as much as human skin. The separation of 'you' and 'the soft animal of your body' into grammatical subject and object (l. 4) arguably makes it easier to envisage these as separate entities. One might imagine the soft down of a goose, since the reference to 'soft animal' is the first line in 'Wild Geese' which might plausibly gloss its title, and a reference to wild geese later in the poem (ll. 12–13) appears to propose them as a model for the reader. At the same time, prototype theory suggests that we will imagine, or mentally 'token', a prototypical soft animal,

---

[23] In *New and Selected Poems*, vol. 1 (Boston, MA: Beacon Press, 1992), p. 110; first published in *Dream Work* (1986).

[24] Perception is termed 'enactive' because it is considered to be something we do with our bodies: we perceive the world by active enquiry and exploration. In other words, we *enact* our perceptual experience. See Alva Noë, *Action in Perception* (Cambridge, MA: MIT Press, 2004).

such as a fluffy puppy or kitten.[25] Other poems by Oliver may prime readers to imagine non-human animals, since they use the adjective 'soft' to describe birds or animals.[26] Furthermore, those creatures Oliver describes as soft are often small and vulnerable, for example the prey of 'The Owl Who Comes', or the duckling pulled to its death by the title character of 'Turtle'.[27] Imagining such soft animals together with 'the soft animal of your body' may generate a more palpable awareness of the body's vulnerability. So, for this reader at least, the poem produces a sense of touching softly, touching something vulnerable, and so touching gently, with special care. This apprehension of a need to be kind and gentle is strengthened by the contrast in the poem between 'let[ting] the soft animal of your body / love what it loves' and 'walk[ing] on your knees / for a hundred miles through the desert', an evocation of crawling whose strangeness means it is likely to produce a strong sensorimotor simulation of its own, a powerful kinesic impression of the discomfort of a harshly treated body.

Sensorimotor responses to 'the soft animal of your body' may also include softening one's body by relaxing the muscles. The reader might also breathe more gently, as tends to happen when we soften the abdominal muscles. Arguably readers are primed to associate this line with breathing by links Oliver makes elsewhere between breathing and themes which are to the fore in 'Wild Geese', such as our 'place' in the world, our status as part of nature, or the ethics of what we should do with our lives. For example, in 'Stars' Oliver implies that all we can do is to keep breathing in and out, in our 'places'.[28] In 'Sunrise', she suggests that breathing deeply, over and over, is somehow an ethical act, an alternative to giving oneself up to die at the stake,[29] recalling the contrast in 'Wild Geese' between salvation through physical mortification and 'let[ting] the soft animal of your body' do as it will (ll. 1–5). She equates not breathing fully with not living fully.[30] 'Sleeping in the Forest' seems to associate the slow, deep breathing of the sleeping poet 'rising and falling' with the breathing of the natural world, specifically the insects and the birds.[31] *Rules for the Dance: A Handbook for Writing and Reading Metrical Verse* opens with a section on breath which states that it is 'our own personal tie with all the rhythms of the natural world, of which we are a part' (p. 3). Oliver's writing

---

[25] On prototypes, see Eleanor Rosch, 'Cognitive representation of semantic categories', *Journal of Experimental Psychology*, 104.3 (1975), 192–233; George Lakoff, *Women, Fire, and Dangerous Things: What Categories Reveal about the Mind* (Chicago, IL; London: University of Chicago Press, 1987). A blogpost provides evidence of these particular animals coming to the mind of at least one other reader. 'I only have to let the soft animal of my body love what it loves. That's all? That's harder than the first two, harder than anything. It sounds so appealing, so cozy, like a kitten cuddling in your lap or a dog snoozing gently in the sun. Soft, warm, relaxed, loving what you love, not thinking about anything else', https://maryoliverchallenge.wordpress.com/2015/06/28/what-is-the-mary-oliver-challenge-2.

[26] For an example which also echoes 'Wild Geese' in other ways, see the sparrow in 'Just Lying on the Grass at Blackwater', *New and Selected*, vol. 2 (Boston, MA: Beacon Press, 2005), pp. 64–5; originally published in *Blue Iris* (2004).

[27] 'The Owl Who Comes', *New and Selected*, vol. 2, pp. 52–3; 'Turtle', *House of Light*, pp. 22–3.

[28] *New and Selected*, vol. 2, p. 127; originally published in *West Wind* (1997).

[29] *New and Selected*, vol. 1, pp. 125–6; originally published in *Dream Work* (1986).

[30] 'Have You Ever Tried to Enter the Long Black Branches', in *New and Selected*, vol. 2, pp. 141–4 (142); originally published in *West Wind* (1997).

[31] *New and Selected*, vol. 1, p. 181; originally published in *Twelve Moons* (1979).

thus invites us to form associations—in our kinaesthetic as well as conceptual intratextual memories[32]—between breathing and a set of themes which will be at stake in 'Wild Geese', increasing the likelihood that we might respond to the phrase 'the soft animal of your body' in part through a change in breathing.[33]

So, 'soft animal of your body' might produce a variety of sensorimotor responses suggesting softening and relaxation, vulnerability and fragility, and kindness and gentleness. This complex combination could be regarded as an emergent property: were one to list the properties of a 'soft animal', one might include 'needs looking after' but probably not relaxation, and one would not produce anything which 'feels' like the combination which emerges in the poem. As I suggested in relation to 'Wings', the emergence of such properties through multiple sensorimotor experiences is particularly suited to Oliver's themes: while 'Wild Geese' refers to our continuity with nature (our place in the 'family of things'), the expression 'the soft animal of your body' can give readers a complex sense of what this continuity might feel like because it invites sensorimotor imaginings focused on different parts of the human and natural worlds.

Once again, an emergent property stems from combining sensorimotor simulations rather than either comparing those focused on a metaphor topic and vehicle or imagining 'one thing through another', metaphor topic through metaphor vehicle. Indeed there is not even a clear separation between tenor and vehicle, subject and object: sensorimotor responses to the 'soft animal of your body' might involve both the reader's own body and those of other animals. The emergence of 'properties' results from engaging in a range of imaginary sensorimotor experiences, focused on different positions, such as the owner of a soft body and the toucher of a different soft body. Whereas Carston's analysis of poetic metaphors indicates that we keep examining a single 'coherent' image until we find enough to satisfy us about the metaphor topic, I am suggesting that we might instead engage in multiple ways with more than one 'picture' and from more than one perspective.

## PAINTING AND POETRY: NATALIA WRÓBEL'S *LIKE A NEEDLE IN THE HAYSTACK OF LIGHT* AND OLIVER'S 'LIKE A NEEDLE / IN THE HAYSTACK / OF LIGHT'

I close this chapter with a quotation from Oliver alongside a painting by Natalia Wróbel which takes that quotation as its title and more generally dialogues with

---

[32] Guillemette Bolens, *The Style of Gestures: Embodiment and Cognition in Literary Narrative* (Baltimore, MD: The Johns Hopkins University Press, 2012), esp. pp. 50–65, 123–66; originally published as *Le Style des gestes: corporéité et kinésie dans le récit littéraire* (Lausanne, Switzerland: Editions BHMS, 2008); see also the Introduction and Chapter 3 in this volume.

[33] It seems that at least some readers respond this way, since the line is cited on a number of websites with reference to various relaxation and breathing practices. For example, http://beingjackbutler. com/relaxing-into-our-animal-nature, www.heartofvillageyoga.com/restorative-yoga-benefit, www. bristolmassagetherapy.co.uk/meet-the-team/sarah-thorne, http://mindfulrelaxation.com/fee-schedule. I first encountered the poem read aloud at a Buddhist retreat focused on embodied practices including breathing meditation, and softening of the breath was among my own responses to it.

Oliver's poetry, cited as an inspiration for the series to which the painting belongs.[34] Invoking linguistics is more surprising in the analysis of painting than of literature; however, as noted above, relevance theory rejects a model of communication grounded in the explicit meanings which language can (in rare cases) achieve, focusing just as much on 'vague' communication and offering a paradigm of it (Mary's seaside gesticulations) in which the sensory is central. Furthermore, as I have discussed, poems can engage the body in ways crucial to the cognitive responses they produce: there is therefore no simple distinction between poetry and visual art in terms of whether they invite sensorimotor responses. However, the two genres and individual artefacts under consideration engage the body differently, and these specificities can be usefully articulated within the framework of the relevance theory model of communication and cognition.

## Mindful

Every day
　I see or I hear
　　something
　　　that more or less

kills me
　with delight,
　　that leaves me
　　　like a needle

in the haystack
　of light.
　　It is what I was born for—
　　　to look, to listen,

to lose myself
　inside this soft world—
　　to instruct myself
　　　over and over

in joy,
　and acclamation.
　　Nor am I talking
　　　about the exceptional,

the fearful, the dreadful,
　the very extravagant—
　　but of the ordinary,
　　　the common, the very drab,

the daily presentations.
　Oh, good scholar,
　　I say to myself,
　　　how can you help

---

[34] http://nataliaswrobel.com/section/384250-Embrace-Series-click-to-view-series.html.

but grow wise
    with such teachings
        as these—
            the untrimmable light

of the world,
    the ocean's shine,
        the prayers that are made
            out of grass?[35]

**Figure 7.1.** Natalia Wróbel, 'Like a Needle in the Haystack of Light', 2013, oil paint on canvas, 30 × 30 inches

[35] 'Mindful' from *Why I Wake early: New Poems*, by Mary Oliver (Beacon Press Boston, Copyright © 2004 by Mary Oliver; reprinted by permission of The Charlotte Sheedy Literary Agency Inc.).

Oliver's 'like a needle / in the haystack / of light' (ll. 8–10), a simile, might at first glance seem to be a single 'coherent' image—a depiction of 'one thing through another'—that would be susceptible to analysis along the lines suggested by Carston (to the extent that the lexicalized meaning of the similar expression 'needle in *a* haystack' did not limit sensorimotor exploration of Oliver's simile). However, because the simile is unravelled over a succession of short lines (a poetic form typical of Oliver), readers are more likely to consider each line before turning to the following one, and so to explore any image suggested by the words up to that point without yet taking into account what comes next. In other words, we might first imagine being 'like a needle' before later incorporating other imagining involving 'the haystack of light'. In addition, the positioning of the nouns 'needle', 'haystack', and 'light' emphasizes them, encouraging us to consider each in turn. Thus a full relevance theory account of emergent properties and poetic images would need to consider poetic form, an aspect of style which 'arises...in the pursuit of relevance'.[36] In 'Mindful', poetic form makes it more likely that we will engage in multiple sensorimotor imaginings which, as in the other cases studied, can combine to produce complex emergent properties.

The poem's title, 'Mindful', evokes a complete attention to—and awareness of—one's experience.[37] After the initial claim that the poet's own sensory experience occasions a rapturous delight, the reader is told that, when the poet is overcome by this delight, she is 'like a needle'. For me at least, this prompts a sense of centredness, tautness, and rigidity in the body. The poet's complete focus on her experience—her mindfulness and delight—are embodied in the 'centredness' of a thin needle: the likely stillness of somebody completely focused on looking and listening 'feels like' being as taut or rigid as a long thin needle. The needle's sharpness might contribute to this sense of focus, as the already thin object is further centred in the point at its extremity. Then, in the next line, the words 'in the haystack' activate the lexicalized or proverbial meaning of 'needle in a haystack' as something tiny relative to the area in which it is located and therefore almost impossible to find, and which one would be foolish to try to find:[38] the poet is small within the vastness of what she perceives, and it would be senseless to try to separate her from it. Taken together with the sensorimotor imagining prompted by the previous line, this gives rise to a strange sense of being not only centred and taut but also lost in a larger whole. The addition of the words 'of light' in the following line means we can, I think, imagine being taut, erect, and centred but also merging with a mass of light— thus shimmering and perhaps quivering. (Any sense of merging or quivering will be further reinforced by the following lines, in which the looking and listening are glossed as 'los[ing] myself' inside a world described as 'soft', an adjective

---

[36] *Relevance*, p. 219.

[37] 'fully aware of the moment, whilst self-conscious and attentive to this awareness', www.oed.com/view/Entry/118740?redirectedFrom=mindful#eid [accessed 4 August 2016].

[38] '*needle in a haystack* and variants: something that would be immensely difficult to find. Usually taken as an example of something it is foolish to attempt to find. Chiefly in proverbial phrases, as *to look for a needle in a haystack*', www.oed.com/view/Entry/125771#eid35043081 [accessed 31 July 2016].

which can suggest a fuzziness, an indeterminacy of the edges between self and world.) One might also feel blinded by the dazzle, a sensation which fits well with the impossibility of locating the 'needle in the haystack', but which shifts the position one occupies in relation to it, making one feel like the person looking as well as the object lost; in this sense, too, there is a kind of separateness combined with merging.

In 'Mindful', then, the dialectic of individuation and merging which has been detected in Oliver's shifts between observation and ecstasy is present in the very moment of revelation or 'delight'. The expression 'like a needle / in the haystack / of light' invites multiple sensorimotor imaginings which can combine to produce emergent properties. These in turn give a sense of what concomitant merging and individuation might feel like: something akin to centredness or rigidity or tautness together with blurring or merging or quivering. I turn now to Wróbel's *Like a Needle in the Haystack of Light* which, I will suggest, shares Oliver's interest in concomitant merging and individuation but explores it in ways which make different calls on our bodies.[39]

*Like a Needle* combines broad expansive brushstrokes with focused thin and strong lines where Wróbel has pressed down hard on the canvas. Wróbel sometimes separates colours from each other in distinct blocks, but elsewhere layers one colour over another so that they partly merge, as in the yellow on top of orange towards the centre of the upper-left quarter. So arguably there is a sense of something like centring and separateness but also merging and continuity. This is likely to come to the fore particularly for those viewers who take up Wróbel's invitation to consider her painting in relation to Oliver's poetry and who might therefore find in it something like the dialectic of centring and merging which is so important in Oliver's work in general as well as in the line cited in particular. Similarly, the lens of Oliver's portrayal of 'merging' strengthens a sense in Wróbel's painting of something like gentleness and conflict, or gentleness and movement: the painting combines intense movement, bright colour, and thick texture with areas of more restful light or muted colour as found particularly in the upper-right quarter of the painting.

Even without the relationship to Oliver's work, Wróbel's title arguably accentuates any sense of merging and centring which viewers get from the painting itself. While Wróbel, in sharp contrast to Oliver, is a painter of the abstract rather than the concrete, the title of her painting draws attention to her thin, hard strokes because they are not unlike needles; it is these lines which most express a centring or most point to a 'rigid', hard action by the artist. At the same time, because the brushstrokes emanate in an apparently disordered way in multiple directions, and because of the many yellows and reds, we may perceive in these colours something like hay in a haystack, although they are more vivid than in an actual

---

[39] As with Oliver's poems, my response to Wróbel's painting is intended to correspond to what relevance theory would term Wróbel's 'informative intention' but is not the only one which would do so. For instance, my knowledge of Oliver is more attuned than any kinaesthetic memory of painting so, while Wróbel renders both of these accessible contexts, as relevance theorists might put it, I can create more 'cognitive effects' with the first than the second.

haystack. The blues and greens and whites incorporate into the painting the colours of sky and grass found around a haystack, bringing them together with the reds and yellows, as if a dazzling haystack were merging with its surroundings. Viewers might be reminded of the haystacks painted by Van Gogh and Monet, which also often use strong thick 'wavy' or 'quivering' strokes, and also merge the borders between haystack and sky, yet still leave the borders in place, the sky and grass beyond the haystack: the 'shimmering' of Impressionist painting is accentuated to the point of abstraction, the point where object and surrounding landscape merge.

This dazzling and merging of separate entities, combined with a strong centring, arguably recalls what I have described in Oliver's poetry. However, Wróbel is not implicated in it in the way that Oliver is: the 'merging' and 'centring' seem to be primarily 'out there in the world', realized in the colours of haystack and sky. Of course, painting and lyric poetry in general differ in that the 'I' is more obviously present in the latter. And, whereas in Oliver's poem it is 'me' who is 'like a needle', Wróbel's extract from Oliver unsurprisingly—given the likely length of titles of paintings—does not include this first-person pronoun, instead leaving it to the viewer to decide what it is that resembles 'a needle in the haystack of light' (the painting? the painter?). The viewer might infer an 'I', particularly if they have read Oliver's poetry or perhaps Wróbel's comments on meditation and focus, but equally they might not, especially since the lexicalized sense of a 'needle in a haystack' normally refers to an object of our gaze rather than to the human subject herself, and since—as discussed above—Wróbel's painting might be thought to bear some limited resemblance to a depiction of a haystack, albeit in a highly abstracted form.

However, while 'merging' and 'centring' do not implicate Wróbel as they do Oliver, both Wróbel's thick expansive brushstrokes and her thin 'needle-like' ones draw attention to what the artist has done with her body. As David Freedberg and Vittorio Gallese have argued, works of art do not need to depict bodies—or even to be figurative—to elicit phenomenological responses: one way in which they do so is through the traces they bear of a painter's actions.[40] What Wróbel 'shows' us, in part at least, is what she has done with her body. While for Oliver 'like a needle in the haystack of light' is a simile for the focused or 'mindful' poet, Wróbel—who conceives painting as a 'moving meditation'[41]—makes the focus more physical or kinesic and invites us to feel something of how it was 'felt' in her body.[42] For me at least, the embodied response to Wróbel's combination of focused and emanating brushstrokes involves a sense of something like centred strength and expansive dynamism, energy in the body together with intensity in its relationship to the canvas

[40] 'Motion, emotion and empathy in esthetic experience', *Trends in Cognitive Sciences*, 11.5 (2007), 197–203.

[41] For example, http://nataliaswrobel.com/news.html.

[42] For the viewer whose knowledge of Oliver means that the painting raises a question about the place of the human subject in relation to the 'haystack of light', this embodied response may become the object of conscious reflection and take on a particular significance; however, research into phenomenological responses suggests that, whether or not this is the case, it operates on a pre-conscious level.

or to the 'haystack', 'needle', and 'light'.[43] In any event, viewers get some sense of what Wróbel's body did and what it may have felt like—a sense more or less precise depending on how attuned our kinaesthetic knowledge of painting is, but a sense available to us all in some degree, insofar as we have all done things with our hands and bodies, made movements which are focused or expansive, hard or soft. Thus bodies—and their relationship to the 'needle in the haystack of light'—become important in a way different from their role in the kind of sensorimotor imagining which Oliver's images invite.

We can describe this in relevance theory terms as constituting a different kind of showing, or as inviting sensorimotor responses focused more on actions of showing than on objects shown. In this sense, relevance theory provides a framework for articulating the specificity of response that different artworks invite, and situating them within a plausible model of human communication and cognition. Conversely, the painting—and its comparison to the poem—offer relevance theory an extended sense of what the showing end of the showing–meaning communicative spectrum can entail and how the body can be involved. Wróbel's painting, through the type of sensorimotor response it elicits, draws attention to the range of ways in which showing might involve the body. Showing can constitute drawing attention not only to what is outside oneself (a 'haystack', light, colour) but also to how it feels to show it. To an extent, Oliver does this too (by encouraging us to look as she looks and listen as she listens), and similarly Peter is invited to look and sniff as Mary does; however, this aspect of communication is more to the fore in the painting.

In conclusion, I hope to have shown that relevance theory offers a fruitful framework for focusing on sensorimotor imagining. Currently scholars are making many and varied intellectual efforts to go beyond post-structuralism and beyond the 'linguistic turn', in particular to analyse the senses and the emotions. Relevance theory's contribution to this work might be its account—grounded in a plausible model of human cognition and communication—of how impressions and emotions can be produced at the micro-level of the sentence or gesture or action. In this chapter, by focusing on sensorimotor responses, I hope to have enhanced relevance theory accounts of showing and particularly of emergent properties. At the same time, I have suggested that they offer a way to articulate some of what goes on when we respond to poetic or visual artefacts, in particular when Oliver's readers 'deepen their journey into the leaves and the sky' and, more generally, when readers encounter poetic images and feel emerging a constellation of emotions or impressions which 'go beyond the words' of the poem.

[43] Wróbel has more than once selected as titles for her paintings lines from Oliver's poetry which invoke (as well as light or fire) precisely an intensity of relationship to the world, for example *Be Ignited, or Be Gone* (a line from 'What I Have Learned So Far') and *Another One of the Ways to Enter Fire* (from 'Sunrise').

# Interlace 8

*Timothy Chesters's chapter shares many of Kathryn Banks's preoccupations: the role of 'weak' implicatures, the 'lingering of the literal', the focus on the way ad hoc concepts and their emergent properties arise in language which is palpably figurative, and above all the sense that the triggering of kinesic effects may be integral to the communicator's intention. This chapter also explores the 'deflationary account of metaphors' proposed by relevance theory, and its critique of the norm of literalness from which metaphor was always supposed to derive its power.*

*The case studies chosen in these two chapters are starkly contrasted: on the one hand, the shifting but easily assimilated flow of Mary Oliver's poems, which seek a communality of feeling without suppressing the needle-like identity of the self; on the other, the voice of Emily Dickinson, whose explosively juxtaposed phrases render the sense of a life that 'had stood—a Loaded Gun— / In Corners—'. Between them, these two kinesic styles invite one to undo the distinctions of a formalist poetics or rhetoric, the attempt to locate (and pin down) pop-up 'metaphors', 'similes', and other figures, together with the unargued assumption that such figures are of sharply different kinds, and trigger different types of cognitive effects. Abandoning the code model of communication means abandoning the niceties of such text-specific terminologies which only ever, when one comes down to it, have a heuristic function. By contrast, the terminologies of the open, inferential mode proposed by relevance theory and kinesic analysis rely not on coding and decoding but on evidence of the kinds of inference that utterances, poetic and otherwise, can make happen in the audience's cognitive environment.*

*Speaking of which: Timothy Chesters's choice of a poem featuring a fly as his opening example is of course not entirely innocent. We haven't asked him whether he was intentionally echoing the long-legged fly of Elleke Boehmer's opening chapter, but we didn't need to: if it wasn't his specific intention, it is at least a plausible inference in our common cognitive environment, and one that gains in relevance by yielding a range of rewarding cognitive effects. From Yeats's delicate insect, hovering above the stream of consciousness out of which seismic changes in the world can emerge, to the obstinate buzzing of Dickinson's fly, witness to a terminal cessation of consciousness, the trajectory is only virtual. Yet both of them make salient, in the embodied form of a tiny non-human agent, something we might have missed but need to know: something that emerges from the margins of awareness to assert its unexpected relevance.*

# 8

# The Lingering of the Literal in Some Poems of Emily Dickinson

*Timothy Chesters*

## INTRODUCTION

The poetry of Emily Dickinson has been thought of as reserving a special place for literalness, for meaning just what you say and nothing more, despite the 'more' that so many of her images seem on the brink of offering.[1] Dickinson criticism has sometimes characterized this retreat into the literal as a refusal of transcendence.[2] Unlike her older contemporary Emerson, say, for whom the whole world was 'emblematic', Dickinson keeps back some portion of the humble, material world that remains stubbornly, untransferably itself.[3] Take the fly of 'I heard a Fly buzz – when I died –':

> I heard a Fly buzz – when I died –
> The Stillness in the Room
> Was like the Stillness in the Air –
> Between the Heaves of Storm –
>
> The Eyes around – had wrung them dry –
> And Breaths were gathering firm
> For that last Onset – when the King
> Be witnessed – in the Room –
>
> I willed my Keepsakes – Signed away
> What portion of me be
> Assignable – and then it was
> There interposed a Fly –

---

[1] For a different view, see Wendy Barker, *Lunacy of Light: Emily Dickinson and the Experience of Metaphor* (Carbondale, IL: Southern Illinois University Press, 1987).

[2] See, for instance, Elissa Greenwald, 'Dickinson among the realists', in Robin Riley Fast and Christine Mack Gordon (eds) *Approaches to Teaching Emily Dickinson* (New York: The Modern Language Association of America, 1989), pp. 164–9 (especially p. 167); Shira Wolosky writes of Dickinson's 'stymied correspondences' in 'Emily Dickinson: being in the body', in Wendy Martin (ed.) *The Cambridge Companion to Emily Dickinson* (Cambridge: Cambridge University Press, 2002), pp. 129–41.

[3] 'The world is emblematic. Parts of speech are metaphors, because the whole of nature is a metaphor of the human mind'; Ralph Waldo Emerson, *Nature and Selected Essays*, edited by Larzer Ziff (New York: Penguin, 2003), p. 53.

With Blue – uncertain stumbling Buzz –
Between the light – and me –
And then the Windows failed – and then
I could not see to see –[4]

What is the 'Fly' supposed to represent in this celebrated poem? It must stand as an analogy for something, one would think. Of all the things to which the speaker might have attended in her dying moments, and now in her posthumous recollection of them, why *this* lowly detail if not that it hints at something larger? In other respects, certainly, the poem is not shy of suggesting equivalences: the subsequent lines describe the 'Stillness of the Room' as *like* 'the Stillness of the Air'; and this atmospheric, storm-punctuated stillness itself seems pregnant with some broader, spiritual possibility. For if air is the fly's element, it is also and significantly that of the human soul—that 'portion' of the poet that is not 'assignable', and now awaits the 'King' (of Heaven) who will arrive to bear it up. The poet seems here to exploit the familiar metaphorical association between spirit and breath: the 'Breaths… gathering firm' among those present in the room anticipate the speaker's final exhalation, and the release of her spirit on its journey to another world. Perhaps, then, the reader is meant to see the 'Fly'—notably slant-rhymed, on its second appearance, with 'me'—as an emblem of the poet's soul. Of course this symbolic resonance would not be without its ironies: in place of the soul-as-Psyche—that is, the soul-as-butterfly—Dickinson offers instead its degraded, humdrum cousin, butting clumsily at the window.[5]

Is this all? It is tempting to extend the range of metaphorical equivalences further. Looking beyond the fly-as-soul, some readers have suggested that the insect may be intended to signify truth (the 'Fly' seems to displace and depose the expected 'King', and thus the comforting illusions of religion) and/or possibly mortality.[6] All three seem plausible 'weak implicatures' for 'Fly', and ways might even be found to reconcile them: in each case this squalid, carrion creature interrupts (is 'interposed' in) and so ironizes a scene of good Christian death.[7] And yet, however the reader satisfies her need for a symbolic equivalence, another dimension of the 'Fly' continues to insist. In 'Blue – uncertain stumbling Buzz' the poet delivers a synaesthetic shock quite unlike anything else in the poem, such that it seems less appropriate here to talk of a poetic 'image' than of a tangle of not only visual but kinaesthetic and—especially—aural impressions too. The poem's structure suggests that this appeal to the sensorimotor content of the concept FLY ought

---

[4] Emily Dickinson, *Complete Poems*, edited by Thomas H. Johnson (London: Faber and Faber, 1970), pp. 223–4.

[5] The contemporary poet Alice Oswald returns to this image in her remarkable poem 'Flies': 'This is the day the flies fall awake mid-sentence / and lie stunned on the window-sill shaking with speeches'; *Falling Awake* (London: Jonathan Cape, 2016), p. 4. My thanks to Terence Cave for pointing out this parallel.

[6] 'Mortality, in the person of the monumentalized and actual Fly, possesses the grandeur of Truth defeating illusion'; H. Vendler, *Dickinson: Selected Poems and Commentaries* (Cambridge, MA: Harvard University Press, 2012), p. 268.

[7] For a discussion of 'weak implicatures', see Introduction, pp. 10–11.

not to be underestimated. It is the impression with which the poet begins ('I heard a Fly buzz') and, whereas her sight may fade at the end of the poem ('I could not see to see'), the one which has lingered longest in her memory. Whatever broader significance readers might wish to lend it, there remains a literal fly, a fly-as-simply-fly, that the symbolic business of the poem does not quite succeed in tidying away.

This chapter will consider a number of further instances of what might be called, to borrow Robyn Carston's phrase, the 'lingering of the literal' in the specific context of Dickinson's metaphors.[8] Rather than viewing this as a phenomenon peculiar to Dickinson herself, it will be argued instead that this lingering or 'buzz' of the literal often characterizes metaphor-processing in general. Dickinson has not invented but is simply exploiting, with all the gifts at her disposal, an already existing feature of human communication and cognition.

## LITERALNESS: A DEFLATIONARY ACCOUNT

What is the role of literal meaning in metaphorical utterances? For example, is it possible to grasp the sense of a speaker's metaphor without some form of circuit via a literal paraphrase? Not according to most traditional accounts. Central to these has been the so-called 'norm of literalness'. In the classical rhetorical tradition, metaphor is viewed as a creative deviation from the default, literal meaning. Metaphor is an ornamental adjunct, a 'happy extra trick' (in I.A. Richards's phrase) performed in place of a more prosaic literal utterance which, from the point of view of meaning, might have served the speaker just as well.[9]

Implicit in this view is a theory of metaphor comprehension as a two-step process. First, and by default, listeners assess the truth value of a proposition (e.g. 'Juliet is the sun') as it is understood literally; only then, having been obstructed in the attempt to make the proposition literally true, do they widen their search to include the possibility that the speaker is suggesting some form of resemblance (Romeo must regard Juliet as being in some way *like* the sun). Even Grice commits to something like this view when he describes metaphorical utterances as blatant violations of his maxim of truthfulness ('Try to make your contribution one that is true').[10] For him, too, understanding metaphors seems to imply assessing then rejecting the literal meaning of the utterance. To this extent Grice might be thought both to inflate and deflate the role of metaphor in human communication. He inflates it by regarding metaphors as different in kind from literal utterances—qualitatively distinct figures of speech insofar as they flout his first Quality maxim.

---

[8] Robyn Carston, 'Ad hoc concepts, literal meaning and mental images', *Proceedings of the Aristotelian Society*, 110 (2010), 295–321.

[9] I.A. Richards, *The Philosophy of Rhetoric* (Oxford: Oxford University Press, 1936), pp. 89–138 (p. 90). Richards intends the phrase ironically, as part of a broader problematization of the literal/metaphorical distinction.

[10] H. Paul Grice, *Studies in the Way of Words* (Cambridge, MA: Harvard University Press, 1989), p. 27.

At the same time, he effectively downplays the force of metaphorical utterances by retaining the classical view that their meaning is ultimately reducible to a literal paraphrase. Metaphor contributes nothing, in Gricean terminology, to 'what is said': its difference from the literal equivalent amounts at most to a sprinkling of ancillary ('perlocutionary') effects.

The norm of literalness can be considered a major casualty of relevance theory's account of metaphor.[11] Central to that account is the idea that listeners infer speaker intentions not according to a criterion of literal truthfulness, but rather as part of their search for *relevance*.[12] According to relevance theorists, there is no evidence to suggest that, in reaching an optimally relevant interpretation of Romeo's 'Juliet is the sun', listeners must first assess and then dismiss as untrue the literal meaning of the utterance; indeed, listeners may not access the literal, encoded concept (SUN) at all.[13] Certainly it would be possible to imagine contexts for this utterance in which the speaker's intention might be construed literally: the context of a pagan religion, for example, in which certain privileged individuals (in this case Juliet) are considered incarnations of astral bodies, or some such. In most cases, however, the literal interpretation of 'sun' (SUN) remains just one candidate among an array of 'ad hoc' concepts (SUN*, SUN**, SUN***) capable of becoming more or less salient as plausible construals of speaker intention, combined with contextual factors, allow. Thus we might suppose that Romeo, as he seeks to alter our perception of Juliet, wishes us to attend to the sun's radiance (SUN*), to its warmth (SUN**), to its being a source of vitality and growth (SUN***), or some combination of these. With each of these interpretations listeners settle on a conceptual representation that is both broader and narrower than the encoded ('literal') concept: broader because the category SUN has now been extended to include people among its members, narrower because only certain features of SUN yield implications which help to satisfy the presumption of relevance. The crucial point here is that no one conceptual representation on this spectrum, including the literal one, can claim the priority of 'default' in relation to any of the others. Metaphors are not literal meanings accessorized; as this example shows, the search for relevance often bypasses some aspects of literal meaning altogether. Instead each concept emerges as a function of online pragmatic adjustments arising within the search for relevance.

Ad hoc adjustments of this kind are not a feature of metaphor alone. According to relevance theorists, cases of hyperbole and 'loose use' operate in a similar way. Consider these everyday examples cited by relevance theorists:

---

[11] Aside from Richards's influential essay, for a further critique (with which relevance theory is also partly in sympathy) see Donald Davidson, 'What metaphors mean', *Critical Inquiry*, 5 (1978), 31–47.

[12] Here, as throughout this volume, 'relevance' is used in its technical sense, where achieving relevance depends on optimally balancing cognitive effects with processing effort. See in particular Deirdre Wilson and Dan Sperber, *Meaning and Relevance* (Cambridge: Cambridge University Press, 2012), pp. 47–83.

[13] This much-cited example was first discussed by Stanley Cavell; see his 'Aesthetic problems of modern philosophy', in Max Black (ed.) *Philosophy in America* (Ithaca, NY: Cornell University Press, 1965); reprinted in Stanley Cavell, *Must We Mean What We Say?* (Cambridge: Cambridge University Press: 1976), pp. 73–96.

(1)  This water is boiling!
(2)  Holland is flat.[14]

Suppose that the hyperbole in (1) is uttered by a speaker unwilling to enter a newly poured bath. At no stage in the comprehension process is a listener likely to suppose that the speaker intends him to infer that the temperature of the water is exactly 100°C: indeed, assessing the plausibility of this literal interpretation would seem an egregious waste of cognitive resources. Instead the expectation of relevance is likelier to guide the listener towards an ad hoc concept BOILING*: implying that the water is too hot for the purpose of taking a bath. Similarly, suppose that two friends are discussing possible destinations for a cycling tour. Only in exceptional contexts (e.g. if one of the friends were conducting a geological survey) would a listener infer that a speaker of (2) intends us to conclude that Holland is a perfect 180° plane. Instead the cyclist in this case knows (and his friend knows he knows) that he is being ushered towards a view of Holland as FLAT*: a suitable place for a gentle bike ride. In each of these cases, as in the metaphor 'Juliet is the sun', the utterance cues a pragmatically adjusted construal of a key concept (SUN, BOILING, FLAT), most elements of whose strictly literal, encoded content never enter the communicative picture.

The ubiquity of ad hoc concept construction in human communication raises the question of whether metaphors should properly be considered special types of utterance at all. Deirdre Wilson and Dan Sperber think not:

> We see metaphors as simply a range of cases at one end of a continuum that includes literal, loose and hyperbolic interpretations. In our view metaphorical interpretations are arrived at in exactly the same way as these other interpretations. There is no mechanism specific to metaphors, no interesting generalisation that applies only to them. In other terms, linguistic metaphors are not a natural kind, and 'metaphor' is not a theoretically important notion in the study of verbal communication.[15]

It is not difficult to see why Sperber and Wilson term their position a 'deflationary' account of metaphor. There is, they would claim, nothing 'extra' (or for that matter tricky) about Richards's 'happy extra trick': by placing metaphors on the 'literal–loose–metaphorical' continuum, relevance theory robs them of any distinctiveness relative to other forms of speech. That said, however deflationary their claims, one could argue that relevance theorists nonetheless restore to metaphor a power of expressive nuance it lacked in the traditional account. The array of ad hoc concepts to which metaphors, like other forms of linguistic expression, are able to give rise is exactly as vast as the range of human intentions could potentially permit. Untethered from the supposedly literal default of most human exchange, metaphor operates on the infinitely calibrated gradient of plausible construal. To this extent we might say that it is not metaphor that the relevance theory account deflates, but the norm of literalness once thought the greatest source of its effects.

---

[14]  Similar examples are discussed in Wilson and Sperber, *Meaning and Relevance*, pp. 97–122.
[15]  *Meaning and Relevance*, p. 97.

## THE LINGERING OF THE LITERAL

Before moving on to the implications of the relevance-theoretic position for poetic metaphor, let us consider a further everyday example. Given the hypothesis outlined above, what happens to the literal content of ROBOT in the following exchange?

> (3) *Sally*: Talk it over with John. He's a sensitive guy.
> *Mary*: John is a robot.

On the relevance theory account, Sally's interpretation of Mary's retort is likely to involve an ad hoc concept (ROBOT*) both broader and narrower than the literal ROBOT. It will be broader because ROBOT*, unlike ROBOT, is capacious enough to include John as a member; it will be narrower because, guided by the search for relevance, Sally attends only to those features of the encoded concept germane to this exchange, that is to say the lack of empathy or social skills she thinks Mary ascribes to John. Whatever the precise content of Sally's interpretation, one thing seems certain: any 'excess' content of ROBOT simply does not arise within the comprehension process just described. Imagine that, returning to eavesdrop on their conversation a minute or two later, we overhear the two women discussing whether John was assembled in Taiwan, or how to locate the wind-up key halfway up his back. This would come as a surprise; we should suspect them of joking, of playing with words. Why? Because normally Sally and Mary, in cooperating to form ROBOT*, will have discarded all non-relevant encyclopaedic features of the encoded concept, if indeed these ever occurred to them at all.[16] We should expect the literal robot to have been scrapped, retaining no onward traction in their cognitive environment.

But is this always so? In a recent attempt to refine the deflationary account, Robyn Carston has identified certain instances in which the encoded content of a metaphorical expression can appear to persist longer than is usual—a phenomenon she calls 'the lingering of the literal'.[17] Take the following example:

> Life's but a walking shadow, a poor player
> That struts and frets his hour upon the stage
> And then is heard no more.
> (Shakespeare, *Macbeth*, V. v. 24–6)

Although listeners know from the beginning of these lines that Macbeth intends this image as a metaphor for 'life', the words he speaks still produce a vivid impression of a ham actor performing briefly on a stage. In this case it seems that the metaphorical character of Macbeth's utterance, unlike 'John is a robot', does not fully eclipse its literal content. Why should this be so? According to Carston it is because, rather than resolve each component of the metaphor one by one, listeners

---

[16] On the encyclopaedic features of concepts, see Introduction, pp. 7–8.

[17] In 'Ad hoc concepts, literal meaning and mental images', p. 305. For further discussion, see also Robyn Carston, 'Metaphor and the literal/non-literal distinction', in K. Jaszczolt and K. Allan (eds) *The Cambridge Handbook of Pragmatics* (Cambridge: Cambridge University Press, 2012), pp. 483–4.

mentally 'hold over' the literal content of the image for reasons of efficiency. Interpreting each metaphorical component ad hoc concept by ad hoc concept (SHADOW*, POOR PLAYER*, STRUTS*, HOUR*, STAGE*, and so on) would come at too great a cognitive cost. Instead an audience would be more likely to sustain the literal content so as to submit it globally for processing downstream. Thus in Macbeth's speech we could expect listeners to attend first to the global, literal image of the poor player; only then would they 'extract relevant information about life that is plausibly attributable to Macbeth at this stage of the play': its short span, its pointlessness, its self-deluding qualities, and so on. In this way Carston proposes a distinction between two 'modes' of metaphor-processing in which 'Mode 1'—the construction of ad hoc concepts—temporarily gives way to a 'Mode 2' procedure involving what Carston calls the 'framing' or 'meta-representation' of the literal.[18]

What conditions determine the choice of one or the other mode? Carston has some suggestions about likely conditions for Mode 2. First, she proposes that a literary metaphor would be more likely to elicit 'meta-representation' than would a face-to-face exchange. This is because the participants in a quick-fire conversation would not expect to enjoy the luxury of holding over the encoded concept for processing later on. Second, she claims that the literal is also liable to linger in extended metaphor or allegory, where sequences of metaphors have room to develop the kind of forward and backward literal priming we see in the example from *Macbeth*. Finally she suggests that, even without such extension, particularly novel metaphors are more likely to switch on Mode 2 than conventional ones, citing this example from Emily Dickinson:

> My life had stood – a Loaded Gun –
> In Corners –

The obscurity of Dickinson's metaphor effectively blocks the pre-reflective formation of a new ad hoc concept, for which the reader has not yet been offered sufficient evidence. Here again it seems that, as Carston puts it, 'an explicit, deliberate process [is] engaged, which assesses the implications and associations carried by this conceptual representation and selects those that might plausibly characterize a human life, specifically a life that "HAD STOOD IN CORNERS"'. Novel or difficult metaphors join literary and extended ones as the three kinds most likely to elicit Mode 2 'framing' of this kind.

In addition to extended and/or literary metaphors requiring 'meta-representation', Carston also identifies a similar phenomenon at work in mixed metaphors. She offers the following everyday example:

(4)  Mary: If you find a student with a spark of imagination, water it.

Even though the cognitive apparatus has supposedly suppressed the literal sense of 'spark' in its search for a relevant speaker-intended propositional meaning

---

[18] By 'meta-representation' in this context Carston means a mental 'holding-over' or 'putting into quotation marks' for the purposes of further processing.

(something like: 'If you find a student with the beginnings of an active and passionate imagination'), most listeners will still rebel against the incongruity of watering a spark. Why? Because it seems that some of SPARK's previously unactivated, literal properties have survived the earlier adjustment to an ad hoc concept (SPARK*), and it is precisely these that seem incongruous with 'water'. Empirical findings in psycholinguistics seem to confirm this jarring effect. Paula Rubio-Fernández has shown that we are relatively slow to deactivate what she calls non-metaphor-consistent information (e.g. encyclopaedic associates not carried over into the ad hoc concept) compared with the speed at which we suppress, for example, the non-relevant content of a homonym such as 'bank'/'bank'.[19] Although Carston does not develop the idea, mixed metaphors—indeed, serial metaphors in general—might be taken as further evidence that the literal sometimes lingers.

## 'ONLY, YOUR INFERENCE THEREFROM': DICKINSON AND THE LITERAL

To claim that literalness occupies a special place in Dickinson seems counter-intuitive in a work so venturesome in metaphor. Several of her poems open with striking cases of the type 'X is a Y' (e.g. 'Prayer is the little implement'; 'Risk is the hair that holds the tun', 'Power is a familiar growth'), with the remaining lines given the task of explication. Here is another example:

> Fame is a bee.
>     It has a song –
>     It has a sting –
>     Ah, too, it has a wing.[20]

This little poem offers a sense of a metaphorical meaning not ready-made but in-the-making.[21] This 'online' character is already suggested in the progressive modulation 'song'–'sting'–'wing', each of Dickinson's trademark dashes forming a miniature cognitive launchpad to the next rhymed word in the sequence. The final line, especially ('Ah, too . . .'), suggests a speaker still apprehending the full implications of her thought. At first sight line 1 appears somewhat opaque—not because it is literally untrue, but rather because the reader is uncertain where relevance is to be sought. The remaining lines guide the reader through a step-wise adjustment of the concept BEE via a nested sequence of secondary metaphors. Line 2 begins the task by drawing attention specifically to SONG, or rather to a pragmatically modified version of that concept (SONG*): the reader interprets the speaker as meaning neither that fame nor bees literally sing but—more loosely—that fame proclaims itself, just as the bee announces its own presence with its buzz. Here the poem

---

[19] Paula Rubio-Fernández, 'Suppression in metaphor interpretation: differences between meaning selection and meaning construction', *Journal of Semantics*, 24 (2007), 345–71.

[20] Dickinson, *Complete Poems*, p. 713.

[21] That is, speaker and reader collude in producing what Terence Cave calls a 'passing theory'. See Chapter 9, especially pp. 171–2.

names what relevance theorists would call an 'emergent property': songfulness is not normally considered an attribute of either FAME or BEE, but has nonetheless become salient in the process of pragmatic adjustment that each concept undergoes in the presence of the other. Then, line 3 specifies a further aspect of BEE to which the reader should attend. Unlike SONG, STING in this case constitutes an encyclopaedic feature of the head-concept BEE: through it we infer the speaker's view of fame as potentially dangerous to its possessor (STING*). Finally, in line 4, the reference to the bee's 'wing' concludes the explication: fame is liable to take flight at any moment; it has an evanescent quality liable to fade (WING*). Dickinson could have expected this last property of fame to become especially salient for a reader familiar (as she certainly would have been) with Virgil's winged 'Fama', the goddess of rumour.

In spite of such cases, it still may be no accident that when seeking an example of 'the lingering of the literal' Robyn Carston should have hit upon Dickinson. Precisely because Dickinson seems so invested in the force or—as we sometimes find—weakness of her metaphors, her verse routinely foregrounds literal meaning even (especially) in contexts that, rhetorically speaking, we would describe as analogical. On certain occasions, such as in 'My Life had stood – a Loaded Gun', the literal persists as an effect of 'meta-representation' (Mode 2 processing). But Dickinson's poetry also contains numerous other instances of literal lingering, as we shall see. In some more explicit cases, the literal seems to assert itself very directly against the analogical dimension of poetry in general; in others, the extent of the lingering effect—and the boundary between Carston's two modes—is far harder to determine.

At its most explicit, the lingering of the literal in Dickinson can take the form of an outright provocation—to read for similitude only to find it wilfully obstructed:

> As if some little Arctic flower
> Upon the polar hem –
> Went wandering down the Latitudes
> Until it puzzled came
> To continents of summer –
> To firmaments of sun –
> To strange, bright crowds of flowers –
> And birds, of foreign tongue!
> I say, As if this little flower
> To Eden, wandered in –
> What then? Why nothing,
> Only, your *inference* therefrom![22]

In its playful insistence on the act of speaking ('I say') and comprehension ('What then?'), this poem trades out loud on our expectation that poets say one thing so as to mean another. Strictly speaking, these lines are built around something closer to a simile (though as well as suggesting similitude 'As if some little Arctic flower' also conveys a powerful hint of the counterfactual), not a metaphor; and, according

---

[22] Dickinson, *Complete Poems*, p. 86.

to relevance theory, similes do not prompt the construction of ad hoc concepts but leave the literal content of the comparator intact (LITTLE ARCTIC FLOWER). Nonetheless, by the end of the poem Dickinson achieves an effect not dissimilar to the 'meta-representation' of 'My Life had stood – a Loaded Gun'. Dickinson knows her readers will expect an equivalent for the little Arctic flower. Some may anticipate an ironic self-portrayal: perhaps this delicate Northern bloom will be revealed to be a proxy for the speaker herself, stumbling puzzled and sunstruck upon her own exotic visions.[23] In the event, however, 'as if' sets up the expectation of a 'so then' which never arrives, throwing the reader back at the poem's close upon the work of 'inference'. The implied intonation and phrasing is strangely at odds in these concluding lines. The emphasis ('*inference*'—underlined in the manuscript) is Dickinson's own, and appears to mark a mock-triumphant appeal to some clinching term of art. For a relevance theorist, the term is of course strikingly apt, since the search for inferences and implications that help to satisfy expectations of relevance is precisely what guides the interpretation process in general, and the construction of ad hoc concepts in particular. Yet at the same time 'why nothing' and 'only, your inference' seem gleefully deflationary. 'Mere' inference is all I leave you, reader, the poet seems to say: you work out my meaning. Unless one also counts the strange, lingering image of a tiny plant, perhaps walking on its stem or roots, 'wandering' south into Eden…[24]

Whereas 'As if some little Arctic flower' prolongs the literal image by eliding the analogy altogether, other poems achieve a similar effect by merely deferring it until the very end:

> I stepped from plank to plank
> So slow and cautiously;
> The stars about my head I felt,
> About my feet the sea.
>
> I knew not but the next
> Would be my final inch, –
> This gave me that precarious gait
> Some call experience.[25]

The metaphorical kernel of this poem is a comparison between a 'precarious gait' and 'experience'. A Lakoffian reading would probably begin (and possibly end)

---

[23] On the intimacy between the poet and sunlight in Dickinson's 'imaginative garden', see Barker, *Lunacy of Light*, pp. 104–6.

[24] That plants should walk (rather than, say, roll, spin, or fly) is of course another 'inference' of a different order, derived from our pre-conscious sense of how human and human-like bodies move across space. Terence Cave discusses a similar inference fleetingly prompted by the ambiguous road-sign 'Heavy Plant Crossing'; see Terence Cave, *Thinking with Literature: Towards a Cognitive Criticism* (Oxford: Oxford University Press, 2016), pp. 93–4. None of this is to deny that the reader's cultural archive is also put to work: it is possible that Dickinson's repeated reference to 'wandering' (ll. 3 and 10) in proximity to 'Eden' is supposed to recall the final lines of Milton's *Paradise Lost* ('They, hand in hand, with wandering steps and slow, / Through Eden took their solitary way').

[25] Dickinson, *Complete Poems*, pp. 416–17.

there, explicating Dickinson's conceit as an elegant expansion of LIFE IS A JOURNEY.[26] And yet the poem itself does not begin there; it begins with a 'literal' description— of a particular precarious gait in a particular setting—which is not going to be assigned a metaphorical function until the poem's final lines.[27] (We might contrast this structure with Macbeth's 'Life is…a poor player', where the poor player is known to function metaphorically from the start.) So what does the reader do on a first reading, as he processes the image of the poet stepping gingerly across the sea? Even though he is not yet warned of the comparison with 'experience', he is unlikely to entertain this image as a *purely* literal one. This is a poem, and moreover an Emily Dickinson poem: he expects some metaphorical equivalence to be brought in sooner or later; what is more, he knows (from poems like 'As if some little Arctic flower…') that Dickinson knows that he expects this. For this reason there may be grounds for saying that the reader 'meta-represents' the literal content of the poet's walk across the planks, holding it over in anticipation that it will yield metaphorical relevance downstream. When the last lines' comparison with 'experience' ultimately confirms this expectation, the reader can begin to process the workings of the metaphor in full. This procedure really gets underway upon *re*-reading, at which point it can be determined that 'planks' are the stages of life, perhaps, 'stars' and 'seas' its unfathomable mysteries, the 'final inch' the calamity awaiting a misstep or poor decision, and so forth. Short poems know they will be re-read, and countless numbers invite this procedure, in which the image-framing, 'mind's-eye' work of Mode 2 hands over to the inferential routines of Mode 1.

But there may be more to say about the particular quality of the literal that lingers in 'I stepped from plank to plank', even on re-reading. Even once we know for sure that the fate of the poet's steps is to be eventually taken up into metaphor, her balancing act continues to demand what Rubio-Fernández calls our 'attentional resources'. It is perhaps worth asking how. So far I have been using the language of 'imagery', as if it were self-evident that the speaker's 'precarious gait' forms some kind of picture in our heads. But should we really talk of an image here? Possibly: of a frail American woman, perhaps, holding her skirts as night and tide close in. And yet the opening stanza also has an immersive force that is as much kinesic and proprioceptive as it is visual, as so often when we observe another person poised at the edge of a cliff or tall building, or walking the plank.[28] Dickinson's technique itself makes being dizzy less a matter of 'seeing stars' than

---

[26] For a Lakoffian approach to Dickinson's poetry (and to this poem in particular), see Margaret Freeman, 'Metaphor making meaning: Dickinson's conceptual universe', *Journal of Pragmatics*, 24 (1995), 643–66; see also, by the same author, 'A cognitive approach to Dickinson's metaphors', in G. Grabher, R. Hagenbüchle, and C. Miller (eds) *The Emily Dickinson Handbook* (Amherst, MA: University of Massachusetts Press, 1998), pp. 258–72. For a clear discussion of the divergences between the relevance theory and conceptual metaphor accounts, see Carston, 'Metaphor and the literal/non-literal distinction', pp. 484–90.

[27] Helen Vendler comments that the apparent literalness of this poem only subsides with the word 'inch' in line 6 (rather than the expected 'step'), after which point 'we know we are in allegory'; *Dickinson*, p. 369.

[28] On the activation and sustained qualities of kinesic effects in the verse of another American woman poet, Mary Oliver, see Kathryn Banks, Chapter 7 in this volume.

of feeling them. In 'The stars about my head I felt / About my feet the sea', the chiasmus of 'Stars'... 'felt'... 'feet'... 'sea' strives for balance at the very moment the speaker is most in danger of losing hers. The poet's 'precarious gait' registers in the reader's mind-body as something 'felt' as well as seen: the literal lingers in his bones.

Where exactly does this leave the final metaphor? I'd like to suggest that the salience of the literal may explain the speaker's faintly attenuated commitment to her closing conceit: not 'that precarious gait / I call', or 'we call', but *some* call experience'. 'I stepped' but 'some call': the speaker is evidently pleased with the clinching metaphor, but not so pleased that she is willing to lay claim to it as she does the first-person 'image' that dominates the poem. It seems tempting to conclude that, for Dickinson, the poem's gift to the reader need not be so much a clever metaphor—only a matter for others' 'inference'—as the momentary immersion in a 'literal' sea-walk or, in the earlier poem cited, the journey of a 'literal' 'artic flower'. But this may be to pit too hastily the literal against the metaphorical. What is most suggestive about Carston's account is that the quality of attention required for 'meta-representation'—Mode 2 processing—may make a 'literal' description not less, but all the more keenly experienced for arising in an atmosphere of metaphoricity. The image in the 'mind's eye' is sharpened, rather than dimmed, by the knowledge that it is 'only a metaphor'.

The poems considered so far have featured instances of Carston's 'meta-representation'. Another type of literal lingering in Dickinson comes closer to the cases of mixed metaphors invoked briefly earlier. This arises in poems involving what we might call serial metaphors (X is a P, X is a Q, X is a Y, and so on):

> Grief is a Mouse –
> And chooses Wainscot in the Breast
> For His shy House –
> And baffles quest –
>
> Grief is a Thief – quick startled –
> Pricks His Ear – report to hear
> Of that Vast Dark –
> That swept His Being – back –
>
> Grief is a Juggler – boldest at the Play –
> Lest if He flinch – the eye that way
> Pounce on His Bruises – One – say – or Three
> Grief is a Gourmand – spare His luxury –
>
> Best Grief is Tongueless – before He'll tell –
> Burn Him in the Public square –
> His Ashes – will
> Possibly – if they refuse – How then know –
> Since a Rack couldn't coax a syllable – now[29]

---

[29] Dickinson, *Complete Poems*, p. 387.

Serial metaphors pose a special challenge to the relevance-theoretic account. However complex, extended, or developed, most of the images considered in the relevance theory literature are singletons: 'my surgeon is a butcher', 'life is a poor player', 'fame is a bee', 'my life is a loaded gun', and so on. Were one to isolate each of the five metaphors offered in this poem—'Grief is a Mouse', 'Grief is a Thief', 'Grief is a Juggler', 'Grief is a Gourmand', 'Best Grief is Tongueless'—and ask for a relevance-theoretic account of each one, one might expect to come away satisfied. But things become more complex the moment we shift the focus of analysis from the single, autonomous metaphor to a series of metaphors operating over a poem as a whole.

In 'Grief is a Mouse' it seems intuitively right that a full understanding of this sequence would require more than just the sum of these five relevance-theoretic accounts, lined up in a row. Why? Because what needs explaining is the way in which the various metaphorical vehicles relate not just to grief, but also to the other members of the sequence. Dickinson has segmented the poem—in its stanzaic division—into what do indeed appear to be five discrete images. On one plausible reading each new metaphor might be interpreted as correcting, even cancelling, the one that precedes it, as if the poet were casting around for the image that best captures what it is like to grieve. This would be an instance of the rhetorical strategy *correctio* ('X, no not X, Y'). On a quite different reading we might infer an intention to build a cumulative, or even composite, metaphor: such that grief is a mouse and a thief and a juggler and so forth, or perhaps some weird hybrid of all these. It seems that bundled up with our answer to these questions will be some important local factors, for example what we consider to be the extent of the poet's commitment to each of her utterances—conjectural or declarative. But our answer will also rest more generally on the kind of life readers think metaphors lead.

Five metaphors for 'grief', then: as mouse, as thief, as juggler, as gourmand, and ('best') as victim of a public burning. One might expect that their rough distribution of a metaphor-per-stanza prompts the reader to process them discretely, one at a time. Although some Mode 2 processing may play a role here, these being both novel and minimally extended metaphors, Mode 1 dominates, as the reader constructs a series of ad hoc concepts likely to make sense of 'Grief is an X' (MOUSE*, THIEF*, JUGGLER*, etc.). Note how far the poet herself collaborates in this (as in 'Fame is a bee') by cueing the necessary adjustments in each case. For instance, the lines immediately following 'Grief is a Mouse' help to specify MOUSE* as something elusive and unwelcome dwelling at the very heart of one's being, not easily expelled. In 'Grief is a Juggler', JUGGLER* becomes somebody who performs for the powerful, and puts on a brave face for fear of revealing his vulnerability, and so on. The impression left by this succession of ad hoc concepts is of an invitation to approach the poet's subject by several distinct paths: not quite Wallace Stevens's 'Fourteen Ways of Looking at a Blackbird', but five different ways of imagining how it feels to grieve.

And yet this is not quite the whole story. Let's return to the first image of the mouse. On the Mode 1 ad-hoc-concept-by-ad-hoc-concept reading just proposed, we should normally expect the non-relevant encyclopaedic properties of this image to drop away once the reader embarks on processing the subsequent—seemingly distinct—metaphor 'Grief is a Thief'. But this is not quite what happens. The thief is furtive and wary; he is 'quick startled'; he 'pricks his ear'...like a mouse. Previously irrelevant encyclopaedic properties of MOUSE (restiveness, an acute sense of hearing) suddenly resurface in stanza 2. It does not end there. Looking forward to the third stanza, we find that the juggler is 'boldest at the Play' for fear that if he 'flinch', watching eyes will '*pounce* on his bruises'. Here the choice of 'pounce' serves to make newly salient another encyclopaedic feature of the earlier 'mouse': it may become the prey for a cat. What is going on here? Since there was no thought of mouse-ears until the thief, and none of pouncing cats before we reached the juggler, it seems that each image in the sequence has reactivated a previously dormant encyclopaedic property of MOUSE. The extent of this reactivation may even be wider than I've suggested so far. To my mind at least, the initial mouse image may even persist into the fourth stanza to suggest a particular kind of 'gour-mand': the kind which has not only 'chosen' but *gnawed* its way into its host's wainscot-breast. No doubt colluding in this sense is the familiar metaphor of grief as an emotion that 'gnaws' at the heart of the griever. And yet 'gnawing' is not spe-cifically implicated in either 'mouse' or 'gourmand'; it emerges as a result of the lingering of the literal.

If we take seriously the idea of the lingering literal in this poem, we can no longer speak of Dickinson's metaphors as producing a sequence of discrete ad hoc concepts, each cancelling the last. Across these ad hoc concepts loiters an increasingly composite suggestion of something else besides: of something fast-moving, nervous, and furtive. Insofar as it grows out from the encoded, supposedly discarded, components of the initial image, 'mouse', this is a literal something. But what exactly is the form that it takes? As in 'I stepped from plank to plank', it would be wrong to speak narrowly of *imagery* here. The Anglo-Saxon verb cluster at the heart of these stanzas—'quick startled', 'pricks', 'flinch', 'pounce'—carries information that seems more sensorimotoric than visual: I would propose that the literal lingers in this poem above all as a *movement*, and one not so much seen as felt in the bones or, more precisely, the muscles. Another of Dickinson's poems captures the poet's own receptivity to exactly this kinesic force:

> I never hear the word 'escape'
> Without a quicker blood,
> A sudden expectation,
> A flying attitude.[30]

Back to 'Grief is a mouse', and the effect is startling. We've become accustomed via a whole set of other, lexicalized metaphors to thinking of grief as something heavy (etymologically, heaviness is of course the literal kernel of words like 'sad' or 'grave'); but here on the contrary the 'attitude' conveyed across this poem is that of something light on its feet, twitchy, and primed for flight. Dickinson has created a

---

[30] Dickinson, *Complete Poems*, p. 40.

poem in which a supposedly distinctively human emotion is conveyed in a micro-drama of limbic, animal life.

## CONCLUSION

Dickinson left behind no formal poetics, and reconstructing even an informal one from her letters is no easy task. The word 'metaphor', for instance, occurs in her correspondence only once, and then in the playful, harum-scarum context of a Valentine letter addressed to George H. Gould, a friend of her brother's, and published in *The Indicator*, Amherst's monthly newspaper:

> I am Judith the heroine of the Apocrypha, and you the orator of Ephesus. That's what they call a metaphor in our country. Don't be afraid of it, sir, it won't bite. If it was my Carlo now! The Dog is the noblest work of Art, sir. I may safely say the noblest—his mistress's rights he doth defend—although it may bring him to his end—although to death it doth him send![31]

Metaphors don't bite—a deflationary account if ever there was one. Perhaps Dickinson's Valentine flirtation should not be taken too seriously. Her mock-reassurance as to the harmlessness of metaphor is a send-up—if not of Gould himself (he was by all accounts a brilliant student) then of the rather stolid, prosaic New England industrialists among their contemporaries at Amherst. The joke evokes, in order to mock, the view that metaphor represents a dangerous transgression of real-world constraints—a danger that seems only heightened through Dickinson's own identification with Judith, slayer of Holofernes. And yet if we do take Dickinson seriously for a moment, and follow her thought to the end, we find a phenomenon quite close to the one explored in these pages. The final three sentences feature a striking instance of the lingering of the literal. No sooner does Dickinson promise that her metaphors won't bite—itself a metaphor—than the literal content of 'bite' suddenly and comically interposes itself once more: the dog that does not bite becomes suddenly 'my Carlo', Dickinson's own pet Newfoundland. That the dog of all creatures should be considered, however comically, the 'noblest work of Art' may confirm the intuition of this chapter. For in the handful of poems considered here, the boldest elements of Dickinson's writing are those in which, even at its most metaphorical, literal meanings most doggedly insist.

---

[31] Emily Dickinson, *The Letters of Emily Dickinson*, edited by Theodora Ward and Thomas H. Johnson, 3 vols (Cambridge, MA: Harvard University Press, 1986), I, p. 92.

# Interlace 9

*These final two chapters, written by the editors, are not designed as a formal conclusion: the arguments and modes of analysis adopted by the other contributors are exploratory and open-ended, and the same remains true for these chapters. Answering to and at times echoing the jointly written Introduction, they serve rather as a double framing device. Chapter 9, beginning with detailed lyric effects of the kind analysed in Chapters 6–8, reflects in its own way on issues arising from the whole set of essays (ostension, inference, the array of implicatures, kinesis and the situatedness of cognition, 'intertextuality', emergent properties, the lyric and the narrative modes of relevance, to name only the most salient). It also argues for the value of relevance theory as a model that insists on the temporal dynamics of communication, as illustrated, for example, by the way that implicatures are endorsed or dropped ('cancelled') as a function of their perceived relevance. This temporal mode of analysis eschews formal labels and categories, together with the metaphor of literary discourse as a 'space'; it erodes the boundaries between rhetorical figures, and indeed between the literal and the figurative as such. Antithesis and 'paradox', it reminds us, are effects of our human logical bias, and are often unhelpful in exploring the untidy but astonishingly effective instruments of cognition that millions of years of evolution have bequeathed to us. That is the sense, above all, in which this essay sketches out a 'passing theory' of literary understanding.*

*The chapter ends with a short transition to Chapter 10, which has its own function as a reflective overview, this time from an authoritative relevance-theoretic standpoint. That final chapter thus requires no further interlace.*

# 9

# Towards a Passing Theory
# of Literary Understanding

*Terence Cave*

## INTRODUCTION

Relevance theory offers a dynamic model of communication where, as communicative utterances are constantly updated by the speaker, they demand a corresponding activity of adjustment on the part of the listener. As opposed to code models, it also makes full allowance for the unstated. In the communicative stream, the audible words (the sound-stream) cannot specify everything that is or might be meant. The spreading patterns they activate are never fully specifiable in verbal language for reasons given by Sperber and Wilson and subsequently developed by Robyn Carston in her discussion of the 'eternal sentences' problem: it simply isn't possible to imagine an exhaustively articulated verbal sequence that would capture all conceivable implicatures.[1] Language is radically underspecified because it is radically mobile, subject to the constraints of time. Hence relevance theory is an account of language on the wing, on the hoof, on the run, and of the strange cognitive pyrotechnics that arise from its passage, like the imaging of particles colliding in the Large Hadron Collider.

In the case of literary utterances, the potential time-scale of this reciprocal communicative activity is expanded in more than one sense. In the first place, literature slows the reader down, allows for reflective time as a matter of principle; that may indeed be one of the reasons why it has become such a major feature of human cultural evolution. Second, real-world urgency is suspended: the decoupling that is germane to literature in all its forms (and is one of its defining features) allows for leisurely extensions that would be catastrophic, for example, for a couple seeking to edge their way out of a tight marital corner. It allows for the writing and reading of sonnets and haikus, for an evening at the theatre, or for sleepless nights with Proust or Hilary Mantel or Karl Ove Knausgård. Third, the sheer length of a literary utterance may be considerable, as some of those examples self-evidently indicate. And finally, indefinite amounts of historical and cultural time may

---

[1] Dan Sperber and Deirdre Wilson, *Relevance: Communication and Cognition* (Oxford: Blackwell, 1995; 1st ed., 1986), pp. 91–3; Robyn Carston, *Thoughts and Utterances: The Pragmatics of Explicit Communication* (Oxford: Blackwell, 2002), pp. 2–3.

supervene between the moment of utterance and the moment of understanding and interpretation. We therefore need to ask two questions: How do incremental effects operate within the virtual time of utterance? And how does one effect become a platform or trigger for others? This chapter will look at how such effects manifest themselves in literary texts, at both the microscopic and the macroscopic scale. It will use as a leitmotif the notion of a 'passing theory', derived from Donald Davidson's brilliant essay on malapropism.[2] I have given the phrase a different (or at least a broadened) sense, but the question of malapropism is relevant here, too, together with the idea that the listener or reader's understanding of an utterance is always provisional, unfolding as it does in time.

## STEPPING STONES

My first example is an 'authentic' one, a fragment of dialogue heard in a local street. Two late-thirties men in business suits walk past, in the opposite direction to mine, so I only catch a tiny fragment of their conversation on the wing. One says to the other: 'He can't handle it; [short pause] he can't hack it.' The second phrase is accompanied by a vigorous downward right lower-arm movement, the hand flat at ninety degrees to horizontal, pivoting at the elbow, the kind of movement one makes when chopping (wood with an axe, meat with a cleaver, etc.).

The shift from 'handle' to 'hack' in this utterance is clearly critical. An expressive direction is established, then confirmed and intensified. 'Handle' is a lexicalized figure, a metaphor or a metonym; the rhetorical distinction between these two figures is in this case hard to maintain. We have here, in fact, a striking illustration of the proposition advanced by relevance theorists that metaphor and other figures can be analysed as instances of 'lexical broadening (or narrowing)': the notion of doing something with your hands is broadened to include a wide range of cases of performing a task successfully; or one might consider the shift from manual dexterity to psychological dexterity as an instance of the relation of natural or cultural contiguity which is a distinctive feature of metonymy. Whichever it is, it's certainly lexicalized; but it's not quite dead (as in the phrase 'a dead metaphor'). It arguably triggers a mental representation of 'handling' in its bodily sense: to make this salient, one need only compare 'handle' to more basic words like 'do'.

'Hack' is also lexicalized, in the sense that is most relevant here: it is synonymous with 'handle' (it carries approximately the same propositional content), and the shift from one to the other is also facilitated by the phonology of the two words (they alliterate). However, this colloquial sense of 'hack' is much more recent, and the speaker treats it as an incremental echo. You can handle something gently or tactfully, whereas those adverbs would make poor collocations with 'hack'.

[2] Donald Davidson, 'A nice derangement of epitaphs', in Ernest Lepore (ed.) *Truth and Interpretation: Perspectives on the Philosophy of Donald Davidson* (Oxford: Blackwell, 1986), pp. 433–46. By 'passing theory', Davidson means (roughly) the rapid construction of ad hoc suppositions that may be reinforced or discarded as the utterance proceeds. The precise sense he gives the expression is of course dependent on a complex set of philosophical arguments which I cannot attempt to reproduce here.

In addition, the speaker's hand gesture ostensively communicates a set of kinesic implicatures in which 'hacking' retains its literal sense. There are consequently emergent properties here: the concept HANDLE mediates the emergence of the properties associated with HACK, hence the formation of the ad hoc concept HACK*.

In short, (i) there is a rising intensity in this utterance, audible in the speaker's voice as well as in the eye-catching muscular activity accompanying the utterance of 'hack'. (ii) The shift 'handle–hack' is kinesic: this is embodied language of the kind that is often accompanied by more or less salient body movements. (iii) There is what one might call a transitional effect which is key to how the sequence works. I suggest that this transitional or 'passing' effect is in fact widespread in figurative uses of language, and indeed more generally in communicative-expressive uses of language.

Let us now consider a literary example, taken from Gerard Manley Hopkins's sonnet 'The Starlight Night':

> The grey lawns cold where gold, where quickgold lies![3]

The postponement of 'cold' in this line allows an immediate reduplication effect with 'gold'. The effect is similar to that of the 'handle–hack' dyad, but this time the synonymy is created only by the juxtaposition and the assonance; it is not available in the lexicon. On the other hand, 'gold' affords a new transition to 'quickgold', which is again a lexical construction, a neologism or catachresis or ad hoc figure: the reader infers 'quicksilver' as a lexical affordance for 'quickgold'.

But there is a further shift here. As soon as the implicature 'quicksilver' has been activated, the reader is impelled to adjust her evaluation of the sequence in favour of the mutually reinforcing implicatures of 'grey' and 'cold'—grey, cold, silver [moonlight]. And that in turn leads to a reappraisal of what 'gold' is doing here. At another level, once the line has been grasped and referred to the context of the sonnet as a whole, its mode of operation becomes not primarily perceptual, but conceptual, value-laden: gold is the traditional figure for rare and hidden value (hidden because it needs to be mined). This is a sonnet about the spiritual value immanent in the created world.

Note that this is not a static amalgam of figures, or a conceptual blending that can be represented diagrammatically. There is (again) a kinesic leaping movement from one lexical and figurative stepping stone to the next. Hopkins's line is an utterance in full flight, like the 'handle–hack' sequence, but at a higher level of complexity. Its continuity is associative. It isn't limited to the semantic domain of metaphor: the acoustic grouping of like items lasts just long enough to allow the semantic association to catch on. The 'logic' that affords this semantic association, furthermore, is situational, not rationalistic or analytic. Yet it isn't vague or indefinite. A spreading activation pattern is set in motion as new elements are added to the sequence, but those new elements also constrain the communicated effect: they establish a cumulative set of coordinates which fix the possibilities of

---

[3] Gerard Manley Hopkins, *The Poetical Works of Gerard Manley Hopkins*, edited by Norman H. MacKenzie (Oxford: Clarendon Press, 1990), p. 140.

meaning that a close reader will be left with by the end of the line. The delicate balance between proliferation and constraint is crucial to poetry, and (arguably) to 'good', 'successful' poetry.

## COLLOCATIONS AND CONTIGUITIES

This sketch of what one might call the 'cognitive momentum' of a single line leaves a good deal to be said about what it is that provides the momentum. To begin to address that issue, we might glance briefly at the linguistic phenomenon of collocation.[4] Collocations are robust constraints specifying which words can be juxtaposed in a given language and which can't. They are internalized (used unreflectively) by native speakers, but it may be difficult or even impossible to explain to a non-native speaker why a given collocation isn't allowed. Native speakers of English might say 'I'll take a quick look at the draft report while I'm on the fast train to London', but they never say 'I'll make a fast look at the draft report while I'm on the quick train to London.' They use the expressions 'walk tall' and 'fly high', but not 'walk high' and 'fly tall'.

It would be easy to assume that collocations are constrained by pure convention, that they are simply a phrasal instance of the supposedly arbitrary conventions governing lexical usage more generally. Yet it is intuitively evident that 'tall' and 'high' in standard uses of those adjectives belong to different sensorimotor maps. Tall things display vertical axes and have their feet on the ground; high things are not earthbound; they typically exhibit (relative) freedom from the constraints of gravity. So a 'tall mountain' is not seen in the same embodied perspective as a 'high mountain' (or more often 'the high mountains', conceived in terms of the sense of being on top, high up). 'Quick' connotes alertness rather than speed in itself, and is in special cases used of living things, as its etymological sense suggests ('the quick and the dead'; hence also 'quicksilver', 'quickgold'); 'fast' (the adjective) is typically a property of vehicles rather than of agents. These connotations may be partly lexicalized, or at least lexicalizable, but it would be hard to capture all of them in a dictionary without extensive lists of examples. They map the sensorimotor world differently in different natural languages, since there are many ways of mapping the same spectrum of sensorimotor responses, but one can assume, I think, that a map in that sense (a virtual set of categories) is involved in all cases. Which would explain why collocational constraints are robust without being reducible to rules.

The constraints of collocation, then, are a fundamental aspect of the linguistic infrastructure. Similar constraints operate also for coinages, whether of single words or phrases: they can be transgressed or bypassed by skilled users of a language

---

[4] The account I give here is inflected both by the literary contexts I am concerned with and by the broader set of arguments in play in this volume. For a more technical overview, see Tomas Lehecka, 'Collocation and colligation', in J.-O. Östman and J. Verschueren (eds) *Handbook of Pragmatics* (Amsterdam: John Benjamins, 2015; DOI 10.1075/hop.19.col2); Gill Philip, *Colouring Meaning: Collocation and Colligation in Figurative Language* (Amsterdam: John Benjamins, 2011), explores the ways in which collocation operates in the figurative domain.

(poets, rappers, stand-up comedians, clever story-tellers, and others), who push the boundaries in ways that appear satisfyingly creative to other users. But the elasticity only goes so far: neologisms have to take their place in some plausible way in the natural linguistic ecology. Some work, some don't. 'Gobsmacked' seems to have entered the English language in the second half of the twentieth century, and—like it or not—it has been enormously successful. It is a word with powerful motor resonances that include the gesture of clapping one's hand to one's mouth in surprise ('I'm speechless, dumbstruck'), together with the implication of a blow delivered by another agent. It is these resonances, rather than a figurative mode of expression demanding a strictly inferential analysis, that seem to do the communicative work in this and similar cases. We may add here a false collocation which has become standard (that is to say, is no longer perceived as false): 'I was literally gobsmacked.' The standard sense of the procedural[5] 'literally' (insisting that a given expression is meant in its literal, not figurative sense, as in 'I was literally elbowed out of the way') has nowadays been broadened to promote the revival of the literal sense of an expression that has been eroded through frequent use, as in this wonderful authentic example quoted on the BBC Radio 4 Today programme: 'Now that she's been promoted, the world is literally her oyster.'[6]

For a relatively conservative speaker, this last example will require an abruptly revised passing theory accompanied by perlocutionary amusement or annoyance (since the effect was presumably not intended by the speaker); in other words, it closely resembles malapropism, which is the instance on which Davidson hangs his notion of a passing theory. If it is used often enough in the broadened sense, 'literally' will require a decreasing degree of adjustment until it becomes an accepted procedural expression belonging to the class that includes 'like' ('I like pushed him to do it'), which ensures that cognitive momentum is sustained and indeed enhanced despite the introduction of relatively unfamiliar or disconcerting terms.

This excursion into adjacent territories is designed to demonstrate that the robustness of collocations on the one hand and, on the other, the amused or irritated revision of a passing theory required by malapropism, transgressive collocation, or ad hoc collocation, are mirror images of one another. In continuous everyday speech between native speakers, robustness becomes a kind of dynamic elasticity, a casual acrobatics that makes light work of grammatical, lexical, and phonological lapses, incoherences, incomplete utterances, and the like. In poetry, where there is a contract of trust between reader and poet such that the poet can expect enhanced

---

[5] This term is borrowed from debates in relevance theory circles about the value of a conceptual–procedural distinction. It was originally proposed by Diane Blakemore in her study *Semantic Constraints on Relevance* (Oxford: Blackwell, 1987); for a brief account, see Carston, *Thoughts and Utterances*, pp. 160–4. Procedural expressions are those whose function is not to communicate concepts but to indicate the way in which the concepts in question are to be interpreted (a simple example would be the different functions of definite and indefinite articles in English). It is generally acknowledged that the distinction is not clear-cut and that many lexical items have both a conceptual and a procedural function.

[6] I failed to take a note of the date on which this broadcast went out (perhaps in 2015?), and equally cannot guarantee that I have remembered the exact wording. But the crucial elements ('literally' plus the oyster) are certainly authentic.

acceptance of the unexpected ('poetic licence'), the passing theory will need to be constantly rebooted as it feeds on an enriched diet of procedurals, motor reson-ances, and sensory supplements (this diet, and the reader's ability to digest it, will of course always be culturally variable).

One further point needs to be clarified here. I said that the cognitive momentum of 'the grey lawns cold, where gold...' was associative and situational. The associ-ation of two near-homonyms is not in itself situational: presumably, the contexts in which a child learns the words 'cold' and 'gold' are likely to be quite different. The association is opportunistic, seizing on one of the innumerable accidents of language to encourage the reader to adopt a passing theory that encompasses the meanings of the two words and their most likely situational cluster of associations (including, in the wider context of the poem, the reflection of light, beauty, precious substances). 'Gold', in other words, is primed to display emergent properties. These processes are, one must suppose, enabled by a variety of procedural memory, an unreflective memory of both real-world experiences and their embodiment in other poems, other canonic expressions; and if this cognitive model is correct, they must to a sufficient extent be available to both poet and reader (speaker and lis-tener), constituting a mutually manifest context. If that were not the case, the expectation of relevance would, for the reader, not be met: however relevant the poet thought a given phrase or sequence was, the reader would perceive it as arbi-trary or meaningless.

One could say, then, that there is a requirement for both perceived (and poten-tially reflective) relevance and embodied or situational relevance. The word 'require-ment' here only means that those conditions are necessary (or at least sufficient) if the line is to modify the cognitive environment of the reader. But it is also the case that the poet does some requiring, too, in the sense that poetry often challenges readers to make additional efforts to recover relevant contexts. As I have already suggested, in fact, the cognitive momentum of Hopkins's line (in the context of the whole poem) is initiated and sustained by an agent who does unexpected things and expects you to trust him[7] to have relevant reasons for doing them. This could be described, from the reader's position, as having a passing theory of the author.

## PASSING ECHOES

Hopkins's poetry is full of echoes: the six-syllable segment '...cold, where gold, where quickgold' contains two echoes of the syllable '*old', and one repetition each of 'where' and 'gold'. The echoes are both acoustic and semantic: the sense of '*old', and indeed of 'gold' itself, mutates with the shifting micro-context of the line.[8] 'Where' is perhaps better treated as a procedural expression: the repetition

---

[7] I use the gender appropriate for Hopkins, not for an anonymous speaker.

[8] The asterisk is designed to indicate that the syllable in question is not to be read as the lexical item *old*, the sense of which, if it occurs at all to the reader, will no doubt be immediately filtered out ('cancelled in context', as the relevance theory phrase goes), since it contributes nothing relevant to the emergent 'passing theory'.

tells you insistently that the semantic gold is to be found in this line, as well as in the nocturnal scene the poem conjures up. Although the density of acoustic repetition (rhythmic as well as phonetic) is exceptional in Hopkins's work, the effects themselves are common to poetry across a wide range of cultures. Cradle-songs, work-songs, medieval alliterative verse, and many other varieties of poetry are marked by the same echoic effects. At the most general level, ostensively organized echoic devices—patterns of rhyme or assonance, isometric structures, use of refrains, and the like—could indeed to be said to be what makes poetry recognizable as such.[9] Classical rhetoric, too, always made plenty of space for echoic effects, whether of sound, lexis, or sense (conduplicatio, anaphora, adnominatio, anadiplosis, epistrophe, epizeuxis, and so on).

We return here to a topic broached in the Introduction. Suppose that speaker A asks, 'Where's Charlie?'; speaker B responds, 'Charlie's gone home', and A says, 'Gone home?' Or take this sentence: 'My childhood days are gone—gone!'[10] In each of those instances, there is an immediate and palpably ostensive repetition of a word or phrase. In the first example, the echo may (depending on context) be a mark of surprise, annoyance, or even contempt; in the second, the iteration is likely to imply an emotive resonance, a sense of finality, as well as an insistence on the non-triviality of the remark: the speaker wants her listener to take her seriously, feel the force of her pathos. Or again, as in the examples of irony cited in the Introduction, the echo of what is normally a positive assertion is contextually understood to have a negative implicature: 'That's fantastic. Just fantastic' (note that the implicature would be triggered here in spoken dialogue by the use of a flat tone which is at odds with the hyperbolic 'fantastic', written as 'fantastic!').

As we remarked in the Introduction, verbal irony is related to varieties of tacit quotation or allusion that have been widely studied in literary works. Another way of putting it would be to say that verbal irony is at the sharp end of the spectrum of echoic utterances, the end with the greatest tension, conflict, or reversal of meaning;[11] at the other end, what is perceived as a possible echo (of something previously said, of a single word even) fades out into a mere accident of language use, since language is in practice made up of a finite set of elements where the same elements are bound to recur. Even if we set aside these 'weak' instances and specify that the echo must in some sense be ostensive or marked (a principle we shall come back to shortly), the spectrum itself is a broad one: the local echoic effects that

---

[9] On pattern recognition as a fundamental aspect of the reading process, see Brian Boyd, *Why Lyrics Last: Evolution, Cognition, and Shakespeare's Sonnets* (Cambridge, MA: Harvard University Press, 2012); pattern recognition as a feature of brain function is also a recurrent theme in Paul Armstrong, *How Literature Plays with the Brain: The Neuroscience of Reading and Art* (Baltimore, MD: The Johns Hopkins University Press, 2013).

[10] This example was first used by Sperber and Wilson, *Relevance*, p. 219; it was taken up again by Adrian Pilkington in a section on epizeuxis (see *Poetic Effects: A Relevance Theory Perspective* (Amsterdam: John Benjamins, 2000), pp. 123–31).

[11] For an illuminating analysis of varieties of literary allusion, citation, and quotation in Renaissance literature (when literary 'imitation' was a common, and widely debated, practice), see Thomas M. Greene, *The Light in Troy: Imitation and Discovery in Renaissance Poetry* (New Haven, CT; London: Yale University Press, 1982), pp. 44–6. Greene regards ironic and adversarial ('agonistic') allusion and citation as the mode in which the writer distances herself most expressly from the quoted or cited text.

characterize Hopkins's line or my invented examples are also apparent at higher levels of organization (where 'higher' simply means 'on a larger scale'). A broad distinction can be made here between echoic effects (whether local or global) which are internal to an utterance or text, and those that are external. The latter would, in the literary field, characteristically be echoes of other (usually comparable) texts; but of course the echoed utterance might also be non-literary.

Echoic effects are above all a way of marking structure: musical works demonstrate that function in its most tangible (audible) form. As I remarked earlier, marked structure is a distinctive feature of all literary forms, even modern ones where the refusal to mark structure is understood by the reader or spectator as a deliberate absence of echoic marking. At another level again, it is also a feature of aesthetic framing: whether the work of art purports to refer to the world or other art-works or both, it is saying 'look again at this', 'listen again to this'.

This is in one sense a truism. What would we gain by thinking of all these different kinds of effect as 'echoic'? Let's take a series of specifically literary examples. At the largest possible scale, Dante's *Divine Comedy* 'echoes' Virgil's *Aeneid*: we know that because Dante is guided in his journey through Hell and Purgatory by Virgil's ghost. This fictional Virgil, a pagan poet who walks and talks in the Christian afterlife, is about as ostensive as you can get when writers signal their echoic effects. By contrast, Virgil's own *Aeneid*, which is very much closer to the Homeric epics in virtually every other respect, features no such ostensive signal: Aeneas visits the underworld, but Homer isn't there (it seems). For any ancient or modern reader familiar with the cultural encyclopaedia of the Graeco-Latin world, the signal simply isn't necessary, any more than I need to make an ostensive signal when I drive past you in the pouring rain, wind down the window, and say 'Hop in' (although winding down the window could of course count as a signal, since it affords my speech-act). There is plenty of evidence that Henry James's *The Portrait of a Lady* intentionally (if not ostensively) echoes George Eliot's *Daniel Deronda* both in the character of Gwendolen and in her disastrous choice of a husband, similarities that are likely to be recognized by an informed reader. Further down the line, however, the similarities may, although striking, possibly be accidental: the current (2016) storyline in *The Archers* in which Helen is offered a kitchen knife by her controlling husband Rob and told to kill herself, but stabs and nearly kills him instead, is arguably an echo of Frank Wedekind's *Lulu*, where Schön gives Lulu a gun to shoot herself with; Lulu shoots him instead, and ends up in jail. The people who write soap-opera scripts are likely to be familiar with modern European literature, especially theatre, and the configuration is striking. But we are clearly here moving down the spectrum to the point where the echoic effect is a function of what particular readers happen to have read, and what becomes cognitively salient for them at a given moment. As it happens, the controlling husband and the wife who causes him harm are both present in *Daniel Deronda*, and a similar thread emerges in the second series of the television drama *Indian Summers*, where Alice's refusal to open the car in the final episode leads (as she knows it will) to her husband's death. These echoes in the popular modern media cannot be said to be ostensive in any standard sense of the word, but they have the effect of creating a cognitive network of references that places at the focus of attention a present-day concern for the plight of women trapped by abusive husbands.

The domain of the echoic, whatever the level at which it operates, self-evidently includes the wear-and-tear effects that are referred to as conventions, topoi, clichés, and the like. In a relevance theory perspective, such phenomena would be acknowledged as the literary equivalent of a general linguistic phenomenon, apparent also in the widely discussed case of 'dead' metaphor. In that perspective, what would be salient is the mutually manifest context within which the speaker and the audience calculate (whether reflectively or pre-reflectively) the degree of wear and tear and its effect on the overall expressive dynamics of the utterance. There can never be such a thing as an intrinsically outworn echoic reference, since the speaker may find ways of rehabilitating or refreshing the echo, or use its very dilapidation as an expressive effect (ironically echoing, perhaps, those who use such references). Thus Robert Burns's famous line 'My love's like a red, red rose' is echoic at various levels: it uses an intrinsic echo ('red, red') to give an expressive lift to the utterance; it refers by implication to a whole tradition of such love-poems and their echoic comparisons; and it also suggests, by its very use of the conventional, the idiom of a popular song, an echo of the everyday.

The passing effect of the echoic 'red' in this line demonstrates that the slightest manipulation of a well-worn expression can make a vast difference. It also shows that what is at stake in many such cases is not an abstract mental procedure but (as in the examples we began with) a sensorimotor effect. Not only is the sensory redness of the rose insistently offered to our attention; the repetition is also rhythmic, and the passing motor beat of the rhythm (three stressed syllables in a row) is reinforced acoustically by the alliteration of 'red' with 'rose' as well as with itself. That analysis is entirely within the domain of a first-stage critical study of literature, except that it completely changes the frame of reference of such readings: it makes sense of the effects as part of an overall cognitive perspective, rather than taking them to be conventional aspects of a folk reading. Wear and tear, indeed, is not restricted to the realm of poetry: it is also apparent in poetics, calling for a refamiliarizing mutation.

It is essential to emphasize that the effects we are speaking of here are dependent not only on the recognition of a literary domain in which texts echo or refer to one another, but also on the degree to which a given expressive formulation is kinesically relayed to another reader (perhaps one from a quite different time and culture). In other words, the quality of reading as an experience of the world is always at stake in the domain of the echoic, whether in the tiny refracted echoes afforded by lyric poems or in the more substantial and wide-ranging instances referred to earlier: *Lulu* and *The Archers*, *Daniel Deronda* and *The Portrait of a Lady*, *Indian Summers*. The echoic has a cognitive purpose, one which would be negated if the echo became a mere abstract or 'textual' reverberation. The cognitive purpose shifts with the passing of time and cultural context, as well as with the individual perspectives afforded by authors, but it always presupposes a relation to the experienced world: an extra-textual relation, one might say.

That relation is equally at work where novels ostensibly draw attention to the cultural wear and tear that leads characters to confuse a textual world (other novels) with authentic experience. In such cases, the outworn fictional convention is used as the springboard—the affordance—for a leap into an experience of special intensity: a revelation or recognition. Edith Wharton's story 'The Long Run' stages a jaded middle-aged man (Halston Merrick) narrating the story of how he pusillanimously failed to grasp the opportunity offered him by an intelligent and beautiful married woman (Paulina Trant). He meets her bold move (she comes to him openly, with her suitcase packed) with a string of gendered commonplaces of the type 'I would fail in my duty as an honourable man if I let you ruin your reputation in this way.' At the time, he believes in them himself, and thinks that her response ('There was no other way') to his implied reproach 'If only you hadn't come to me here!' was itself 'like some hackneyed phrase in a novel that she had used without any sense of its meaning'.[12] Later, however, Merrick sees in a flash of insight that she had set up this scene in the expectation that he would behave exactly as he did:

> I remember, in particular, starting up in bed one sleepless night as there flashed into my head the meaning of her last words: 'There was no other way'; the phrase I had half-smiled at at the time, as a parrot-like echo of the novel heroine's stock farewell. ... As the idea came to me it was as if some ironic hand had touched an electric button, and all my fatuous phrases had leapt out on me in fire.   (pp. 352–3)

The irony and the echoic effect are repeated three years later when, after the accidental death of Paulina's husband, Merrick visits her with the intention of proposing marriage: 'But there, between us, was the memory of the gesture I hadn't made, forever parodying the one I was attempting! There wasn't a word I could think of that hadn't an echo in it of words of hers I had been deaf to' (p. 354).

Cognitively speaking, there is a lot going on in this denouement. Merrick's passing theory of what Paulina Trant had meant by her phrase, or rather of the preset implicatures it affords when correlated with standard novels, turns out to be wrong. He is the one who speaks in clichés; he is the cardboard figure of the 'honourable man' who is really only a coward. Once that inversion has retrospectively taken effect, it can't be undone. Merrick has finally acquired the epistemic vigilance that Paulina had exercised all along, but the consequence is that any proposal he makes to her now would be fatally undermined by the echoic irony of its formulation: he would be parroting back to her, in a context from which risk has now been excluded, the very words she used when the stakes were at their highest. And what the reader *feels* here, triggered by the delayed readjustment of a passing theory, is the reverberation of a double disaster: a vision of two lives ruined.

The echo-chamber that is particular to this story could easily be expanded by including Wharton's 'Autres temps...', which offers another variant of this whole-life story, together with another retrospective unmasking of inauthenticity, or Henry

---

[12] Edith Wharton, 'The Long Run', in *The New York Stories of Edith Wharton*, edited by Roxana Robinson (New York: The New York Review of Books, 2007), pp. 350–1 (the story was first published in 1912).

James's better-known (but by comparison overheated and melodramatic) story 'The Beast in the Jungle'. American readers of the period when these stories were published would certainly have recognized the affinities, and thus the array of implicatures that flow from their mutual repositionings. Few writers have captured better than Wharton and James the ironies lurking behind echoed codes and conventions; few have more powerfully manipulated apparently banal utterances to display the moral and existential undertow on which they are borne, implicatures recognized always too late by speakers and listeners as they are dragged down to their ruin.

Expand the echo-chamber again and it will inevitably include Flaubert, whose fascination with outworn speech conventions was such that he compiled a *Dictionnaire des idées reçues*. Flaubert is often regarded as a pessimistic writer, even a nihilistic one, but his relentless unmasking of the conventional is perhaps best viewed as a marker or limit-case for the calibration of all the most fine-tuned implicatures that can be coaxed out of the finite set of words and expressions available to him.[13] Wider again, and we are in the storyworld of *Don Quixote*, where the error of thinking that a set of codes can implement a lived reality is so richly handled that, more than almost any other fiction of its day (Shakespeare is as ever the obvious exception), it delivers an overwhelming sense of the human and the humane: the spring of irony releases that sense by ensuring in advance that the reader won't be deceived by a conventional fiction.

In such ways, echoes and the echoic are intrinsic to the literary canon, the very function of which is to comprise a large and resonant echo-chamber. Instead of focusing exclusively on the ideological construction and deconstruction of canons (although worrying about such things may also be a constituent of the epistemic vigilance that good readings demand), one might indeed claim that a canon is precisely what affords the possibility of cognitively rich echoes.

At the broadest level, then, the relevant point here, the point that makes relevance theory helpful for us, is that in the large and permissive thought-world that we are calling 'literature' there will always be on the reader's or spectator's side a calculus of echoic effect. Whether the effect is triggered will depend in part on the writer's ostensive posture; but it also depends on a whole suite of modes of cognitive attentiveness (the word 'cognitive' is of course more or less redundant in this phrase, but I leave it ostensively in to keep us on track), which are themselves dependent on the possibilities afforded by what the reader knows, her personal 'encyclopaedia'.

This account might seem to give too much credit to reflective modes of awareness, and potentially to a kind of literary cleverness: the prize goes to the literary buff who can detect the greatest number of 'echoes', or the least obvious ones. That objection is met by recalling that the process we are talking about here is one fundamental to all language use; its effects (together with the audience's calculus of those effects), even where they are subsequently subject to a reflective analysis, are

---

[13] See also Guillemette Bolens (Chapter 3 in this volume) on the subliminal echoes that mark the kinesic trajectories of *Madame Bovary*.

pre-reflective. They are also intimately connected, as are all cognitive processes, with the embodied responses that are relayed by language and thus also by literature.

Although the communicative resources of a given culture necessarily operate within the general constraints and possibilities of human cognition, the poetics of the echo is culturally bound and therefore shifts according to the historical and cultural point of reference. Renaissance theories of *imitatio* and the reading expectations they imply allow for much more salient echoic practices (rewritings of Petrarchan sonnets, Horatian odes, Sophoclean or Senecan tragedy, Terentian comedy, and many other similar forms of *imitatio*) than is the case in the modern period.[14] In modern poetics, the term which has most often been used to designate an inclusive category of close or putative textual encounters is 'intertextuality'. The success of this term, its pervasiveness in modern critical language, is such that one is obliged to ask why it should not be used instead of the relevance theory term 'echoic'.

The first answer would be that it first arose in a theoretical context that expressly sought to remove from the critical scene all traces of the author and her intentions.[15] Textuality, it was argued, was neutral, relieved of the humanistic assumptions that had surrounded the notion of a literary 'work'; intertextuality was a dialogue of texts, not of people. The word has since been used so widely that, for most users, it has lost these associations, or carries them only as weak implicatures. It is clearly convenient (otherwise it wouldn't have been so successful), above all, perhaps, because it is so conveniently neutral in the ordinary sense of that word. It makes no overt cultural assumptions,[16] and is only marginally metaphorical: it gestures, perhaps, towards a space in which 'texts' can meet and mingle. Yet its neutrality and its near-abstraction are liable to erase the situational and kinesic energies that course through intertextual encounters. The term 'echoic' is more dynamic, more rooted in general language use (as in the 'handle–hack' example). It is also temporal: an echo occurs in a time-frame dictated (in nature) by the speed of sound, an interval which can imaginatively be dilated ('broadened', to use the relevance theory expression) to encompass even the obscure reaches of historical time ('an echo from the past'). It is like a Doppler effect: as it fades, or is amplified, or replaced by other echoes, its movement through cultural time and space is marked. And above all, we think of echoes predominantly as voiced sound; there can be purely physical echoes, of course (the echo of an explosion in the mountains), but the echoic is situated in the domain of the speaking or singing voice.

---

[14] Robert Herrick's collection of poems entitled *Hesperides*, discussed by Raphael Lyne as an 'array' of voices (Chapter 2, pp. 44–8), provides a clear example of the way in which poems in Renaissance collections and cycles echo one another while also echoing earlier poetry in the same generic tradition.

[15] It is generally agreed that the term was first used in two essays published by Julia Kristéva in 1966–7 and then disseminated more widely in her major work *Sèméiotikè. Recherches pour une sémanalyse* (Paris: Tel Quel, 1969). The later outgrowth of terminology built around the notion of 'text' (hypertext, paratext, etc.) was of course largely the work of Gérard Genette, who systematized modern poetics within this perspective.

[16] But clearly it makes some cultural assumptions—those, broadly, of our own day, and of the 'western' academic consensus.

Echo can indeed be personified, turned into a myth, a metamorphosis that would be hard to imagine for the formal term 'intertextuality'.[17]

## TOWARDS A PASSING THEORY OF NARRATIVE

Before proceeding to further macro-examples of what in this chapter I have called a 'passing theory', it may be helpful to recall Roman Jakobson's famous opposition between the syntagmatic and the paradigmatic axis of communication. The syntagmatic axis is the constantly evolving forward-moving thread of syntactic and logical relation; the paradigmatic axis is constituted by the synchronic possibilities available at each point, expressed as the field of synonymous and related terms and metaphorical (or more broadly figurative) substitutions. Both are present in all forms of communication, but in everyday language and pragmatic, function-related discourse, the syntagmatic is dominant, while in literary discourse, especially lyric poetry, the paradigmatic moves into the foreground.[18] This opposition may be reframed in cognitive terms as a trade-off between sequence and simultaneity. It is precisely the point of a 'passing theory' to preserve the balance between these two poles, which must necessarily intersect: there can be no question here of an excluded middle, only of a point of intersection on two virtual gradients. The brain 'knows' a very large number of things (including of course not only lexical items, but also traces of sensorimotor responses, rhythms, sounds, experiential echoes: episodic, procedural, and semantic memories) that it can potentially bring to bear at a given moment if the appropriate retrieval systems are triggered. Augustine's famous model of the reading of a hymn (itself a remarkably precocious passing theory) is designed to display just this point of intersection, although in a metaphysical rather than a purely cognitive perspective:

> What holds for the whole hymn holds for the individual parts of it too, and the individual syllables, and for the longer performance (of which the hymn is only a part): and in a whole human life, the parts of which consist of all the actions of that human individual; and in the whole age of the children of men, the parts of which consist of the lives of every human being.[19]

Following Augustine's example, I propose now to explore this set of issues (broadly, the relation between sequence and simultaneity) with the instruments of literary

---

[17] On the use of this term, see also, in this volume, the Introduction (p. 17), and in particular the contributions of Boehmer (Chapter 1) and Williams (Chapter 6), who both use the term in what I would regard as the 'weak' sense (the one compatible with the principles of relevance theory).

[18] Jakobson calls this '[the projection of] the principle of equivalence from the axis of selection into the axis of combination'; see Roman Jakobson, 'Closing statement: linguistics and poetics', in Thomas A. Sebeok (ed.) *Style in Language* (Cambridge, MA: The MIT Press, 1960), pp. 350–77 (p. 358).

[19] St Augustine, *Confessions*, edited and translated by Carolyn J.-B. Hammond (Cambridge, MA: Harvard University Press, Loeb Classical Library, 2016), ch. XI, p. 255. The word that Hammond here translates as 'hymn' (Latin 'canticum') is often translated elsewhere as 'psalm'; it can also refer more widely to a 'song' or a 'poem'.

rather than conceptual analysis, and my examples will be taken this time from the more expansive literary configurations of narrative fiction.[20]

David Mitchell's novel *Cloud Atlas*[21] consists of five collocated narrative strands. Four of these are divided into two segments, the break often coming at unexpected and apparently arbitrary moments (one segment ends in the middle of a sentence). The first segment and the ninth form a complete narrative unit, as do the second and the eighth, the third and the seventh, the fourth and the sixth. The fifth is a complete sequence, placed in the centre of the novel's structure, which thus forms a kind of palindrome (although only in formal terms: if you chose to read the novel in reverse order of the segments, the effect would be different). The specificity of this structure implies a coherence which the collocations themselves don't immediately deliver: they are first experienced as breaks, as unfinished business, to an extent that exceeds the standard interlace of romance fictions. The fissures are salient because they are also temporal: the fictional time of the novel is extended first across two centuries of the recent past (as seen from the reader's present moment), then with increasingly large gaps into the distant future. As the palindrome passes through its return sequence, furthermore, it suggests that these fictions of the future are only eventualities, calculations of outcomes that could still be undone. In this sense, the sequential axis is both circular and self-questioning; what emerges above all is not an outcome but a virtual simultaneity. This emergence is afforded primarily by two narrative procedurals.[22] Most prominently, the very different central characters of the five fictional strands are associated through a birthmark that suggests that they are something like reincarnations (since there is no genetic line between them). But the title of the book also turns out to be the title of a musical work composed in the second and eighth segment, heard in the third, and turned into a commercial logo in the fourth; it connotes shifting patterns that may be interpreted in different ways, like shapes in the clouds. Hence the novel seeks to bring off a simulation of the intersecting dimensions of simultaneity and sequence, although of course it can only do this as a trade-off, which is ideally carried out in the reader's cognitive experience of reading it (as in Augustine's model). In such ways, *Cloud Atlas* deploys in the mode of narrative fiction the capturing of a passing theory that we observed in microscopic form in Hopkins's poem: the virtual complete set of implicatures can never be entirely present at a single moment, and their imaginative entropy is even evoked by the notion of a 'cloud atlas'; yet the novel ambitiously turns us continually back on the circle it describes so that the implicatures are progressively amplified rather than dissipated.

[20] The aim here is not to propose even in the sketchiest form a revised narratology drawing on relevance theory and other cognitive approaches. Despite a preliminary disclaimer, Gregory Currie's *Narrative & Narrators: A Philosophy of Stories* (Oxford: Oxford University Press, 2010) provides some solid critical starting-points for such a project (for the disclaimer, see p. vii). One of the problems one faces here is that the narratology of the last half-century has been resolutely formalist, a methodology that, implicitly if not explicitly, presupposes a code model of language and communication. Whether a resolutely anti-formalist narratology is possible remains to be seen.

[21] David Mitchell, *Cloud Atlas* (London: Hodder & Stoughton, 2004).

[22] The procedurals I refer to here, as my commentary indicates, belong to the mixed class of lexical items and expressions that have a conceptual as well as a procedural function (see above, note 5).

This is clearly, one might argue, a special case. But it is only special because it displays the character of the totalizing narrative fiction with a special reflective urgency.[23] Traces of a similar relation between sequence and simultaneity are apparent everywhere in the canon of the novel and may indeed be regarded as necessary effects of the cognitive status and function of the novel. There are even more extreme forms of apparently unmotivated collocation, such as the two intertwined narrative strands in William Faulkner's *The Wild Palms*, where the reader is faced with inferring associations in the absence of any clear authorial clues. There are cases like Flaubert's *Éducation sentimentale*, where simultaneity is built into the sequence through the repetition of similar scenarios (Frédéric's amorous and economic fiascos) and firmly buckled in place at the close: Frédéric and a friend, having searched their memories for significant moments, decide that the best thing that had happened to them was a visit to a prostitute that had taken place before the beginning of the fictional narrative itself and is not otherwise recorded therein. In a procession behind Frédéric, like the ghostly kings in *Macbeth*, stand the failed heroes of fictions from *Don Quixote* to Flaubert's own *Madame Bovary*, who achieve a strange sequential simultaneity by making salient the fungibility of the imagination.[24] Inversely, there is the fictional time that is redeemed through Proust's extraordinary act of narrative and cognitive prestidigitation, whereby the reader also becomes engaged in a sequence of unplanned procedural memories as a trigger for the recovery of episodic memory. Edith Wharton's placing of the two references to La Bruyère's *Les Caractères* like bookends or parentheses encapsulating Lily's failed life as a single moment is more discreet (see Chapter 5 in this volume), but it serves the same function of ensuring the intersection of sequence and simultaneity that is crucial for a cognitive grasp of what an utterance means, and what 'the whole life of man' (in Augustine's terms) might be taken to mean.

We could add rich Shakespearean examples here, not least the remarkable moments of simultaneity as sequence on which the late romances turn, or Wagner's *Ring*. From current novels written in English, Peter Carey's *Oscar and Lucinda*, with its tiny collocated chapters focused on particular moments and its overarching double helix of narrative sequence, would lend itself wonderfully to a cognitively inflected analysis. As a final example, however, I choose instead a novel serendipitously published as this chapter was being written, Elleke Boehmer's *The Shouting in the Dark*.[25] Less flamboyantly experimental than *Cloud Atlas* or *The Wild Palms* (or *Cymbeline*, come to that), it nonetheless has a strikingly original structure in which collocation creates the cognitive momentum.

---

[23] I use 'totalizing' to indicate the formal completeness of the novel as a printed work encompassing a single narrative complex, as opposed to the serial or episodic oral narrative, the continuous romance, and the soap opera. And I use 'reflective' in the cognitive sense, as opposed to the late twentieth-century notion of the 'self-reflexive text': although Mitchell's novel is in an obvious sense self-aware, its ultimate import is not that of a self-referring fiction, advertising the 'constructedness' of its mimetic strategies.

[24] On the failure of communication in *Don Quixote* and *Madame Bovary*, see Guillemette Bolens (Chapter 3 in this volume); the theme is also developed by Wes Williams (Chapter 6).

[25] Elleke Boehmer, *The Shouting in the Dark* (Dingwall: Sandstone Press, 2015).

*The Shouting in the Dark* is a biographical fiction spanning the childhood and adolescence of a South African girl with Dutch parents living in the province of Natal (now KwaZulu-Natal). It is divided into chapters virtually all of which have single-word thematic or conceptual titles ('Monsters', 'Sleep', 'Flights', 'Verandah', 'Parsley'). Each of these is quite distinct, focusing on a particular aspect of the young person's experience: being bullied (not least by 'the father', 'the mother', and the family doctor) because of her body-shape; suffering from insomnia that again lets her in for coercive medication; the experience of travelling between the Netherlands and South Africa in the company of a mother who suffers embarrassing panic attacks when flying; listening from an upper window as the father sits on the verandah drinking and telling his endlessly repeated stories of wartime in the Allied navy to the old friends who occasionally visit him; an episode near a ravine where the family dog nearly gets taken by a huge vulture-like bird. The collocation of these scenes and episodes appears to belong to the genre of poetic life-writing rather than standard narrative fiction. Some of them are samples of a recurring pattern; the gradual movement towards adolescence and early adulthood is secondary and at times almost imperceptible. Yet the almost imperceptible counts for a great deal in this novel. Markers are put down that have a slow-burn effect across the whole span of the story: the young Durban gardener of Ella's childhood is eventually replaced by another who becomes the first object of her erotic arousal; the mother's sense of exile from her homeland, and the father's nostalgia for wartime heroics, compensated for by a hyperbolic attachment to the police-state politics of his adopted country, form the double counterpoint for the sense of rootedness in Africa that emerges in Ella's consciousness and becomes the grounding of an active political engagement.

Collocation, in other words, provides the cognitive momentum in this story for emergent narrative properties: Ella's politics is an effect of the way the story is presented rather than a narrative strand as such. It is true that, at the outermost level, the novel establishes from its opening pages all the conditions for a page-turner: the adult Ella, at risk in South Africa because of her political activities, is refused Dutch citizenship and ordered to leave the Netherlands because 'the father' never registered her as his child. A corresponding closing chapter partially closes the circle, although the novel is highly underspecified, and one needs to draw on knowledge of the fall of the apartheid regime in order to imagine Ella's possible futures. The interface between these different strategies, the point at which sequence becomes simultaneity, consequently obliges the reader to engage in a constant recalibration of the novel's thrust and import, which could be defined as the projection in biographical terms of the whole South African question as it emerged and mutated, slowly and painfully, in the later twentieth century. What is implied and what emerges, in other words, is Africa itself or, using relevance theory conventions for ad hoc concepts with emergent properties, AFRICA*.

## CONCLUSION

This chapter has sought to bring together the micro-analysis of particular utterances with a broader-scope reflection on the cognitive principles that operate over whole sets of utterances. As we have said earlier, not least in Interlace 6, these two polarities are in no sense antithetical: everything that happens at one end of the scale can and does also happen at the other, although the human attention span is such that short lyric poems afford condensed and near-simultaneous apprehension of effects, whereas the more extended time span of fictional narrative is in general less demanding at the local level, and may indeed need to compensate for the reader's failure to remember all the details of a previous reading episode. The constraints of memory, in other words, are inevitably at work in the time-bound, ephemeral passage of verbal events through the reader's cognitive focus.

The relevance theory heuristic which has presided over all the essays in this volume can thus be explored in various different directions. It offers a persuasively constructed thought-world that is well suited not only to the apparently banal exchanges of everyday communication (what the implicatures of Vibeke's remark to Vladimir may have been when he dropped the vase, what Aaron inferred from Shama's under-specified remark about the weather, or even from the way she sniffed the air) but also to the most dense and allusive of literary utterances. It operates at close quarters, but also over long stretches of continuous prose, over both close reading and what has been called 'distant reading'.[26] It insists that we attend to authors and their intentions, without claiming that our inferences about these are more than a best guess, an optimal approximation (optimal relevance, one might say, is always a refined approximation); and it provides a highly flexible instrument for thinking about how readers, whether reflectively or unreflectively, supply what is needed to make sense of literary utterances.

Having reached this point in the book, the point at which the literary specialists have had their say, we now move to an essay from the other side of the disciplinary table (a more appropriate metaphor, for us, than 'frontier' or 'divide'). It will not provide a conclusion in the sense of a finally agreed set of arguments, but rather a retrospective view that also evaluates where we have got to in the enterprise of rethinking literature and literary criticism through the lens of relevance theory.

---

[26] See Franco Moretti, *Distant Reading* (London: Verso, 2013).

# 10

# Relevance Theory and Literary Interpretation

*Deirdre Wilson*

## INTRODUCTION

Since *Relevance: Communication and Cognition* was first published in 1986, the suggestion that it might have implications for literary interpretation has been welcomed and resisted in roughly equal measures. In an early review, Alastair Fowler described the book as having a potentially revolutionary impact on literary studies:

> If the theory of communication sketched in *Relevance* is as significant as I take it to be... contemporary methods of criticism all need to be thought through afresh.[1]

Ten years later, responding to a collection of papers on the implications of relevance theory for stylistics and rhetoric,[2] Keith Green commented that so far, the impact of relevance theory on literary studies had been 'minute' in comparison with its effect on other disciplines, adding that this should come as no surprise, since

> Anything that a relevance theorist can say about a literary text... can be, and most probably has been, said by conventional literary criticism.[3]

The essays in this volume represent the first sustained attempt by literary scholars to explore the impact of relevance theory on their own critical practice. In this concluding chapter, I will reflect in general terms not only on what relevance theory might contribute to literary studies, but also on how it stands to benefit from a careful consideration of the process of literary interpretation and the concerns of literary critics.

Assuming that the interpretation of literary works is not entirely *sui generis*—that it draws on the same basic cognitive and communicative abilities used in ordinary face-to-face exchanges—it seems reasonable to expect a theory such as relevance theory, which is primarily concerned with the interpretation of ordinary utterances, to shed light on the interpretation of literary utterances too. The essays

---

[1] Alastair Fowler, 'A new theory of communication', *London Review of Books*, 30 March 1989, p. 17.
[2] *Language and Literature*, 5 (August 1996).
[3] Keith Green, 'Butterflies, wheels and the search for literary relevance', *Language and Literature*, 6 (May 1997), 134.

in this volume draw on the basic assumptions of relevance theory (the idea that communication and cognition are governed by the search for relevance, that relevance is definable in terms of cognitive effects and processing effort, and that a key component of the interpretation process is a relevance-guided comprehension heuristic). They also make free use of theoretical notions from relevance theory (the analysis of ostensive communication as involving the expression and recognition of intentions, the distinction between explicit and implicit communication, the notions of loose use and ad hoc concepts, of attributive and echoic use, and so on), the aim being to develop a type of literary criticism which, to use Terence Cave's terms, is not only 'cognitively informed' but also 'cognitively inflected': that is,

> A literary criticism worthy of the name, resisting integration into extraneous agendas for which literature would provide mere illustrative examples, but at relevant points inflected by frames of reference, terminology, conjectures, and the like drawn from across the spectrum of cognitive disciplines.[4]

It is perhaps worth emphasizing that although the concerns of relevance theorists and literary critics overlap in many respects, they do not coincide exactly. The goal of relevance theory is to produce a cognitively plausible, empirically testable theory of a certain type of communication—ostensive communication—and to investigate how it manifests itself in both verbal and non-verbal behaviour. When relevance theorists draw on literary works, their focus tends to be on finding evidence for or against particular theoretical claims rather than producing rich and nuanced interpretations of individual utterances in context. As the essays in this volume illustrate, in producing such interpretations, the pragmatic abilities studied by relevance theorists interact with a wide range of contextual factors and other cognitive abilities on which relevance theorists have no particular expertise, and on which they have much to learn from literary scholars.

The questions that relevance theorists set out to answer include, for instance, 'What is communication?', 'How is communication achieved?', 'What role do contexts play in communication, and how are they constructed in the course of comprehension?', 'How are metaphorical, metonymic and ironical uses of language understood?', 'What are stylistic and poetic effects?', and so on. Some of these questions have also interested literary scholars, whose intuitive answers often chime with those suggested by relevance theorists. So far, however, the systematic theoretical answers imported into literary studies from other disciplines have rarely done justice to aspects of literary interpretation of which literary scholars themselves are well aware.

To take just one illustration, structuralism, which had a strong influence on twentieth-century literary theory, is committed to the code model of communication, and yet this model has little to say about the type of communication found in literary works. According to the code model, what is communicated is a 'message' or 'meaning' which can be rendered as a proposition (or a small set of propositions)

---

[4] Terence Cave, *Thinking with Literature: Towards a Cognitive Criticism* (Oxford: Oxford University Press, 2016), p. vi.

and duplicated in the minds of communicator and addressee; however, as literary scholars are well aware, the thoughts communicated by a literary text are often too rich and vague, too complex and subtly interlinked to be treated as a meaning or message of this type. Moreover, according to the code model, communication is a yes–no matter: a thought is either communicated or it is not; however, as literary scholars are again well aware, the interpretation of literary works often calls for some creative input from the reader, so that different readers arrive at different interpretations for which they must share some of the responsibility themselves. Although structuralists often highlighted the insufficiencies of the code model, they failed to replace it with an alternative model. Relevance theory, which accommodates a much broader range of ostensive acts and offers a much richer set of answers to the above questions, might well provide a more promising alternative.

So far, the aspect of relevance theory that has perhaps been most attractive to literary scholars is its analysis of figurative utterances and their role in the creation of stylistic and poetic effects. In later sections, I will draw some of the threads of our discussions together by reassessing this aspect of the theory in the light of the case studies presented in this volume. The aspect of relevance theory that has so far been of most *concern* to literary scholars has been its treatment of 'non-propositional' phenomena—images, emotions, sensorimotor processes—and their role in the interpretation of literary works. I will go on to reassess this aspect of the theory in the light of our discussions, and suggest that a broader notion of inference than the one adopted in early work in relevance theory might help to provide a more unitary account of the full range of 'non-propositional' effects. First, I will briefly recall some central aspects of the theory outlined in the Introduction, and introduce a distinction between *comprehension* and *interpretation* which will be useful in later sections.

## COMMUNICATION, COMPREHENSION, AND INTERPRETATION

Central to relevance theory's account of communication is the notion of an *ostensive act*, designed to attract the addressee's attention and convey a certain *import*. As outlined in the Introduction, the notion of an import is broader than the notion of a meaning or a message in two main respects. In the first place, the import of an ostensive act consists not of a single proposition (or small set of propositions) but of an *array of propositions*, which may amount to a simple meaning or message at one extreme, but be indefinitely rich and complex at the other. In the second place, the propositions in this array may not all be equally *manifest*[5] to the individual: that is, some of them may be more salient or strongly evidenced than others, and hence more likely to be entertained and accepted as true. By rejecting the idea that

---

[5] 'A proposition is *manifest* to an individual at a given time to the extent that he is likely to some positive degree to entertain it and accept it as true'; Dan Sperber and Deirdre Wilson, 'Beyond speaker's meaning', *Croatian Journal of Philosophy*, 15 (2016), 132.

what is communicated must be a simple meaning or message, we can account for the fact that not all the import of a literary work may be equally manifest to both writer and reader at a given time, that different parts of it may become more or less manifest to different readers at different times, and that some of the responsibility for constructing a satisfactory overall interpretation may lie with the reader as well as the writer.

The import of an ostensive act may be conveyed by either *showing* or *telling*.[6] By *showing* you a photograph of my garden, I provide you with direct perceptual evidence for a vast array of propositions; by *telling* you about my garden, I provide direct linguistic evidence not of the array of propositions itself but of my intention to convey it. Showing and telling may combine, as when I tell you about my garden using a tone of voice or facial expression that displays something of my emotional attitude. As noted in the Introduction (section on 'Replacing the Code Model of Communication'), when sensorimotor or emotion-reading mechanisms are involved in the comprehension process, the array of propositions made manifest by an ostensive act may be richer and more fine-grained than when purely linguistic evidence is provided.

The most basic claim of relevance theory is that although human cognition and communication are both geared to the search for relevance, ostensive acts raise expectations of relevance not raised by other stimuli. The addressee of an ostensive act is therefore entitled to presume that it will yield enough implications (and other cognitive effects), at a low enough processing cost, to satisfy the expectations of relevance it has raised. The relevance-guided comprehension heuristic is an automatic procedure for identifying the intended import of an ostensive act:

> The hearer takes the conceptual structure constructed by linguistic decoding; following a path of least effort, he enriches this at the explicit level and complements it at the implicit level, until the resulting interpretation meets his expectations of relevance; at which point, he stops.[7]

As noted in the Introduction (section on 'The Explicit and the Implicit'), since identifying the intended import of an utterance involves following a path of least effort, the outcome of the comprehension procedure depends on which disambiguations and reference assignments, which lexical narrowings and broadenings, which contextual assumptions and implications are most salient at the point where the addressee has to make a choice. The communicator is responsible for structuring the utterance or discourse so as to raise the right expectations of relevance and make the intended import salient enough to be selected by an addressee using the comprehension heuristic. If the resulting overall interpretation is relevant in the expected way, the addressee is entitled to assume (of course at a risk) that this is the one the communicator intended.

---

[6] See Kathryn Banks (Chapter 7) for an interesting discussion of the relation between showing and telling.

[7] Dan Sperber and Deirdre Wilson, 'The mapping between the mental and the public lexicon', in Peter Carruthers and Jill Boucher (eds) *Language and Thought: Interdisciplinary Themes* (Cambridge: Cambridge University Press, 1998), p. 192.

In identifying the intended import of an ostensive act, the addressee necessarily has to go beyond it. As we chat at a party, you ask me if I grew up in England and I tell you that I grew up in Cornwall. My reply explicitly communicates that I grew up in Cornwall and strongly implicates that I grew up in England. By telling you explicitly that I grew up in Cornwall, I cause you more processing effort than if I had merely said 'Yes', and this encourages you to look for an array of further implications (perhaps about the particular type of childhood I had) to offset this extra effort and thus increase the relevance of my utterance. By implicating that I grew up in England, I specifically answer your question, and therefore have good reason to think that this information will be relevant to you. However, I may have no clear idea *how* it (or the more specific information that I grew up in Cornwall) will be relevant: that is, what implications (and other cognitive effects) it will enable you to derive. Yet these are the implications that will satisfy your expectation of relevance. As Sperber and Wilson put it,

> what our theory of relevance implies is that one of the speaker's intentions (and a crucial one) is that the hearer, by recognising the speaker's intentions, should be made capable of going beyond them and of establishing the relevance of the utterance for himself. This general intention of being relevant gives the crucial guide to recovery of the meaning, references and inferences (if any) intended by the speaker. A successful act of comprehension (which is what is aimed at by both speaker and hearer) is one which allows the hearer to go beyond comprehension proper.[8]

This suggests that it is worth distinguishing *comprehension* from *interpretation*, where comprehension is the process of recognizing the intended import of an ostensive act, and interpretation includes the broader process of drawing one's own conclusions as part of the overall search for relevance. When the intended import consists of a wide array of propositions, there may be no clear cut-off point between comprehension and interpretation. While some propositions in the array will be strongly communicated (in the sense that the communicator made it strongly manifest that she intended to make these specific propositions manifest), others may be more weakly communicated, so that an addressee who decides to accept them must take some responsibility for their truth. As communication becomes weaker, comprehension shades off into interpretation, and communication is no longer a yes–no matter but a matter of degree.[9]

As comprehension shades off into interpretation, the borderline between authorial intentions and unintended implications becomes increasingly blurred. In a recent interview, Philip Roth explicitly disavows an interpretation of his novel *The Plot Against America* put forward in a *New York Times* review:

*Philip Roth:*  That book was helped by a column in the *New York Times* by Frank Rich. (This was at the time Bush became President.) He said what I was doing

---

[8] Dan Sperber and Deirdre Wilson, 'Mutual knowledge and relevance in theories of comprehension', in Neil Smith (ed.) *Mutual Knowledge* (London: Academic Press, 1982), p. 78.
[9] On strength of communication, see Dan Sperber and Deirdre Wilson, 'A deflationary account of metaphors', in Raymond Gibbs (ed.) *Metaphor in Language and Thought* (Cambridge: Cambridge University Press, 2008), sect. 7.

was writing a kind of allegory about the Bush administration. And those years felt so powerless in the face of what they were up to that the book caught on. I had no intention at all of writing an allegory of the Bush administration.

*Mark Lawson:*   Can you understand, though, the fact that many readers and critics read that allegory into it—does that have any validity, or are they wrong?

*Philip Roth:*   No, they're not wrong. It isn't the way that *I* read the book, but each person makes use of the book in his or her own way.[10]

Roth is clear that the allegorical interpretation is not part of the intended import of the novel, although he has no objection to readers constructing it on their own initiative. Indeed, in an article written before the book was published, he anticipates the possibility of an allegorical interpretation and rejects it:

> Some readers are going to want to take this book as a *roman à clef* to the present moment in America. That would be a mistake.[11]

Frank Rich acknowledges this warning, but finds an allegorical interpretation hard to resist:

> As long as there's no explosive evidence to rain on that parade, Mr. Roth is entirely right to say that *The Plot Against America* cannot be squared with 'the present moment in America.' But what makes this book terrifying in its sly, even insidious way is that you can't read it without imagining how the combustible elements of our own home front might ignite if the present moment does not hold.[12]

The distinction between comprehension and interpretation helps in analysing this exchange. On the one hand, as Frank Rich points out, the allegorical interpretation adds significantly to relevance of the book for many readers, who are bound to notice these parallels for themselves. On the other hand, Philip Roth denies that the allegorical interpretation is part of the intended import, while acknowledging that 'each reader makes use of the book in his or her own way'. This fits well with the idea that in identifying the intended import of an ostensive act, the addressee must necessarily go beyond it and draw some conclusions that the communicator need not necessarily either anticipate or endorse.

## FIGURATIVE UTTERANCES AND STYLE

> In true poetry it is...impossible to express the meaning in any but its own words, or to change the words without changing the meaning.[13]

> The infallible test of a blameless style is its *untranslatableness* in words of the same language without injury to the meaning.[14]

---

[10] Mark Lawson, interview with Philip Roth, *Front Row*, BBC radio, June 2011.
[11] Philip Roth, 'The story behind *The Plot Against America*', *New York Times*, 19 September 2004.
[12] Frank Rich, 'President Lindbergh in 2004', *New York Times*, 23 September 2004.
[13] A.C. Bradley, *Oxford Lectures on Poetry* (London: Macmillan, 1909), p. 19.
[14] Samuel Taylor Coleridge, *Biographia Literaria* (New York: Leavitt, Lord & Co, [1817] 1834), p. 267.

The essays in this volume amply illustrate the point made in these quotations, that some of the most striking effects of literary works depend on lexical, syntactic, or prosodic properties which contribute to the intended import without directly affecting the linguistically encoded meaning of the text. Timothy Chesters (Chapter 8) discusses the following passage from Emily Dickinson:

> I stepped from plank to plank
> So slow and cautiously;
> The stars about my head I felt,
> About my feet the sea.

As his analysis shows, the syntax and prosody of the last two lines affect the interpretation in a way that bypasses their encoded meaning:

> In 'The stars about my head I felt / About my feet the sea', the chiasmus of 'Stars'...
> 'felt'...'feet'...'sea' strives for balance at the very moment the speaker is most in danger of losing hers.[15]

A long-standing aim of relevance theory has been to show that stylistic and poetic effects traditionally associated with figurative utterances arise naturally in the pursuit of relevance, and call for no special treatment not required for the interpretation of ordinary literal utterances.[16]

Two aspects of the theory are helpful in this respect. First, as noted in the Introduction (section on 'Relevance, Communication, and Cognition'), relevance is a potential property not only of ostensive acts but of any external stimulus or internal representation—linguistic, sensorimotor, or conceptual—that provides an input to cognitive processes; thus, a visual scene, a piece of behaviour, a facial expression, or use of a particular linguistic form may all be relevant to an individual at a given time. This makes it possible to see how the presence of a certain word or phrase, a certain syntactic structure or prosodic feature, may contribute directly to relevance by reducing processing effort or increasing cognitive effects. In some cases, the effects are achieved at a purely sub-attentive level, while in others, a certain aspect of linguistic form may seem relevant enough to attract attention and lead on to further reflection.

Second, apparently unmotivated departures from routine provide tentative cues to ostension. This is a special case of the more general point that the manner in which an action is performed may suggest that it is ostensive. Compare the manner of a tennis player routinely serving in a match with the slower, more effortful, less natural-seeming manner of the same player teaching a class how to serve. Such apparent inefficiencies in behaviour can be explained on the assumption that the player is not simply serving but showing the class how to serve in a way most likely to get the intended import across. Traditional handbooks of rhetoric provide taxonomies of apparently unmotivated departures on the level of lexical, syntactic,

---

[15] Timothy Chesters, this volume, p. 160.
[16] *Relevance*, ch. 4, sect. 5–9; Dan Sperber and Deirdre Wilson, 'Rhetoric and relevance', in John Bender and David Welbery (eds) *The Ends of Rhetoric: History, Theory, Practice* (Stanford, CA: Stanford University Press, 1990).

or prosodic properties; but beyond noting that they add a certain 'vividness', 'liveliness', or 'beauty' to the text, they say little about the resulting effects on interpretation. From a relevance theory perspective, such departures fall together with a much broader class of tentative cues to ostension, encouraging a search for further aspects of the intended import that might help to satisfy expectations of relevance. Timothy Chesters's interpretation of the chiasmus in Emily Dickinson beautifully illustrates this point and shows, moreover, that the intended import cannot be decoded, but only inferred.

Repetition (of a word, a phrase, a syntactic structure, or lexical feature) provides a further tentative cue to ostension. In her contribution to this volume, Guillemette Bolens (Chapter 3) shows that the verb *se traîner* is repeatedly used in *Madame Bovary* to apply to several different types of referent (the movement of dust across a floor, voices lingering or dying away, Emma dragging herself across a room or spinning out a useless existence), conveying different nuances each time. In the English translation, where *se traîner* is rendered by a series of different words ('creep', 'draw out', 'linger', 'drag', 'drawl', 'spin out'), an array of implications made manifest by the original are lost. What English readers would miss, even if the translation perfectly captured the nuances of each use of the verb *se traîner* in the original, is precisely the fact that the same word was used to convey these nuances throughout. As Bolens puts it,

> It is through style in Flaubert's novel that the verb *se traîner* becomes relevant, as its repetition and specific use progressively call for attention. Whether applied to sound and voice, or to movement and gait, this verb is about the sensation of an energy that is gradually drained out by meaninglessness and a slow motivational collapse.[17]

The use of *se traîner* in *Madame Bovary* is a special case of a more general point taken up by several contributors: that words are often used to convey 'ad hoc' (unlexicalized) concepts which are broader or narrower than the linguistically encoded meanings (see Introduction, section on 'The Figurative and the Literal'). Most approaches to pragmatics treat the encoded 'literal' meaning as a default, to be considered first and abandoned only if it proves unsatisfactory. By contrast, relevance theory suggests that in many circumstances a looser interpretation will be easier to construct than a strictly literal one, and will be accepted as long as it satisfies expectations of relevance. Raphael Lyne's discussion of 'Corinna's going a Maying' (Chapter 2 in this volume) illustrates this point.[18] Here are two lines from early in the poem:

> Nay! Not so much as out of bed?
> When all the Birds have Mattens seyd.

Based only on the knowledge that birds sing and that Matins is a religious service held early in the morning, it is easy enough to interpret 'all the Birds have Mattens seyd' loosely as implying not much more than that the dawn chorus is over, and

---

[17] Guillemette Bolens, this volume, p. 61.    [18] Raphael Lyne, this volume, p. 38.

this might satisfy a reader familiar with the pastoral genre. However, as Lyne goes on to show, the accumulation of religious vocabulary throughout the poem provides a tentative cue to ostension, encouraging a search for richer implications based on a more literal interpretation of these terms. In this case, a loose interpretation may be the first to come to mind, and the move towards a more literal interpretation takes more effort.

The claim that metaphor is a type of loose use has been part of relevance theory from the start. The analysis of loose use (and lexical narrowing and broadening in general) in terms of ad hoc concepts is more recent, and although this improves on earlier analyses in many respects, it has been seen as problematic in others.[19] In particular, it is not clear how well the ad hoc concept approach deals with 'extended metaphors', as in the following passage from *Macbeth*:

> Life's but a walking shadow, a poor player
> That struts and frets his hour upon the stage
> And then is heard no more.

Robyn Carston, who has discussed this issue in some detail, suggests that replacing the literal meaning of each metaphorical use of a word in this passage with an ad hoc concept might be cumbersome at best, and considers the possibility of an alternative account:

> Are we to suppose that we are forming ad hoc concept after ad hoc concept, WALKING-SHADOW*, POOR PLAYER*, STRUTS*, FRETS*, HOUR*, STAGE*, even UPON*, and so on, replacing each of the literal lexical meanings in the developing interpretation? What appears to me to be going on here is that the literal meaning is not just lingering in the background (remaining activated even once a new metaphorical meaning has been formed), but has taken over from any process of metaphorical adjustment of concepts.[20]

On this alternative account, there are two possible 'modes of processing' for metaphors, one involving ad hoc concept construction and the other a 'meta-representational' mode in which the literal meaning is (so to speak) put into quotation marks and retained for further inspection. This second mode, often strikingly described as involving a 'lingering of the literal', is explored by several contributors. Timothy Chesters summarizes it as follows in discussing the same passage from *Macbeth*:

> Interpreting each metaphorical component ad hoc concept by ad hoc concept (SHADOW*, POOR PLAYER*, STRUTS*, HOUR*, STAGE*, and so on) would come at too great a cognitive cost. Instead listeners are more likely to sustain the literal content so as to submit it globally for processing downstream.[21]

---

[19] Deirdre Wilson and Robyn Carston, 'A unitary approach to lexical pragmatics: relevance, inference and ad hoc concepts', in Noel Burton-Roberts (ed.) *Pragmatics* (Basingstoke, UK: Palgrave Macmillan, 2007), pp. 230–59; Sperber and Wilson, 'Deflationary account of metaphors'.

[20] Robyn Carston, 'Metaphor: ad hoc concepts, literal meaning and mental images', *Proceedings of the Aristotelian Society*, 110 (2010), 308.

[21] Chesters, this volume, p. 155.

Extended metaphors present a genuine challenge to the ad hoc concept approach. Building on ideas put forward earlier in this section, I would like to suggest that what is involved in the interpretation of many extended metaphors is not so much a 'lingering of the literal meaning' as a 'lingering of linguistic form'.

The assumption that constructing an ad hoc concept is more effortful than accepting the encoded 'literal' meaning conflicts with a view often expressed in relevance theory, that pragmatic processes apply 'spontaneously, automatically and unconsciously to fine-tune the interpretation of virtually every word'.[22] Sperber and Wilson comment,

> a word which encodes a given concept can be used to convey . . . another concept that neither it nor any other expression in the language actually encodes. There is nothing exceptional about such uses: almost any word can be used in this way. Quite generally, the occurrence of a word in an utterance provides a piece of evidence, a pointer to a concept involved in the speaker's meaning. It may so happen that the intended concept is the very one encoded by the word, which is therefore used in its strictly literal sense. However, we would argue that this is no more than a possibility, not a preferred or default interpretation.[23]

Indeed, as we saw with 'All the birds have Mattens said' above, a loose interpretation, based on only a few of the implications activated by the linguistically encoded meaning, is often easier to construct than a more literal one.

How can a loose interpretation be easier to construct than a literal one even though the encoded literal meaning is automatically activated on encountering a word? Relevance theory sees the key to utterance comprehension as the search for implications: on this approach, the function of the encoded meaning of a word or phrase is to give easy access to an array of implications that may help to satisfy expectations of relevance. Having found such an array, the addressee is entitled to assume (of course at a risk) that what the communicator intended to convey was not the encoded meaning but an ad hoc concept (which may be broader or narrower than the encoded meaning) that warrants the desired implications. In 'Corinna's going a Maying', for instance, the encoded meaning of 'All the birds have Mattens seyd' gives easy access to an array of implications to the effect that the birds have finished their early morning song. An addressee whose expectations of relevance are satisfied by this array is entitled to assume, without looking more deeply into the encoded meaning, that what the communicator intended to convey was an ad hoc concept, MATTENS SEYD*, which is broader than the encoded meaning and which warrants these implications.[24]

However, the accumulation of religious vocabulary throughout the poem provides a tentative cue to ostension, which will encourage some readers to pay more attention to the exact wording of the text and look for further implications made

---

[22] Deirdre Wilson, 'Relevance theory and lexical pragmatics,' *Italian Journal of Linguistics*, 15 (2003), 273–91.

[23] Dan Sperber and Deirdre Wilson, 'Mapping', pp. 196–7.

[24] On ad hoc concepts and backwards inference, see Sperber and Wilson, 'Mapping'; Deirdre Wilson and Dan Sperber, 'Truthfulness and relevance', *Mind*, 111 (2002), 583–632.

accessible by the encoded meaning. The ad hoc concept MATTENS SEYD** which warrants these implications would still be broader than the encoded meaning, but it would be narrower, with a more restrictive denotation, than MATTENS SEYD*. In each case, what drives the interpretation process is the search for implications made easily accessible by the encoded meaning which help to satisfy the addressee's expectations of relevance. The ad hoc concept is determined by an automatic process of backward inference: it is simply the concept that warrants these implications. On this approach, what is needed to justify a fully literal interpretation of a word or phrase is not the mere fact that its encoded meaning has been activated, but that nothing less than this encoded meaning would warrant the array of implications that satisfies the addressee's expectations of relevance.

Returning to the passage from *Macbeth*, it should be easy on a fairly superficial reading to construct a loose interpretation based on only a few implications activated by the encoded meanings of the metaphorically used terms. However, the accumulation of later references to dramatic performance provides a tentative cue to ostension, which will encourage some readers to pay more attention to the exact wording of the text and search for further implications activated by the encoded meaning. Some classic experiments on language processing suggest that when the exact wording of a text makes a difference to relevance, it tends to be remembered verbatim, whereas when the exact wording makes no difference to relevance, only the 'gist' is retained.[25] With written texts, of course, the reader can always go back to the exact wording when relevant, and through it can gain access not only to the linguistically encoded meaning, but also to the other types of interpretive effect discussed in this section, which depend on lexical, syntactic, and prosodic properties that bypass the encoded meaning.[26] What all these cases have in common is not so much a 'lingering of the literal meaning' as a 'lingering of linguistic form'.

## IRONY, PARODY, AND ECHOING

A further type of interpretive effect which depends on linguistic properties that do not directly affect the encoded meaning arises in the following passage from 'Tam o'Shanter':

> But pleasures are like poppies spread,
> You seize the flow'r, its bloom is shed;
> Or like the snow falls in the river,

---

[25] J.D. Bransford, J.R. Barclay, and J.J. Franks, 'Sentence memory: a constructive versus interpretive approach', *Cognitive Psychology*, 3 (1972), 193–209.

[26] I am assuming here a distinction between 'extended metaphors', which are analysable in terms of ad hoc concepts, and 'allegories' (for instance, Cicero's 'What I marvel at and complain of is this, that there should exist any man so set on destroying his enemy as to *scuttle the ship on which he himself is sailing*'), where the literal meaning remains transparent throughout. For discussion, see Christoph Unger, 'Towards a relevance theory account of allegory', in Agnieszka Piskorska and Ewa Wałaszewska (eds) *From Discourse to Morphemes: Applications of Relevance Theory* (Newcastle-upon-Tyne, UK: Cambridge Scholars Publishing, 2016).

> A moment white—then melts for ever
> Or like the Borealis race,
> That flit ere you can point their place;
> Or like the rainbow's lovely form
> Evanishing amid the storm ...[27]

The encoded meaning of these lines gives easy access to a few fairly strong implicatures (having to do with the transience of sensual pleasure), and a wide array of weak implicatures (derived by bringing together encyclopaedic assumptions about sensual pleasure, on the one hand, and poppies, snow, rainbows, and the 'Borealis race' on the other). But to stop there would be to miss the tentative cue to ostension provided by a shift in style from the playful tone and Scottish diction in the rest of the poem to formal neoclassical English in these eight lines. David Daiches describes the shift as introducing 'a touch of irony';[28] it has also been seen as parodic:

> the 'touch of irony' emerges, I submit, from the parodic element which Burns... introduces. Those who see in this passage only a series of beautiful similes are surely missing part of Burns's intention. ... It is true that each of these comparisons is poetically effective in itself; but more significant is the *accumulation* of similes. Burns is not satisfied with one or two; he piles them on, one after another. ... Moreover, he encloses these similes within an extremely formal, even heavy-handed, rhetorical framework. ... Thus, not only does Burns switch into English poetic diction in this passage, but he calls attention to it by adopting a stiff and artificial structure which parodies grandiose poetics or 'fine writing'.[29]

Relevance theorists would treat this as a case of 'parodic irony', in which the communicator exploits resemblances in linguistic form to convey a lightly mocking attitude to the content of an original being echoed, here 'grandiose poetics or "fine writing"'.[30]

Central to relevance theory's account of irony (see the Introduction, section on 'Echoic Utterances and Irony') is the notion of an *echoic* utterance: that is, one chosen at least partly for its resemblance to another utterance or thought, which is used to show that the communicator has that utterance or thought in mind and wants to convey her own attitude or reaction to it.[31] With verbal irony, the resemblance is crucially one of content, and the communicator's attitude to that content is one of mockery, contempt, or scorn. Here is a depiction by Jane Austen of an exchange between a pretty, good-natured, but profoundly silly woman and her

---

[27] Robert Burns, 'Tam o'Shanter', in *The Complete Works of Robert Burns* (Boston, MA: Phillips, Sampson & Co, 1855), p. 172.

[28] 'Burns is seeking a form of expression which will set the sternness of objective fact against the warm, cosy, and self-deluding view of the half-intoxicated Tam, and he wants to do this with just a touch of irony'; David Daiches, *Robert Burns* (New York: Rinehart, 1950), p. 286.

[29] Allan H. MacLaine, 'Burns's use of parody in Tam o'Shanter,' *Criticism*, 1 (Fall 1959), 312–13.

[30] Deirdre Wilson and Dan Sperber, 'Explaining irony', in Deirdre Wilson and Dan Sperber, *Meaning and Relevance* (Cambridge: Cambridge University Press, 2012).

[31] *Relevance*, ch. 4, sect. 9.

husband, who is described as behaving towards her with 'studied indifference, insolence and discontent':

> 'Oh! my love!' cried Mrs Palmer to her husband, who just then entered the room.—
> 'You must help me persuade the Miss Dashwoods to go to town this winter.'
>     Her love made no answer; and after slightly bowing to the ladies, began complaining of the weather.[32]

The phrase 'her love' ironically echoes Mrs Palmer's term of endearment to her husband, making manifest an array of implications to the effect that her use of the term was worthy of mockery or criticism, that her husband's behaviour falls short of the standards expected of lovers, that there is a lack of reciprocity or gulf in feeling between them, and so on. With parodic irony, illustrated by the passage from 'Tam o'Shanter' above, the communicator expresses an ironical attitude to the content of an echoed utterance (or type of utterance), this time by exploiting resemblances in linguistic form. Not all echoing is ironical, however: one can echo an utterance or thought in order to endorse it, question it, or simply to show that one has it in mind and finds it relevant. As the essays in this volume show, literature is a very rich source of echoes based on resemblances in content, structure, or form.

Kirsti Sellevold (Chapter 5 in this volume) analyses a scene from Edith Wharton's *The House of Mirth* which bears striking parallels to a famous scene from *Pride and Prejudice*. Both involve an encounter between the heroine and a potential suitor (Lily Bart and Percy Gryce in one case, Elizabeth and Darcy in the other) and both involve a blush (from Percy Gryce in one case, and from both Elizabeth and Darcy in the other). Sellevold shows that the parallels and contrasts between the two scenes are strong enough to provide a tentative cue to ostension, which she interprets as indicating a subtly ironical intent:

> Wharton's brilliant allusion to Austen's Pemberley scene...voices an attitude to Austen's marriage plot that is perhaps more humorous than contemptuous. It performs a subtle satire of that novel's depiction of feelings and its eventual happy ending.[33]

As Sellevold points out, some readers might enjoy the scene from *The House of Mirth* without picking up the allusion, while others might notice the parallels and find them relevant without treating them as intentional. The stronger the parallels, and the less likely they are to be accidental, the more justifiable it is to treat the resulting implications as weakly communicated aspects of the intended import.

In a wide-ranging discussion of echoing in literature, Terence Cave (Chapter 9 above) considers a whole spectrum of structural parallels between different literary works.[34] Some are manifestly intended to be noticed and to contribute to the intended import (between the *Divine Comedy* and the *Aeneid*, for instance), while others are much less likely to be so (between a storyline from 'The Archers' and Frank Wedekind's *Lulu*, for instance). As Cave points out, unintended parallels may be highly salient and relevant for particular readers, as the parallels between

---

[32] Jane Austen, *Sense and Sensibility* (Harmondsworth, UK: Penguin, 1811/1969), p. 134.
[33] Kirsti Sellevold, this volume, p. 101.        [34] Terence Cave, this volume, pp. 172–9.

*The Plot Against America* and the political situation at the time of publication were for Frank Rich. What helps to distinguish intended from unintended parallels is not merely that the resemblances are striking in one case and not in the other, or even that they are relevant in one case and not in the other, but that they were manifestly intended to be noticed and to contribute to the intended import in one case and not in the other.

Several contributors to this volume reflect on the relation between echoic effects and intertextuality, a notion which covers some of the same ground and is widely used in literary studies. For instance, Elleke Boehmer (Chapter 1) discusses Yeats's lines 'That the topless towers be burnt / And men recall that face', which echo a famous passage from *Dr Faustus* and also stand in an intertextual relation to that passage.[35] In the framework of relevance theory, recognizing the allusion as a tentative cue to ostension helps readers to identify the unnamed woman in the poem and activates a body of contextual information which they are encouraged to use in inferring the intended import. Wes Williams's discussion of 'invisible guests' in poetry (Chapter 6) is a sustained reflection on echoing and intertextuality in which

> Poets' words both echo and enrich each other across languages and traditions. ... And literature in turn sustains and transforms itself by way of both inference and transference.[36]

It is worth noting that although they cover some of the same ground, the notions of echoing and intertextuality are quite distinct. As Terence Cave points out, intertextuality studies are more concerned with formal relations among texts than with issues of authorial agency or intention, and have little to say about how readers might distinguish intended from unintended resemblances, or identify the attitudes conveyed by the use of echoing in either ordinary utterances or literary texts. In fact, linguists define 'text' much more narrowly than many literary scholars do, and treat ordinary utterances as belonging to discourse rather than text; in that case, relations between two ordinary utterances could not strictly speaking count as intertextual, although they might well be echoic. While the notion of a text might conceivably be stretched to cover ordinary utterances, it is hard to see how it could also cover unspoken thoughts, which do not qualify in any sense as 'text'. Yet as noted in the Introduction, verbal irony often involves an echoic relation between an ordinary utterance and an unspoken thought, and in this case, echoing and intertextuality come apart.

## IMAGES, INFERENCES, AND 'NON-PROPOSITIONAL' EFFECTS

In the last two sections, I have considered a variety of interpretive effects which are 'non-propositional' in the sense that they do not constitute a meaning or message which can be rendered as a single proposition (or small set of propositions). A few

---

[35] Elleke Boehmer, this volume, p. 29.     [36] Wes Williams, this volume, p. 113.

early works on relevance theory suggested that these non-propositional effects, typically associated with figurative utterances, might call for a new type of 'rhetorical' mechanism, distinct from the inferential pragmatic mechanisms used to derive implicatures. As Sperber and Wilson put it,

> In addition to the propositions it expresses or implicates, an utterance may suggest to the hearer certain non-propositional lines of interpretation—for example by evoking images or states of mind—which are precisely characteristic of figurative utterances. ...What seems to be needed is a new type of interpretive mechanism, in addition to the semantic and pragmatic ones already available, which can account for irony, metaphor and figurative interpretation in general.[37]

This idea was quickly dropped in favour of a fully inferential approach to the whole range of ostensive acts; but it is sometimes felt, by both supporters and critics of relevance theory, that the attempt to unify pragmatics with rhetoric may have left out something crucial. The essays in this volume offer a chance to reassess this issue, taking several new factors into account.

The idea that non-propositional effects are associated only with figurative utterances is increasingly hard to defend. In the first place, the theoretical value of a literal–figurative distinction is now widely questioned. Moreover, the essays in this volume underline the importance of sensorimotor mechanisms in understanding both literal and figurative utterances. The literary passages discussed are full of tiny muscle tensings, explosive leaps, gingerly steps, sudden starts and irruptions, violent hand gestures, snatch raids, arrested movements, creeping, dragging, and so on, which have been shown to activate sensorimotor mechanisms even when encountered only indirectly, via a linguistic description.[38] The sensory and kinesic information these mechanisms provide is generally seen as giving rise to non-propositional effects. If a new type of interpretive mechanism is needed to deal with the evocation of 'images and states of mind', it cannot be seen as applying only to figurative utterances.

It might still be claimed that two types of pragmatic mechanism are needed: one properly inferential and used to construct messages or meanings, the other non-inferential and used to create non-propositional effects. For someone who sees inference as involving an 'abstract logic' of the type used in conscious syllogistic reasoning, the case for invoking additional non-inferential mechanisms to account for the full range of interpretive effects might seem overwhelming. But as several contributors to this volume point out, relevance theorists have moved towards a broader conception of inference, allowing for a much wider range of inferential procedures, both conscious and unconscious. As Sperber and Wilson put it,

---

[37] Deirdre Wilson and Dan Sperber, 'On Grice's theory of conversation', in Paul Werth (ed.) *Conversation and Discourse* (London: Croom Helm, 1981), pp. 163–4.

[38] Guillemette Bolens, *The Style of Gestures: Embodiment and Cognition in Literary Narrative* (Baltimore, MD: Johns Hopkins University Press, 2012); Bolens, this volume.

Not all inferences involve step by logical step derivations of explicit conclusions from explicit premises. Arguably, the vast majority of inferences made by humans and other animals do not involve such derivations.[39]

This approach to inference is defended in some detail in recent work by Hugo Mercier and Dan Sperber, who sum it up as follows:

> Cognition involves going well beyond the information available to the senses. All that sensory organs get by the way of information, be it in ants or in humans, are changes of energy at thousands or millions of nerve endings. To integrate this information, to identify the events in the environment that have caused these sensory stimulations, to respond in an appropriate manner to these events, cognition must, to a large extent, consist in drawing inferences about the way things are, about what to expect, and about what to do.[40]

On this broader view, perception and memory both involve a substantial element of inference, the sensorimotor mechanisms are themselves inferential, and the recognition of a communicator's intentions using the relevance-guided comprehension heuristic is an inferential process par excellence.

The output of the relevance-guided comprehension heuristic is an array of propositions taken to constitute the intended import of an ostensive act. The notion of a proposition (like the notion of an inferential mechanism) can be more or less narrowly construed. For someone who sees propositions as closely related to the sentences of a natural language, the case for treating the output of the comprehension heuristic as including not only propositions but also 'images or states of mind' must again seem overwhelming. From the start, however, relevance theorists have argued for a broader construal on which the gap between propositions and natural-language sentences is much greater than is standardly assumed:

> There are always components of a speaker's meaning which her words do not encode.... Indeed, we would argue that the idea that for most, if not all, possible meanings that a speaker might intend to convey, there is a sentence in a natural language which has that exact meaning as its linguistic meaning is quite implausible.[41]

On this approach, there are many thoughts that cannot be directly encoded into words.

With the introduction of ad hoc concepts, it became clear that the gap between language and thought exists not only on the level of whole sentences, but also on the level of individual words. Words are standardly seen as corresponding roughly one-to-one to concepts, so that to communicate a concept, one merely has to utter the word that encodes it. By contrast, as noted in the Introduction (section

---

[39] Sperber and Wilson, 'Beyond speaker's meaning', p. 136.

[40] Hugo Mercier and Dan Sperber, *The Enigma of Reason* (Cambridge, MA: Harvard University Press and Harmondsworth, UK: Penguin Books, 2017); Hugo Mercier and Dan Sperber, 'Why do humans reason? Arguments for an argumentative theory', *Behavioral and Brain Sciences*, 34 (2011), 57–111.

[41] Deirdre Wilson and Dan Sperber, 'Preface', in Deirdre Wilson and Dan Sperber, *Meaning and Relevance* (Cambridge: Cambridge University Press, 2012), p. ix; Robyn Carston, *Thoughts and Utterances: The Pragmatics of Explicit Communication* (Oxford: Blackwell, 2002).

on 'The Figurative and the Literal'), relevance theorists have argued that humans have many more concepts than words, and indeed, that they may create whole swathes of new concepts for very little effort using existing concepts as templates.[42] On this broader construal, concepts are capable of capturing fine-grained differences in perception, action, or emotion in a way that single words cannot, and are communicated not by encoding them but by providing evidence of one's intention to convey them.[43]

To illustrate, consider Kathryn Banks's discussion (Chapter 7 in this volume) of what might be communicated by use of the word 'rippling' in the line 'As I stood like that, rippling' in a poem by Mary Oliver. The encoded concept RIPPLE denotes (let us say) a variety of undulating movements, some of which will be highly salient in the immediate context: 'the shaking of a person experiencing intense joy or pain', the shaking of a heron's wings before it explodes into action, the rippling of water, the undulations of light and darkness against the sky. As Banks puts it,

> So readers...might imagine movements made by the human body in explosive ecstasy; by enormous expansive heron wings interrupting the bird's poise; by undulating waves of water; and perhaps by ripples of light in the sky. The combination of these sensori-motor imaginings gives some indication of what Oliver's experience might be like, of what it might feel like...to merge with nature.[44]

The ad hoc concept RIPPLING* would be constructed by backward inference from a wide array of implications which render different aspects of this complex experience in a rich and fine-grained way, and would figure in the reader's (provisional) interpretation of the poem, to be adjusted and readjusted in the course of further readings.[45]

For communication to succeed, the addressee has to identify the array of propositions that the communicator intended to make manifest or more manifest. Identifying an array of propositions, however, does not necessarily involve enumerating each individual member of the array. In the first place, the members of an array are typically manifest to different degrees: some will be in the forefront of attention, while others may not be mentally represented and entertained in the course of the comprehension process at all, and listing them would tend to distort the structure of the intended import. Moreover, the communicator's intention to make this array of propositions manifest will itself be more strongly manifest in some cases than in others. Often, at most a few members of an array will be enumerated, while the rest must be identified in some other way.

Another way to identify an array is by use of a description. If you ask whether I've had time to tidy my study and I respond by opening the door and showing you the chaos inside, the array of propositions I manifestly intended to convey can be

---

[42] Dan Sperber, *Explaining Culture: A Naturalistic Approach* (Oxford: Blackwell, 1996).
[43] Sperber and Wilson, 'Mapping'; Carston, *Thoughts and Utterances*, chapter 5; Sperber and Wilson, 'Deflationary account of metaphors', sect. 8.
[44] Kathryn Banks, this volume, p. 137.
[45] Terence Cave (Chapter 9 in this volume) illustrates in some detail the dynamics of the literary interpretation process.

described as those that have become perceptually salient to you as a result of my behaviour and that help to answer your question.

A third way to identify the intended import of an ostensive act is by what might be called 'metacognitive acquaintance'. Sometimes we experience a change in our cognitive environment as a result of a communicator's behaviour, and we identify this change as something that the communicator intended to bring about and to have us recognize as part of the intended import. Kathryn Banks describes just such a change as the effect of reading Mary Oliver's line 'As I stood like that, rippling' in the context of the poem as a whole. As a result of reading this line, we are disposed to make a certain kind of inference. The author need not have intended us to make any specific inference; her intentions may have been quite vague and concerned only with the general drift of our inferences, and our understanding may be equally vague without this amounting to a failure of comprehension. What is aimed at in cases of weak communication is a degree of cognitive alignment, not an exact duplication of thoughts. Such cases lie well beyond the scope of the code model.

## THE RELEVANCE OF FICTION

As Neil Kenny notes in Chapter 4 of this volume, literary works may be seen as having both 'internal' and 'external' relevance. Expectations of 'internal' relevance arise in the context of the preceding text and guide the interpretation of subsequent text. For instance, the interpretation of each simile in the passage from 'Tam o'Shanter' above is affected by what has gone before and creates expectations of relevance for what comes after, with the resulting interpretations being mutually adjusted with each other. Similarly, Jane Austen's description of the encounter between the Palmers in *Sense and Sensibility* is interpreted in the light of their previous interactions and creates internal expectations of relevance which will be strengthened, enriched, or adjusted in the light of later encounters.

However, while some fiction (genre novels, romantic or detective fiction) may be written largely to entertain, and have mostly the internal type of relevance discussed above, literary works are generally expected to have more significance than this. And indeed, many literary works achieve what might be called 'external' relevance by having lasting cognitive effects on beliefs and assumptions about the actual world that the reader has independently of the text. This presents a problem both for relevance theory and for literary studies. Works of fiction are not put forward as true descriptions of the actual world, so how can they provide evidence strong enough to achieve lasting effects of this type?[46]

A possible answer suggested by Sperber and Wilson is that an author may be simultaneously performing ostensive acts on two levels: a lower-level act of describing a fictional world, and a higher-level act of showing this world to the reader as

---

[46] For interesting discussion, see Anna Ichino and Gregory Currie, 'Truth and trust in fiction', in E. Sullivan-Bissett, H. Bradley, and P. Noordhof (eds) *Art and Belief* (Oxford: Oxford University Press, 2017).

an example of what is possible, or conceivable.[47] The expectations of relevance raised by the lower-level act would be internal, while the higher-level act would create external expectations of relevance. The title of a work may give a clue to the type of external relevance the author aims to achieve. In *Sense and Sensibility*, for instance, Mrs Palmer might be seen as an example of a person whose good looks and good nature cannot make up for her total lack of either sense or sensibility, and her inter-actions with the other characters may achieve some external relevance as a result.

Sperber and Wilson suggest that literary works typically achieve external rele-vance by strengthening or reorganizing existing assumptions and creating a sense of kinship with the author rather than giving rise to totally new implications. Each of us probably has some evidence that sensual pleasures are ephemeral, but the passage from Burns encourages us to expand this evidence into a richer, more nuanced awareness and to treat this as at least partly shared with the author. As Coleridge puts it,

> Who has not a thousand times seen snow fall on water? Who has not watched it with
> a new feeling, from the time that he has read Burns' comparison of sensual pleasure
>> To snow that falls upon a river
>> A moment white—then gone for ever![48]

The connections we make in reading this passage may also have more lasting cog-nitive effects by increasing the long-term salience of certain assumptions, or help-ing to set up new inferential routines as a result of which, as Coleridge suggests, we may never think of snow, or sensual pleasures, in the same way again. As Neil Kenny points out (Chapter 4 in this volume) in a fascinating reflection on the interactions between immersion, external relevance, and epistemic vigilance in the interpretation of Mark Twain's *Adventures of Tom Sawyer*, certain fictions may encourage us to use inferential routines whose outputs we strongly resist, and this may ultimately undermine rather than reinforce our sense of kinship with the author.[49] This opens up an interesting new area of research in which interdisciplin-ary collaboration between literary scholars, relevance theorists, and psychologists could well produce exciting results.

## CONCLUDING REMARKS

I started this chapter by noting some widely recognized inadequacies of the code model of communication, and suggested that relevance theory's account based on ostension and inference might provide a suitable alternative framework for analys-ing literary interpretation. As the essays in this volume demonstrate, the type of communication achieved by literary works is much more creative and flexible than a purely code-based account would suggest. There is no restriction on the methods

---

[47] See Dan Sperber and Deirdre Wilson, 'Presumptions of relevance', *Behavioral and Brain Sciences*, 10 (1987), 751. The idea that ostensive acts may be performed on two levels should also shed light on allegory, as discussed in footnote 26 above.
[48] Coleridge, *Biographia Literaria*, p. 56.     [49] Neil Kenny, this volume.

a communicator can use, and no limit to what she can convey, as long as she can get the addressee to recognize her intention to convey it. These essays also highlight several topics which cry out for further collaboration between literary scholars and relevance theorists. I will end by mentioning just one.[50]

One of the original features of relevance theory is the prominence it gives to the notion of processing effort, and to the idea that in formulating their utterances, communicators aim (among other things) to strike an optimal balance between the cognitive effects achieved and the processing effort required. Not all communicators are equally successful in doing so, and this is allowed for in the definition of optimal relevance, which refers to the communicator's *abilities*—for instance, to find a suitable formulation in the available time—and *preferences*—for instance, to spend time re-reading and redrafting. As the essays in this volume show, many writers have excellent intuitions about how to formulate their utterances so as to manipulate their readers' expectations of relevance, using minute changes in syntax, prosody, or vocabulary as tentative cues to ostension. Although little is known about the source of these intuitions, or about how an optimal balance between cognitive effects and processing effort is achieved, studying the successive drafts of literary works from this perspective might well provide useful insights for literary scholars and relevance theorists alike.

---

[50] Other interesting directions for future collaboration are explored in Patricia Kolaiti, *The Limits of Expression: Language, Literature, Mind* (Cambridge: Cambridge University Press, 2019).

# Bibliography

Abbott, H. Porter, 'Reading intended meaning where none is intended: a cognitivist reappraisal of the implied author', *Poetics Today*, 32 (2011), 461–87.

Allen, John T., 'Smiles and laughter in *Don Quixote*', *Comparative Literature Studies*, 43.4 (2006), 515–31.

Alvar, Carlos, *Don Quijote: Letras, armas, vida* (Madrid: SIAL Ediciones, coll. Trivium de Textos y Ensayo, 2009).

Anscombre, Jean-Claude and Oswald Ducrot, *L'Argumentation dans la langue* (Liège: Pierre Mardaga, 2nd ed., 1988).

Armstrong, Paul, *How Literature Plays with the Brain: The Neuroscience of Reading and Art* (Baltimore, MD: The Johns Hopkins University Press, 2013).

Atlas, Jay David, 'Intuition, the paradigm case argument, and the two dogmas of Kant'otelianism', in Klaus Petrus and Uli Sauerland (eds), *Meaning and Analysis: New Essays on Grice* (London: Palgrave Macmillan, 2010), pp. 47–75.

Augustine, Saint, *Confessions*, ed. and trans. Carolyn J.-B. Hammond (Cambridge, MA: Harvard University Press, Loeb Classical Library, 2016).

Austen, Jane, *Sense and Sensibility* (Harmondsworth, UK: Penguin Books, 1969).

Barker, Wendy, *Lunacy of Light: Emily Dickinson and the Experience of Metaphor* (Carbondale, IL: Southern Illinois University Press, 1987).

Belfiore, Elizabeth, '"Ter frustra comprensa": embraces in the *Aeneid*', *Phoenix*, 38.1 (1984), 19–30.

Blakemore, Diane, *Semantic Constraints on Relevance* (Oxford: Blackwell, 1987).

Boehmer, Elleke, *The Shouting in the Dark* (Dingwall, UK: Sandstone Press, 2015).

Bolens, Guillemette, *The Style of Gestures: Embodiment and Cognition in Literary Narrative* (Baltimore, MD: The Johns Hopkins University Press, 2012); original version: *Le Style des gestes: corporéité et kinésie dans le récit littéraire* (Lausanne, Switzerland: Editions BHMS, 2008).

Bolens, Guillemette, 'Les simulations perceptives et l'analyse kinésique dans le dessin et dans l'image poétique', *Textimage: Revue d'étude du dialogue texte-image*, 4 (2014), http://archive-ouverte.unige.ch/unige:74799.

Bolens, Guillemette, 'Les simulations perceptives dans la relation aux œuvres d'art littéraires', in Mireille Besson, Catherine Courtet, Françoise Lavocat, and Alain Viala (eds), *Corps en scènes* (Paris: Éditions du CNRS, 2015), pp. 115–25, http://archive-ouverte.unige.ch/unige:76393.

Bolens, Guillemette, *L'Humour et le savoir des corps: Don Quichotte, Tristram Shandy et le rire du lecteur* (Rennes, France: Presses Universitaires de Rennes, 2016).

Bolens, Guillemette, 'Cognition et sensorimotricité, humour et timing chez Cervantès, Sterne et Proust', in Françoise Lavocat (ed.), *L'Interprétation littéraire et les sciences cognitives* (Paris: Éditions Hermann, 2016), pp. 33–55, http://archive-ouverte.unige.ch/unige:84248.

Booth, Wayne, *The Rhetoric of Fiction* (Chicago, IL: University of Chicago Press, 1961).

Boyd, Brian, *Why Lyrics Last: Evolution, Cognition, and Shakespeare's Sonnets* (Cambridge, MA: Harvard University Press, 2012).

Boyer, Pascal, *Religion Explained: The Human Instincts that Fashion Gods, Spirits and Ancestors* (London: William Heinemann, 2001).

Bradley, A.C., *Oxford Lectures on Poetry* (London: Macmillan, 1909).

Bransford, J.D., J.R. Barclay, and J.J. Franks, 'Sentence memory: a constructive versus interpretive approach', *Cognitive Psychology*, 3 (1972), 193–209.

Brown, Harry J., *Injun Joe's Ghost: The Indian Mixed-Blood in American Writing* (Columbia, MO; London: University of Missouri Press, 2004).

Bryson, J. Scott, *The West Side of Any Mountain: Place, Space, and Ecopoetry* (Iowa City, IA: University of Iowa Press, 2005).

Bugan, Carmen, *Seamus Heaney and East European Poetry in Translation: Poetics of Exile* (Oxford: Legenda, 2013).

Burke, Michael and Emily T. Troscianko (eds), *Cognitive Literary Science: Dialogues between Literature and Cognition* (Oxford: Oxford University Press, 2017).

Burns, Robert, *The Complete Works of Robert Burns* (Boston, MA: Phillips, Sampson & Co, 1855).

Burrow, Colin, 'You've listened long enough', review of *Aeneid: Book VI*, trans. Seamus Heaney, *London Review of Books*, 38(8) (2016), 13–14.

Caracciolo, Marco, 'Patterns of cognitive dissonance in readers' engagement with characters', *Enthymema*, 8 (2013), 21–37.

Carston, Robyn, 'Informativeness, relevance and scalar implicature', in Robyn Carston and Seiji Uchida (eds), *Relevance Theory: Applications and Implications* (Amsterdam: John Benjamins, 1998), pp. 179–236.

Carston, Robyn, *Thoughts and Utterances: The Pragmatics of Explicit Communication* (Oxford: Blackwell, 2002).

Carston, Robyn, 'Truth-conditional content and conversational implicature', in C. Bianchi (ed.), *The Semantics/Pragmatics Distinction* (Stanford, CA: CSLI, 2004), pp. 65–100.

Carston, Robyn, 'Metaphor: ad hoc concepts, literal meaning and mental images', *Proceedings of the Aristotelian Society*, 110.3 (2010), 295–321.

Carston, Robyn, 'Metaphor and the literal/non-literal distinction', in Kasia Jaszczolt and Keith Allan (eds), *The Cambridge Handbook of Pragmatics* (Cambridge: Cambridge University Press, 2012), pp. 469–92.

Carston, Robyn and Catherine Wearing, 'Metaphor, hyperbole and simile: a pragmatic approach', *Language and Cognition*, 3.2 (2011), 283–312.

Cascardi, A.J. (ed.), *The Cambridge Companion to Cervantes* (Cambridge: Cambridge University Press, 2002).

Cave, Terence, *Thinking with Literature: Towards a Cognitive Criticism* (Oxford: Oxford University Press, 2016).

Cavell, Stanley, 'Aesthetic problems of modern philosophy', in Max Black (ed.), *Philosophy in America* (Ithaca, NY: Cornell University Press, 1965); reprinted in Stanley Cavell, *Must We Mean What We Say?* (Cambridge: Cambridge University Press, 1976), pp. 73–96.

Cervantes Saavedra, Miguel de, *The Ingenious Hidalgo Don Quixote de la Mancha*, trans. John Rutherford (London: Penguin Books, 2003).

Cervantes Saavedra, Miguel de, *El Ingenioso Hidalgo Don Quijote de la Mancha*, ed. Manuel Fernandez Nieto (Madrid: Biblioteca Nuova, 2006).

Chesters, Timothy, 'Flaubert's reading notes on Montaigne', *French Studies*, 63.4 (2009), 399–415.

Christensen, Laird, 'The pragmatic mysticism of Mary Oliver', in J. Scott Bryson (ed.), *Ecopoetry: A Critical Introduction* (Salt Lake City, UT: The University of Utah Press, 2002), pp. 135–52.

Clark, Andy, *Supersizing the Mind: Embodiment, Action, and Cognitive Extension* (New York: Oxford University Press, 2011).

Clark, Billy, *Relevance Theory* (Cambridge: Cambridge University Press, 2013).

Clark, Billy, 'Before and after Chekhov: inference, evaluation and interpretation', in S. Chapman and B. Clark (eds), *Pragmatic Stylistics* (Basingstoke, UK: Palgrave Macmillan, 2014).

Close, Anthony, *Cervantes and the Comic Mind of his Age* (Oxford: Oxford University Press, 2000).

Coleridge, Samuel Taylor, *Biographia Literaria* (New York: Leavitt, Lord & Co, 1834).

Cosmides, Leda and John Tooby, 'Consider the source: the evolution of adaptations for decoupling and metarepresentations', in Dan Sperber (ed.), *Metarepresentations: A Multidisciplinary Perspective* (Oxford: Oxford University Press, 2000).

Coughlan, Patricia, '"Bog Queens": the representation of women in the poetry of John Montague and Seamus Heaney' (1991), republished in Claire Connolly (ed.), *Theorizing Ireland* (Basingstoke, UK: Palgrave, 2003), pp. 41–60.

Crane, Mary Thomas, 'Illicit privacy and outdoor spaces in Early Modern England', *Journal for Early Modern Cultural Studies*, 9 (2009), 4–22.

Crane, Mary Thomas, 'Cognitive historicism: intuition in early modern thought', in Lisa Zunshine (ed.), *The Oxford Handbook of Cognitive Literary Studies* (Oxford: Oxford University Press, 2015), pp. 15–33.

Crane, Susan, *The Performance of Self: Ritual, Clothing, and Identity During the Hundred Years War* (Philadelphia, PA: University of Pennsylvania Press, 2002).

Creaser, John, '"Times trans-shifting": chronology and the misshaping of Herrick', *English Literary Renaissance*, 39 (2009), 163–96.

Crozier, W. Ray, 'The blush: literary and psychological perspectives', *Journal for the Theory of Social Behaviour*, 46.4 (2016), 502–16.

Crozier, W. Ray and Peter J. de Jong (eds), *The Psychological Significance of the Blush* (Cambridge: Cambridge University Press, 2013).

Culler, Jonathan, *Flaubert: The Uses of Uncertainty* (London: Paul Elek, 1974).

Currie, Gregory, *Image and Mind: Film, Philosophy and Cognitive Science* (New York: Cambridge University Press, 1995).

Currie, Gregory, *Narrative & Narrators: A Philosophy of Stories* (Oxford: Oxford University Press, 2010).

Currie, Gregory and Anna Ichino, 'Beliefs from fiction', unpublished paper, http://gregcurrie. com/images/downloads/beliefsfromfiction.pdf.

Curtius, Ernst Robert, *European Literature and the Latin Middle Ages*, trans. Willard R. Trask (Princeton, NJ: Princeton University Press, 1953; first published in German, 1948).

Daiches, David, *Robert Burns* (New York: Rinehart, 1950).

Darnton, Robert, 'What is the history of books?', *Daedalus*, 113.3 (1982), 65–83.

Darwin, Charles, *The Expression of the Emotions in Man and Animals*, edited by Paul Ekman (New York: Oxford University Press, 1998).

Davidson, Donald, 'What metaphors mean', *Critical Inquiry*, 5 (1978), 31–47.

Davidson, Donald, 'A nice derangement of epitaphs', in Ernie Lepore (ed.), *Truth and Interpretation: Perspectives on the Philosophy of Donald Davidson* (Oxford: Blackwell, 1986), pp. 433–46.

Davis, Todd F. and Kenneth Womack, *Postmodern Humanism in Contemporary Literature and Culture* (Basingstoke, UK; New York: Palgrave Macmillan, 2006).

Davis, Wayne, 'Implicature', in Edward N. Zalta (ed.), *The Stanford Encyclopedia of Philosophy* (Spring 2013 edition), http://plato.stanford.edu/archives/spr2013/entries/implicature.

Deming, Robert H., *Ceremony and Art: Robert Herrick's Poetry* (The Hague: Mouton, 1974).

Derrida, Jacques, *Limited Inc.*, trans. Samuel Weber and Jeffrey Mehlman (Evanston, IL: Northwestern University Press, 1988).

Dezecache, G., L. Conty, M. Chadwick, L. Philip, R. Soussignan et al., 'Evidence for unintentional emotional contagion beyond dyads', *PLoS ONE* 8(6): e67371 (2013), doi:10.1371/journal.pone.0067371.

Dezecache, Guillaume, Hugo Mercier, and Thomas C. Scott-Phillips, 'An evolutionary approach to emotional communication', *Journal of Pragmatics*, 59.B (December 2013), 221–33.

Dickinson, Emily, *Complete Poems*, edited by Thomas H. Johnson (London: Faber and Faber, 1970).

Dickinson, Emily, *The Letters of Emily Dickinson*, edited by Theodora Ward and Thomas H. Johnson, 3 vols (Cambridge, MA: Harvard University Press, 1986).

Ducrot, Oswald, *Les Mots du discours* (Paris: Seuil, 1980).

Elder, John, *Imagining the Earth: Poetry and the Vision of Nature* (Athens, GA; London: University of Georgia Press, 2nd ed., 1996).

Eliot, George, *Daniel Deronda*, edited by Terence Cave (London: Penguin Classics, 1995).

Eliot, T.S., *Collected Poems* (1963; London: Faber, 1974).

Ellman, Richard, *The Identity of Yeats* (New York: Macmillan, 1954).

Emerson, Ralph Waldo, *Nature and Selected Essays*, edited by Larzer Ziff (New York: Penguin, 2003).

Farrell, John, *The Varieties of Authorial Intention: Literary Theory Beyond the Intentional Fallacy* (Basingstoke, UK: Palgrave Macmillan, 2017).

Felski, Rita, *The Limits of Critique* (Chicago, IL: University of Chicago Press, 2015).

Fishkin, Shelley Fisher, *Lighting Out for the Territory: Reflections on Mark Twain and American Culture* (Oxford; New York: Oxford University Press, 1997).

Fishkin, Shelley Fisher, *A Historical Guide to Mark Twain* (Oxford: Oxford University Press, 2002).

Flaubert, Gustave, *Madame Bovary*, edited by Bernard Ajac (Paris: GF Flammarion, 1986, 2006).

Flaubert, Gustave, *Madame Bovary*, trans. Adam Thorpe (London: Vintage, 2011).

Flaubert, Gustave, *Correspondance*, edited by Bertrand Le Gendre (Paris: Editions Perrin, 2013).

Flaubert, Gustave, *Madame Bovary*, trans. Eleanor Marx-Aveling. The Gutenberg Project (2006/12), www.gutenberg.org/files/2413/2413-h/2413-h.htm [accessed 27 June 2016].

Foster, R.F., *W.B. Yeats: A Life*, 2 vols (Oxford: Oxford University Press, 2003).

Fowler, Alastair, 'A new theory of communication', *London Review of Books* (30 March 1989), 16–17.

Fowler, Alastair, 'The formation of genres in the Renaissance and after', *New Literary History*, 34 (2003), 185–200.

Freedberg, David and Vittorio Gallese, 'Motion, emotion and empathy in esthetic experience', *Trends in Cognitive Sciences*, 11.5 (2007), 197–203.

Freeman, Margaret, 'Metaphor making meaning: Dickinson's conceptual universe', *Journal of Pragmatics*, 24 (1995), 643–66.

Freeman, Margaret, 'A cognitive approach to Dickinson's metaphors', in G. Grabher, R. Hagenbüchle, and C. Miller (eds), *The Emily Dickinson Handbook* (Amherst, MA: University of Massachusetts Press, 1998), pp. 258–72.

Frith, Chris, *Making Up the Mind: How the Brain Creates our Mental World* (Oxford: Blackwell, 2007).

Frye, Northrop, *Spiritus Mundi: Essays on Literature, Myth and Society* (Bloomington, IN: Indiana University Press, 1976).

Furlong, Anne, 'A modest proposal: linguistics and literary studies', *Canadian Journal of Applied Linguistics*, 10.3 (2007), 325–47.

Fusaroli, R., N. Gangopadhyay, and K. Tylén, 'The dialogically extended mind: language as skilful intersubjective engagement', *Cognitive Systems Research*, 29–30 (2014), 31–9.

Gerrig, Richard J., *Experiencing Narrative Worlds: On the Psychological Activities of Reading* (New Haven, CT: Yale University Press, 1993).

Gommlich, Klaus, 'Can translators learn two representational perspectives?', in J. Danks, G.M. Shreve, S.B. Fountain, and M.K. McBeath (eds), *Cognitive Processes in Translation and Interpreting* (Thousand Oaks, CA; London; New Delhi: Sage Publications, 1997), pp. 57–76.

Green, Keith, 'Butterflies, wheels and the search for literary relevance', *Language and Literature*, 6 (1997), 133–8.

Green, Mitchell S., *Self-Expression* (Oxford: Oxford University Press, 2007).

Greenblatt, Stephen, *Shakespearean Negotiations: The Circulation of Social Energy in Renaissance England* (Berkeley, CA: University of California Press, 1988).

Greene, Thomas M., *The Light in Troy: Imitation and Discovery in Renaissance Poetry* (New Haven, CT; London: Yale University Press, 1982).

Greenwald, Elissa, 'Dickinson among the Realists', in Robin Riley Fast and Christine Mack Gordon (eds), *Approaches to Teaching Emily Dickinson* (New York: The Modern Language Association of America, 1989).

Grice, H. Paul. *Studies in the Way of Words* (Cambridge, MA: Harvard University Press, 1989).

Guibbory, Achsah, *Literature, Religion and Cultural Conflict in Seventeenth-Century England* (Cambridge: Cambridge University Press, 1998).

Guthrie, Stewart, *Faces in the Clouds: A New Theory of Religion* (Oxford; New York: Oxford University Press, 1993).

Hakemulder, Jèmeljan, *Moral Laboratory: Experiments Examining the Effects of Reading Literature on Social Perception and Moral Self-Concept* (Amsterdam; Philadelphia, PA: John Benjamins, 2000).

Halsey, Katie, 'The blush of modesty or the blush of shame? Reading Jane Austen's blushes', *Forum for Modern Language Studies*, 42.3 (2006), 226–39.

Hampton, James A., 'Emergent attributes in combined concepts', in T. Ward, S. Smith, and J. Vaid (eds), *Creative Thought: An Investigation of Conceptual Structures and Processes* (Washington, DC: American Psychological Association, 1997), pp. 83–110.

Harris, Paul, *Trusting What You're Told: How Children Learn from Others* (Cambridge, MA; London: The Belknap Press of Harvard University Press, 2012).

Heaney, Seamus, *Preoccupations: Selected Prose, 1968–1978* (London: Faber and Faber, 1980).

Heaney, Seamus, 'The impact of translation', in *The Government of the Tongue: The 1986 T.S. Eliot Memorial Lectures and Other Critical Writings* (London: Faber and Faber, 1988), pp. 36–44.

Heaney, Seamus, 'The indefatigable hoof-taps: Sylvia Plath', in *The Government of the Tongue: The 1986 T.S. Eliot Memorial Lectures and Other Critical Writings* (London: Faber and Faber, 1988), pp. 148–70.

Herman, David, 'Narrative theory and the intentional stance', *Partial Answers*, 6 (2008), 233–60.

Herrick, Robert, *The Complete Poetry of Robert Herrick*, edited by Thomas Cain and Ruth Connolly (Oxford: Oxford University Press, 2013).

Hopkins, Gerard Manley, *The Poetical Works of Gerard Manley Hopkins*, edited by Norman H. MacKenzie (Oxford: Clarendon Press, 1990).

Horchak, O.V. et al., 'From demonstration to theory in embodied language comprehension: a review', *Cognitive Systems Research*, 29–30 (2014), 66–85, http://dx.doi.org/10.1016/j.cogsys.2013.09.002 [accessed 27 June 2016].

Horn, Laurence, 'Implicature', in Laurence R. Horn and Gregory Ward (eds), *The Handbook of Pragmatics* (Oxford: Blackwell, 2004), pp. 3–28.

Hutchinson, Stuart (ed.), *Mark Twain: Critical Assessments*, 4 vols (Robertsbridge, UK: Helm Information, 1993).

Ichino, Anna and Gregory Currie, 'Truth and trust in fiction', in E. Sullivan-Bissett, H. Bradley, and P. Noordhof (eds), *Art and Belief* (Oxford: Oxford University Press, 2017).

Jakobson, Roman, 'Closing statement: linguistics and poetics', in Thomas A. Sebeok (ed.), *Style in Language* (Cambridge, MA: The MIT Press, 1960).

Jameson, Fredric, *The Political Unconscious: Narrative as a Socially Symbolic Act* (Ithaca, NY: Cornell University Press, 1981).

Jarvis, Simon, 'Mock as screen and optic', *Critical Quarterly*, 46 (2004), 1–19.

Jeannerod, Marc, *Motor Cognition: What Actions Tell the Self* (Oxford: Oxford University Press, 2006).

Johnson, Mark, '"Keep looking": Mary Oliver's Emersonian project', *The Massachusetts Review*, 46.1 (2005), 78–98.

Johnston, Maria, Review of Seamus Heaney, *The Human Chain*, www.towerpoetry.org.uk/poetry-matters/reviews/reviews-archive/434-maria-johnston-reviews-human-chain-by-seamus-heaney.

Kaschak, Michael P. and Arthur M. Glenberg, 'Constructing meaning: the role of affordances and grammatical constructions in sentence comprehension', *Journal of Memory and Language*, 43 (2000), 508–29.

Kay, Magdalena, *In Gratitude for All the Gifts: Seamus Heaney and Eastern Europe* (Toronto: University of Toronto Press, 2012).

Kolaiti, Patricia, *The Limits of Expression: Language, Literature, Mind* (Cambridge: Cambridge University Press, 2019).

Kristeva, Julia, *Sèméiotikè: Recherches pour une sémanalyse* (Paris: Tel Quel, 1969).

Kukkonen, Karin, 'Bayesian narrative: probability, plot and the shape of the fictional world', *Anglia: Journal for English Philology*, 132.4 (2014), 720–39.

Lakoff, George, *Women, Fire, and Dangerous Things: What Categories Reveal about the Mind* (Chicago, IL; London: University of Chicago Press, 1987).

La Rochefoucauld, Duc de, *Maximes*, edited by Jacques Truchet (Paris: Garnier, 1967).

Lee, Hermione, *Edith Wharton* (London: Pimlico, 2013 [2007]).

Lehecka, Tomas, 'Collocation and colligation', in J.-O. Östman and J. Verschueren (eds), *Handbook of Pragmatics* (Amsterdam: John Benjamins, 2015; DOI 10.1075/hop.19.col2).

Lepore, Ernie and Matthew Stone, *Imagination and Convention: Distinguishing Grammar and Inference in Language* (Oxford: Oxford University Press, 2015).

MacLaine, Allan H., 'Burns's use of parody in Tam o'Shanter,' *Criticism*, 1 (Fall 1959), 308–16.

McDonald, Peter, '"Weird brightness" and the riverbank: Seamus Heaney, Virgil, and the need for translation' (forthcoming).

McKanna, Clare, *The Trial of 'Indian Joe': Race and Justice in the Nineteenth-Century West* (Lincoln, NE: University of Nebraska Press, 2003).

Marcus, Leah S., *The Politics of Mirth: Jonson, Herrick, Milton, Marvell, and the Defense of Old Holiday Pastimes* (Chicago, IL: University of Chicago Press, 1986).

Markman, Keith D., William M.P. Klein, and Julie A. Suhr (eds), *The Handbook of Imagination and Mental Simulation* (New York: Taylor and Francis, Psychology Press, 2009), http://dx.doi.org/10.1016/j.cogsys.2013.09.002 [accessed 27 June 2016].

Marlowe, Christopher, 'Doctor Faustus', *Plays*, ed. Roma Gill (Oxford: Oxford University Press, 1979), 383.

Mercier, Hugo and Dan Sperber, 'Why do humans reason? Arguments for an argumentative theory', *Behavioral and Brain Sciences*, 34 (2011), 57–111.

Mercier, Hugo and Dan Sperber, *The Enigma of Reason: A New Theory of Human Understanding* (Cambridge, MA: Harvard University Press; Harmondsworth, UK: Penguin Books, 2017).

Mill, John Stuart, 'Thoughts on poetry and its varieties', *The Crayon*, 7 (1860), 93–7.

Miller, Chris, 'The Mandelstam syndrome and the "Old Heroic Bang"', *PN Review*, 162 (31.4) (March–April 2005).

Milner, Brenda, Larry R. Squire, and Eric R. Kandel, 'Cognitive neuroscience and the study of memory', *Neuron*, 20.3 (1988), 445–68.

Miłosz, Czesław, 'Ars Poetica?' [1968], in *Selected and Last Poems, 1931–2004* (London: Penguin, 2014).

Mitchell, David, *Cloud Atlas* (London: Hodder & Stoughton, 2004).

Monteith, Ken, *Yeats and Theosophy* (London; New York: Routledge, 2008).

Moss, Ann, *Printed Commonplace-Book and the Structuring of Renaissance Thought* (Oxford: The Clarendon Press, 1996).

Murillo, L., 'Lanzarote y Don Quijote', *Studies in the Literature of Spain*, 10 (New York; Brockport, NY: State University of Brockport, 1977), 55–68.

Neefs, Jacques and Claude Mouchard, *Flaubert* (Paris: Balland, 1986).

Noë, Alva, *Action in Perception* (Cambridge, MA: MIT Press, 2004).

O'Donoghue, Bernard, *Here nor There* (London: Chatto and Windus, 1999).

O'Farrell, Mary Ann, *Telling Complexions: The Nineteenth-Century English Novel and the Blush* (Durham, NC: Duke University Press, 1997).

Oliver, Mary, *House of Light* (Boston, MA: Beacon Press, 1990).

Oliver, Mary, *New and Selected Poems*, vol. 1 (Boston, MA: Beacon Press, 1992).

Oliver, Mary, *Rules for the Dance: A Handbook for Writing and Reading Metrical Verse* (Boston, MA: Houghton Mifflin, 1998).

Oliver, Mary, *Why I Wake Early: New Poems* (Boston, MA: Beacon Press, 2004).

Oliver, Mary, 'Foreword', in Brian Swann (ed.), *Poetry Comes Up Where It Can: An Anthology* (Salt Lake City, UT: The University of Utah Press, 2000), pp. xi–xv.

Oliver, Mary, *New and Selected Poems*, vol. 2 (Boston, MA: Beacon Press, 2005).

Oliver, Mary, www.oed.com/view/Entry/146666?rskey=G3sldR&result=3#eid [accessed 27 August 2016].

Oliver, Mary, www.onbeing.org/program/mary-oliver-listening-to-the-world/transcript/8051#main_content.

Oswald, Alice, *Falling Awake* (London: Jonathan Cape, 2016).

Palmer, Patricia, *The Severed Head and the Grafted Tongue: Literature, Translation and Violence in Early Modern Ireland* (Cambridge: Cambridge University Press, 2014).

Parry, Graham, *The Arts of the Anglican Counter-Reformation: Glory, Laud and Honour* (Woodbridge, UK: Boydell and Brewer, 2006).

Pecher, Diane and Rolf A. Zwaan (eds), *Grounding Cognition: The Role of Perception and Action in Memory, Language, and Thinking* (Cambridge: Cambridge University Press, 2005).

Pfitzer, Gregory M., ' "Iron dudes and white savages in Camelot": the influence of dime-novel sensationalism on Twain's "A Connecticut Yankee in King Arthur's Court"', *American Literary Realism, 1870–1910*, 27.1 (1994), 42–58.

Philip, Gill, *Colouring Meaning: Collocation and Colligation in Figurative Language* (Amsterdam: John Benjamins, 2011).

Phillips, Natalie M., 'Literary neuroscience and history of mind: an interdisciplinary fMRI study of attention and Jane Austen', in Lisa Zunshine (ed.), *The Oxford Handbook of Cognitive Literary Studies* (Oxford: Oxford University Press, 2015), pp. 55–83.

Pilkington, Adrian, *Poetic Effects: A Relevance Theory Perspective* (Amsterdam: John Benjamins, 2000).

Pilkington, Adrian, Barbara MacMahon, and Billy Clark, 'Looking for an argument: a response to Green', *Language and Literature*, 6.2 (1997), 139–48.

Polchow, S.M., 'Manipulation of narrative discourse: from Amadís De Gaula to Don Quixote', *Hispania*, 88 (2005.1), 7–81.

Quinn, Justin, 'Heaney and Eastern Europe', in Bernard O'Donoghue (ed.), *The Cambridge Companion to Seamus Heaney* (Cambridge: Cambridge University Press, 2009), pp. 92–105.

Recanati, François, 'Can we believe what we do not understand?', *Mind and Language*, 12 (1997), 84–100.

Recanati, François, *Literal Meaning* (Cambridge: Cambridge University Press, 2004).

Redondo, Augustin, *Otra manera de leer el Quijote: Historia, tradiciones culturales y literatura* (Madrid: Editorial Castalia, 1997).

Rich, Frank, 'President Lindbergh in 2004', *New York Times*, 23 September 2004.

Richards, I.A., *The Philosophy of Rhetoric* (Oxford: Oxford University Press, 1936).

Riffaterre, Michael, *Production du texte* (Paris: Éditions du Seuil, 1979).

Riquer, Martin de, 'La technique parodique du roman médiéval dans le *Quichotte*', in G. Pierre (ed.), *La Littérature narrative d'imagination* (Paris: PUF, 1961), pp. 55–69.

Riquer, Martin de, *Para leer a Cervantes* (Barcelona: Acantilado, 2010).

Ronsard, Pierre de, *Œuvres complètes*, edited by Jean Céard, Daniel Ménager, and Jean Céard ([Paris]: Gallimard, Bibliothèque de la Pléiade, 1994).

Rosaler, Ruth, *Conspicuous Silences: Implicature and Fictionality in the Victorian Novel* (Oxford: Oxford University Press, 2016).

Rosch, Eleanor, 'Cognitive representation of semantic categories', *Journal of Experimental Psychology*, 104.3 (1975), 192–233.

Roth, Philip, *The Plot Against America* (New York: Random House, 2004).

Roth, Philip, 'The story behind *The Plot Against America*', *New York Times*, 19 September 2004.

Roubaud-Bénichou, S., *Le Roman de chevalerie en Espagne: Entre Arthur et Don Quichotte* (Paris: Honoré Champion, 2000).

Rubio-Fernández, Paula, 'Suppression in metaphor interpretation: differences between meaning selection and meaning construction', *Journal of Semantics*, 24 (2007), 345–71.

Rukhelman, Svetlana, 'The laughter of gods and devils: Edith Wharton and the Coen Brothers on deception, disappointment, and cosmic irony', in David Gallagher (ed.), *Comedy in Comparative Literature: Essays on Dante, Hoffman, Nietzsche, Wharton, Borges, and Cabrera Infante* (Lewiston, NY: Edwin Mellen Press, 2010).

Ryan, Marie-Laure, *Narrative as Virtual Reality 2: Revisiting Immersion and Interactivity in Literature and Electronic Media* (Baltimore, MD: Johns Hopkins University Press, 2015).

Schaeffer, Jean-Marie, *Why Fiction?*, trans. Dorrit Cohn (Lincoln, NE; London: University of Nebraska Press, 2010); original version, *Pourquoi la fiction?* (Paris: Seuil, 1999).

Schaeffer, Jean-Marie, *L'Expérience esthétique* (Paris: Gallimard, 2015).

Schoolcraft, Henry R., *Archives of Aboriginal Knowledge: Containing all the Original Papers Laid Before Congress Respecting the History, Antiquities, Language, Ethnology, Pictography, Rites, Superstitions, and Mythology of the Indian Tribes of the United States* (Philadelphia, PA: J.B. Lippincott, vol. i, 1860; vol. v, 1865).

Scott-Phillips, Thom, *Speaking our Minds: Why Human Communication is Different, and How Language Evolved to Make it Special* (Basingstoke, UK: Palgrave, 2014).

Spenser, Edmund, *The Yale Edition of the Shorter Poems of Edmund Spenser*, edited by William A. Oram et al. (New Haven, CT: Yale University Press, 1989).

Sperber, Dan, *Explaining Culture: A Naturalistic Approach* (Oxford: Blackwell, 1996).

Sperber, Dan and Deirdre Wilson, 'Mutual knowledge and relevance in theories of comprehension', in Neil Smith (ed.), *Mutual Knowledge* (London: Academic Press, 1982), pp. 61–85.

Sperber, Dan and Deirdre Wilson, 'Presumptions of relevance', *Behavioral and Brain Sciences*, 10 (1987), 736–54.

Sperber, Dan and Deirdre Wilson, 'Rhetoric and relevance', in John Bender and David Welbery (eds), *The Ends of Rhetoric: History, Theory, Practice* (Stanford, CA: Stanford University Press, 1990); reprinted in Deirdre Wilson and Dan Sperber, *Meaning and Relevance* (Cambridge: Cambridge University Press, 2012).

Sperber, Dan and Deirdre Wilson, *Relevance: Communication and Cognition* (Oxford: Blackwell, 2nd ed., 1995).

Sperber, Dan and Deirdre Wilson, 'The mapping between the mental and the public lexicon', in Peter Carruthers and Jill Boucher (eds), *Language and Thought: Interdisciplinary Themes* (Cambridge: Cambridge University Press, 1998), pp. 184–200; reprinted in Deirdre Wilson and Dan Sperber, *Meaning and Relevance* (Cambridge: Cambridge University Press, 2012).

Sperber, Dan and Deirdre Wilson, 'Pragmatics, modularity, and mind-reading', *Mind and Language*, 17 (2002), 2–23; reprinted in Deirdre Wilson and Dan Sperber, *Meaning and Relevance* (Cambridge: Cambridge University Press, 2012).

Sperber, Dan and Deirdre Wilson, 'A deflationary account of metaphors', in R. Gibbs (ed.), *The Cambridge Handbook of Metaphor and Thought* (Cambridge: Cambridge University Press, 2008), 84–105; reprinted in Deirdre Wilson and Dan Sperber, *Meaning and Relevance* (Cambridge: Cambridge University Press, 2012).

Sperber, Dan and Deirdre Wilson, 'Beyond speaker's meaning', *Croatian Journal of Philosophy*, 15:44 (2015), 117–49.

Sperber, Dan, Fabrice Clément, Christophe Heintz, Olivier Mascaro, Hugo Mercier, Gloria Origgi, and Deirdre Wilson, 'Epistemic vigilance', *Mind and Language*, 25.4 (2010), 359–93.

Squire, Larry R. and Eric R. Kandel, *Memory: From Mind to Molecules* (New York: Scientific American Library, 1999).

Starobinski, Jean, 'L'Échelle des températures: lecture du corps dans *Madame Bovary*', in Gérard Genette et Tzvetan Todorov (eds), *Travail de Flaubert* (Paris: Seuil, 1983), pp. 45–78.

Starr, Gabrielle, 'Multisensory imagery', in Lisa Zunshine (ed.), *Introduction to Cognitive Cultural Studies* (Baltimore, MD: The Johns Hopkins University Press, 2010), pp. 275–91.

Stewart, J., O. Gapenne, and E.A. Di Paolo, *Enaction: Toward A New Paradigm for Cognitive Science* (Cambridge, MA; London: Bradford Books, MIT Press, 2010).

Trotter, David, 'Analysing literary prose: the relevance of Relevance Theory', *Lingua*, 87 (1992), 11–27.

Twain, Mark, 'The noble red man', *The Galaxy: A Magazine of Entertaining Reading* (September 1870), pp. 426–9.

Twain, Mark, *Mark Twain's Autobiography*, with an Introduction by Albert Bigeloe Paine, 2 vols (New York; London: Harper and Brothers, 1924).

Twain, Mark, *The Adventures of Tom Sawyer*, edited by Peter Stoneley (Oxford: Oxford University Press, 2008).

Unger, Christoph, 'Towards a relevance theory account of allegory', in Agnieszka Piskorska and Ewa Wałaszewska (eds), *From Discourse to Morphemes: Applications of Relevance Theory* (Newcastle-upon-Tyne, UK: Cambridge Scholars Publishing, 2016).

Vaage, Margrethe Bruun, 'On the repulsive rapist and the difference between morality in fiction and real life', in Lisa Zunshine (ed.), *The Oxford Handbook of Cognitive Literary Studies* (Oxford; New York: Oxford University Press, 2015), pp. 421–39.

van Delft, Louis, *La Bruyère moraliste: Quatre études sur les Caractères* (Geneva, Switzerland: Droz, 1971).

Vega Moreno, Rosa E., 'Metaphor interpretation and emergence', *UCL Working Papers in Linguistics*, 16 (2004), 297–322.

Vega Moreno, Rosa E., *Creativity and Convention: The Pragmatics of Everyday Figurative Speech* (Amsterdam: John Benjamins, 2007).

Vendler, Helen, *Dickinson: Selected Poems and Commentaries* (Cambridge, MA: Harvard University Press, 2012).

Vicente, Agustin and Fernando Martínez-Manrique, 'Overhearing a sentence: Recanati and the cognitive view of language', *Pragmatics and Cognition*, 12 (2004), 219–51.

Walton, Kendall L., *Mimesis as Make-Believe: On the Foundations of the Representational Arts* (Cambridge, MA: Harvard University Press, 1990).

Wharton, Edith, *The New York Stories of Edith Wharton*, edited by Roxana Robinson (New York: The New York Review of Books, 2007).

Wharton, Edith, *The House of Mirth*, edited by Martha Banta (Oxford: Oxford University Press, Oxford World's Classics, 2008).

Wharton, Tim, *Pragmatics and Non-Verbal Communication* (Cambridge: Cambridge University Press, 2009).

Williamson, Edwin, *The Half-Way House of Fiction*: Don Quixote *and Arthurian Romance* (Oxford: Clarendon Press, 1984).

Wilson, Deirdre, *Slave of the Passions* (London: Picador, 1991).

Wilson, Deirdre, 'Metarepresentation in linguistic communication', in D. Sperber (ed.), *Metarepresentations: A Multidisciplinary Perspective* (Oxford: Oxford University Press, 2000); reprinted in Deirdre Wilson and Dan Sperber, *Meaning and Relevance* (Cambridge: Cambridge University Press, 2012).

Wilson, Deirdre, 'Relevance theory and lexical pragmatics', *Italian Journal of Linguistics*, 15 (2003), 273–91.

Wilson, Deirdre, 'Relevance and the interpretation of literary works', in A. Yoshimura (ed.), *Observing Linguistic Phenomena: A Festschrift for Seiji Uchida* (Tokyo: Eihosha, 2012).

Wilson, Deirdre, 'Relevance theory', in Yan Huang (ed.), *The Oxford Handbook of Pragmatics* (Oxford: Oxford University Press, 2017).

Wilson, Deirdre and Robyn Carston, 'Metaphor, relevance and the "emergent property" issue', *Mind & Language*, 21.3 (2006), 404–33.

Wilson, Deirdre and Robyn Carston, 'A unitary approach to lexical pragmatics: relevance, inference and ad hoc concepts', in Noel Burton-Roberts (ed.), *Pragmatics* (Basingstoke, UK: Palgrave Macmillan, 2007), pp. 230–59.

Wilson, Deirdre and Robyn Carston, 'Metaphor and the "emergent property" problem: a relevance-theoretic treatment', *The Baltic International Yearbook of Cognition, Logic and Communication*, 3(3) (2008), 1–40.

Wilson, Deirdre and Dan Sperber, 'On Grice's theory of conversation', in Paul Werth (ed.), *Conversation and Discourse* (London: Croom Helm, 1981).

Wilson, Deirdre and Dan Sperber, 'Relevance theory', in Laurence R. Horn and Gregory Ward (eds), *The Handbook of Pragmatics* (Oxford: Blackwell, 2004), pp. 607–32.

Wilson, Deirdre and Dan Sperber, 'Truthfulness and relevance', *Mind*, 111 (2002), 583–632; reprinted in Deirdre Wilson and Dan Sperber, *Meaning and Relevance* (Cambridge: Cambridge University Press, 2012).

Wilson, Deirdre and Dan Sperber, *Meaning and Relevance* (Cambridge: Cambridge University Press, 2012).

Wilson, Deirdre and Dan Sperber, 'Explaining irony', in Deirdre Wilson and Dan Sperber, *Meaning and Relevance* (Cambridge: Cambridge University Press, 2012).

Wilson, Deirdre and Tim Wharton, 'Relevance and prosody', *Journal of Pragmatics*, 38.10 (2006), 1559–79.

Wilson, Robert A. and Lucia Foglia, 'Embodied cognition', in Edward N. Zalta (ed.), *The Stanford Encyclopedia of Philosophy* (Spring 2017 edition), https://plato.stanford.edu/archives/spr2017/entries/embodied-cognition.

Wolosky, Shira, 'Emily Dickinson: being in the body', in Wendy Martin (ed.), *The Cambridge Companion to Emily Dickinson* (Cambridge: Cambridge University Press, 2002), pp. 129–41.

Wordsworth, William, *A Critical Edition of the Major Works*, edited by Stephen Gill (Oxford: Oxford University Press, 1984).

Wróbel, Natalia, http://nataliaswrobel.com/section/384250-Embrace-Series-click-to-view-series.html.

Wróbel, Natalia, http://nataliaswrobel.com/news.html.

Yeats, W.B., *The Poems*, edited by Daniel Albright (London: Dent, 1992).

Zona, Kirstin Hotelling, '"An attitude of noticing": Mary Oliver's ecological ethic', *Interdisciplinary Studies in Literature and Environment*, 18.1 (2011), 123–42.

Zunshine, Lisa, *Why We Read Fiction: Theory of Mind and the Novel* (Columbus, OH: Ohio State University Press, 2006).

# Index of Names

The names of the contributors to this volume are not included here, with two exceptions: Elleke Boehmer and Deirdre Wilson are cited exclusively as the authors of literary fictions and not for their scholarly works.

Authors of scholarly works are only included where a substantive comment is made on their work.

Canonic works referred to by title or eponymous character ('Quixote') appear under the name of their author.

# Index of Concepts and Terms